Worship
Reformed according to Scripture

Revised and Expanded Edition

Hughes Oliphant Old

Westminster John Knox Press
LOUISVILLE • LONDON

Scripture quotations, unless otherwise indicated, are from the Revised Standard Version of the Bible, copyright © 1946, 1952, 1971, and 1973 by the Division of Christian Education of the National Council of the Churches of Christ in the U.S.A., and are used by permission.

Book design by Sharon Adams

First edition
Published by Westminster John Knox Press
Louisville, Kentucky

This book is printed on acid-free paper that meets the American National Standards Institute Z39.48 standard. ∞

PRINTED IN THE UNITED STATES OF AMERICA
    04 05 06 07 08 09 10 11 — 10 9 8 7 6 5 4 3 2

Library of Congress Cataloging-in-Publication Data is on file at the Library of Congress, Washington, D.C.

0-664-22579-9

To the memory of my aunt and uncle
Mr. and Mrs. A. C. Oliphant

Contents

Author's Preface

The book before us has, to be sure, a history. In the summer of 1979 Professor Donald Wardlaw asked me to do a series of lectures on worship for the pastors' institute at McCormick Theological Seminary in Chicago. After some discussion we chose as the subject "The Biblical Roots of Reformed Worship." At the end of the course Wardlaw asked if he might have the manuscript typed up and mimeographed for use in his introductory course on worship the following semester. The manuscript needed considerable work before it could be used for this purpose, and with the editorial assistance and great patience of Mrs. Sue Armendariz, a manuscript was produced for Wardlaw's class in the spring of 1980. To this was given the title *Introduction to Reformed Worship*.

In the spring of 1981 I received an invitation to give a paper at the meeting of the International Colloquium of Calvin Studies held at Calvin College in Grand Rapids. It was at the suggestion of the late Ford Lewis Battles that I was asked to write something on Calvin's theology of worship. The first chapter of this book represents to a large extent a reshaping of that lecture. Professor Edward Dowey of Princeton Theological Seminary offered a number of comments and criticisms from which I have greatly profited.

The chapter on the Reformed discipline of daily morning and evening prayer is a very brief reworking of a considerable amount of research that I have done as a member of the North American Academy of Liturgics committee on the daily office. To Professor William Storey of the University of Notre Dame I owe appreciation for encouraging me to dig deeply into the Reformed approach to the service of daily prayer. Much of the work on prayer I did in connection with my being on General Assembly's task force on prayer. Here I am particularly indebted to the sympathetic support of Dr. James Kirk, director of the Advisory Council of Discipleship and Worship of the Presbyterian Church.

Behind all of my work is the encouragement of my doctor Father at the University of Neuchâtel in Switzerland, Professor Jean-Jacques von Allmen. In the five years I spent under his guidance I got to know a great amount about the Continental Reformed liturgical heritage. To him I am most grateful.

Two things I have been obliged to leave out of this study. I should have very much liked to have treated at length the liturgical contributions of the Middle Ages, both in the Eastern and Western churches. I think there would be genuine worth in a Reformed liturgical scholar treating this period sympathetically. Much happened in this period that is of great value. For example, I would like to have written at greater length about the monastic daily office and the eucharistic theology of the high scholastic theologians. When one sees the variety of thought and practice during the Middle Ages, the work of the Reformers is put in much clearer perspective. I should also have liked to have written about the developments in Reformed worship in more recent centuries. Charles W. Baird I have always regarded as a personal hero. Henry van Dyke was a much beloved cousin in my mother's family. The figure of Alexander Campbell has interested me for years. Here again, many positive things happened. This book was supposed to be brief, and if something of substance was to be said, it seemed necessary to focus on those periods of our liturgical history that were crucial. The editor and I decided to leave aside for the present the subjects mentioned above.

As it now stands, the purpose of the book is to explicate the classical Reformed tradition in regard to worship. The heart of this tradition is the witness of the Reformers to the teaching of Scripture. Professor John Leith, who first asked me to write this book, and I were in agreement that it was appropriate to spend a large part of each chapter presenting the relevant biblical passages. Particular attention has been given to the collegial nature of the Reformed tradition. Because the Reformed liturgical heritage has been shaped by many hands, it seemed important to treat a variety of Reformers. I have given attention to the less well known Reformers of the first generation such as Oecolampadius, Capito, and Bucer, as well as to the English Puritans of later generations. Apart from taking this wide-angle lens, it is really very hard to get the whole picture in focus. More and more I am fascinated by Peter Martyr Vermigli, William Perkins, and Thomas Manton. I did not realize we had such treasures in our attic! Our tradition is not very well known, and what is known is badly misunderstood. My highest hope for the pages which lie ahead is not that they will constitute a "definitive work," but rather that they will inspire a more careful look at the subject treated. What I have written is only a report on what I have discovered up to this point. This is a fascinating field, and there is much yet to be brought to light.

I express appreciation to Christopher Borgert, a member of my congregation, who has now for the last two years acted as my research assistant. He chases down books for me in the library and performs innumerable other services. To him goes the credit for putting together the bibliography and the index. Even more important, he keeps a sharp eye on my spelling and syntax and lets me know whether I have said what I really intended to say.

To my congregation go very special thanks for their being patient with my putting so much time into my research and writing. There is not much in this book that they have not heard, in sermon form. Mrs. Grieke Toebes very kindly read through the manuscript before I sent it to the publisher to see whether it was readable. Our church secretary, Mrs. Peggy Downey, has usually typed up the first draft of whatever I have written. She keeps me up to date on my correspondence and generally keeps me in order. Without such practical saints, there would be no doctors of theology.

Preface to the Expanded Edition

The publisher originally asked me to write a short book about Reformed worship. So I wrote primarily on the liturgical reforms of the Protestant Reformation in the sixteenth and seventeenth centuries. For this to be understandable, I had to speak of the roots of these reforms in Scripture and in the life of the early church. This, however, meant that little was said about the Middle Ages or what has happened from the eighteenth century down to the present. At the time, both the editors and I regretted this but felt that our priority had to be the presentation of the material on the Reformation. Even now, the emphasis needs to be put there, but the additional material should help put the Reformers in clearer perspective.

In the seventeen years since the book was published, it has found its place in the literature on Reformed worship, and the increasing interest in the subject suggests that the time has come to continue the work. I still want to be brief, but I also want to fill in some of the subjects left out of the first edition. Only in the briefest way will I speak of some of the positive things that happened in Christian worship during the Middle Ages. Going on to the eighteenth century, I will give special attention to the way Pietism affected Reformed worship. Herrnhut had almost as much effect on Reformed worship as Wittenberg and Geneva, and surely we owe as much to Jonathan Edwards, John Wesley, and George Whitefield as we do to Richard Baxter, Isaac Watts, and Matthew Henry.

The nineteenth and twentieth centuries have made their contributions as well. It is not quite as clear which of these will be lasting, particularly with regard to the contributions of the twentieth century, but I will put forward a few suggestions.

I express a word of appreciation to John Leith, to whom all of us who value the Reformed tradition are so much indebted. He was the original editor of the series Guides to the Reformed Tradition, in which the first edition of this work appeared. His sponsorship of the Calvin Colloquium at Davidson College provided many of us an opportunity to make public our research. It was he who first asked me to write a volume on Reformed worship. His encouragement was a great inspiration, and his constant recommendation assured its success. Without John Leith my work might well have been buried in obscurity.

Chapter 1

Some Basic Principles

We worship God because God created us to worship him. Worship is at the center of our existence, at the heart of our reason for being. God created us to be his image—an image that would reflect his glory. In fact the whole creation was brought into existence to reflect the divine glory. The psalmist tells us that "the heavens are telling the glory of God; and the firmament proclaims his handiwork" (Ps. 19:1). The apostle Paul in the prayer with which he begins the epistle to the Ephesians makes it clear that God created us to praise him.

> Blessed be the God and Father of our Lord Jesus Christ, who has blessed us in Christ with every spiritual blessing in the heavenly places, even as he chose us in him before the foundation of the world, that we should be holy and blameless before him. He destined us in love to be his sons through Jesus Christ, according to the purpose of his will, to the praise of his glorious grace. . . . (Eph. 1:3–6)

This prayer says much about the worship of the earliest Christians. It shows the consciousness that the first Christians had of the ultimate significance of their worship. They understood themselves to have been destined and appointed to live to the praise of God's glory (Eph. 1:12). When the Westminster Shorter Catechism teaches us, "Man's chief end is to glorify God and to enjoy him forever,"[1] it gives witness to this same basic principle; God created us to worship him. Surely it is here that we must begin when as Reformed theologians we ask what worship is. Worship must above all serve the glory of God.

Some people today justify worship for any number of other reasons. We are told that we should worship because it brings us happiness. Sometimes worship does make us happy, but not always. We are told that we should worship because it will give us a sense of self-fulfillment. Surely worship does fulfill the purpose of our existence, but we do not worship *because* it brings us self-fulfillment. We are often told that we should worship in order to build family solidarity: "The family that prays together stays together." The high priests of the Canaanite fertility religions said much the same thing. All kinds of politicians have insisted on participation in various religious rites in order to develop national unity or ethnic identity. Queen Elizabeth I was not the first or the last who tried to consolidate her realm by insisting that the worship be in some way English. One can always find medicine men and gurus who advocate religious rites for the sake of good health, financial success, or peace of mind. True worship, however, is distinguished from all of these in that it serves, above all else, the praise of God's glory.

Not only did God create us to worship him, but he also commanded us to worship him. The first four of the Ten Commandments concern worship. The first commandment tells us, "Thou shalt have no other gods before me" (Exod. 20:3 KJV). Jesus tells us that the first and greatest commandment is that we are to love God with all our hearts, all our minds, and all our souls. The point is that our worship, our deepest devotion, our most ardent love is to be directed to God rather than to ourselves. Even before loving ourselves or our neighbor or any other worthy human cause, we are to devote ourselves to God. John Calvin (1509–64), one of the leaders of the Protestant Reformation, in his commentary on the Ten Commandments says that the first commandment means that we are "with true and zealous godliness . . . to contemplate, fear, and worship, his majesty; to participate in his blessings; to seek his help at all times; to recognize, and by praises to celebrate, the greatness of his works—as the only goal of all the activities of this life."[2] The second commandment tells us that we are not to use images or idols in our worship, for as the apostle Paul tells us, God is not represented by human art and imagination; God created *us* to be the reflection of his image (Acts 17:22–31). Taking this commandment seriously has been fundamental to the Reformed understanding of worship. If today American Protestant worship services have confused worship with art, or even worse, if we have confused it with entertainment, it is because we have failed to fathom the meaning of the second commandment. The third commandment tells us that we are not to use the Lord's name in vain. *Vain* means "empty." The commandment teaches us to worship God honestly and sincerely, to worship God "in spirit and in truth," to use the words of Jesus. The fourth commandment tells us to remember, or observe, the worship of the Sabbath Day. This commandment makes the preceding three commandments very concrete. Without this commandment it might seem that the law had had in mind something much more subjective than actual services of worship. As we shall see in another chapter, Jesus, too, interpreted this commandment in a very concrete way when he told the disciples to celebrate the Lord's Supper in *remembrance* of him. Throughout Scripture we find commandments to worship God and commandments regarding worship, which are in fact an unfolding and an interpretation of the first four commandments. True worship is an act of obedience to the law of God. Reformed theology with its Augustinian sense for the continuity between the Old and New Testaments has taken very seriously what the first tablet of the law has to say about worship.

This then is the first characteristic of Reformed worship: it is worship that is "according to Scripture." The Reformers did not mean by this a sort of Bible-pounding literalism—although they have often been accused of this. Much more they had in mind that Christian worship should be in obedience to God's Word as it is revealed in Holy Scripture. At the very beginning of the Reformation we find this principle put forth by Martin Bucer (1491–1551), the leading reformer of the city of Strasbourg, one of the first cities of that day actually to attempt liturgical reform. As Bucer put it, only the worship that God asks of us really serves him. Bucer obviously did not understand worship as though it were some sort of creative art, as though the object of worship were to entertain God with elaborate liturgical pageants and dramas. As Bucer and his colleagues understood it, God directs us above all to worship him by the proclamation of his Word, the giving of alms, the celebration of Communion, and the ministry of prayer. This Bucer gathered from the text of Acts 2:42, which tells of the worship of the primitive church: "And they devoted themselves to the apostles' teaching and fellowship, to the breaking of bread and the prayers."

John Oecolampadius (1482–1531), the reformer of Basel, and one of the most highly respected scholars of his age, developed at considerable length what the early Reformed theologians meant by worship that was according to Scripture. As Oecolampadius well understood, the Bible does not provide us with any ready-made liturgies or services of worship. Nevertheless the church should develop services of worship in accordance with whatever specific directions and examples are found in Scripture. When Scripture does not give specific directions, then we should be guided by scriptural principles. For instance, Oecolampadius taught that Christian worship should be simple and without pompous ritual and sumptuous ceremony, because the manner of life Jesus taught was simple and without pretense. As Oecolampadius understood it, the worship of the church should be consistent with such essential principles as justification by faith, prevenient grace, and, above all, Christian love.

This principle, that the worship of the church should be according to Scripture, has suggested to a large extent the arrangement of this book. One cannot readily appreciate what the Reformers had to say about worship unless one sees how they brought it out of the Scriptures. One has to understand their teaching as an interpretation of the Scriptures. We will therefore explore first what the Scriptures have to say about various aspects of worship and then how the Reformers understood the Scriptures. In order to understand what Reformed is, we must understand what Reformed according to God's Word is.

There is more. While the Reformers understood the Scriptures to be their sole authority, they were very interested in how generations of Christians down through history had understood the Scriptures. In the history of Christian worship they found many good examples of how the church had truly understood Scripture. Often the Fathers of the early church had been most faithful witnesses to the authority of Scripture. The Reformers learned from Athanasius about Christian psalmody, from Ambrose about catechetical instruction, from John Chrysostom about preaching, and from Augustine about the sacraments. In these pages we will need to say something about both the way the church through many centuries maintained a faithful witness, and the way the church confused that witness. Otherwise it would be difficult to understand what the reform was all about and why it was necessary.

One often asks why today we should study the Reformers. We study the Reformers for the same reason the Reformers studied the church fathers. They are witnesses to the authority of Scripture. The Reformers studied the patristic commentaries on Scripture because they enriched their own understanding of Scripture. Today we study the Reformers because they throw so much light on the pages of the Bible. They were passionately concerned to worship God truly, and they searched the Scriptures to learn how. We study the Reformers because their understanding of Scripture is so profound.

The second fundamental of Christian worship is that it should be in the name of Christ (Col. 3:17). We begin our worship as Christians by being baptized in his name (Acts 2:38). It is in his name that the Christian congregation is assembled, remembering the promise that when two or three are gathered together in his name he is present with us (Matt. 18:20). Jesus frequently taught his disciples to pray in his name (John 14:14; 15:16; 16:23). That we are to pray in the name of Jesus is a very important principle of Christian prayer. To do something in someone's name is to do it as the agent of someone else. It is to do something in the service of someone else. When we pray in the name of Christ we are praying in his service; we are continuing the ministry of intercession that Jesus himself began on the cross. The preaching and teaching of the apostles was likewise in the name of Jesus (Acts 5:41). It was in the name of Jesus because he commissioned the church to continue that ministry of preaching and teaching which he began. The church is, as Jesus himself put it, to teach "all things whatsoever I have commanded you" (Matt. 28:20 KJV). In the same way, our giving of alms and our good works are to be in the name of Christ (Matt. 18:5; Mark 9:38–41; Acts 3:6). In the upper room at the Last Supper Jesus commissioned the Twelve to act as his agents, "Do this in remembrance of me" (Luke 22:19). How often Jesus had broken bread with them, and how often Jesus had fed the multitude! Now the apostles were to go out and hold the memorial that he had appointed in his name.

Christian worship is in the name of Christ because worship is a function of the body of Christ and as Christians we are all one body. All of our worship must be in him! What an important New Testament concept this is that the church is the body of Christ, and how vividly the first Christians understood that they were all together one body, the body of Christ. They understood their worship to be part of the worship that the ascended Christ performed in the heavenly sanctuary to the glory of the Father (Heb. 7:23–25; 9:25; 10:19–22; 13:15).

If Reformed theology is concerned that worship be according to God's Word and in obedience to God's Word and if Reformed theology has made a point of worship being in the name of Christ and in the body of Christ, it is most surely because it has realized that worship is far more than a human work. Worship is the work of the Holy Spirit. Here is the third principle we would like to advance. The Scriptures are particularly clear about prayer being the work of the Holy Spirit. As the apostle Paul tells us, it is the Holy Spirit who cries out within us when we pray (Rom. 8: 15–27). The apostle tells us that when we pray, "Our Father," it is the Holy Spirit praying within our hearts (Rom. 8:15). The hymns and psalms that are sung in worship are spiritual songs, that is, they are the songs of the Holy Spirit (Acts 4:25; Eph. 5:19). Even the preaching of the church is to be in the Spirit (1 Cor. 12:8). Jesus promised to us that when we present our testimony before the world it is not we who speak but the Holy Spirit who gives us utterance (Mark 13:11). Christian worship is inspired by the Spirit, empowered by the Spirit, directed by the Spirit, purified by the Spirit, and bears the fruit of the Spirit. Christian worship is Spirit-filled.

As far back as the eighth century before Christ, the prophet Amos had insisted that true worship must be holy. It must come from a people whose lives are consecrated to God. God has no interest in the sacrifices of a wicked people or the praises of those who ignore the ethical demands of the law.

> "I hate, I despise your feasts,
>   and I take no delight in your solemn assemblies.
> Even though you offer me your burnt offerings and cereal offerings,
>   I will not accept them,
> and the peace offerings of your fatted beasts
>   I will not look upon.
> Take away from me the noise of your songs;
>   to the melody of your harps I will not listen.
> But let justice roll down like waters,
>   and righteousness like an everflowing stream."
>
>   (Amos 5:21–24)

With these words, Amos announced God's displeasure with the worship of Samaria. Mistreatment of the poor, militarism, the luxury of the rich, bribery in the courts, sexual promiscuity, high interest rates, and oppressive taxes revealed the religious hypocrisy of the kingdom of Israel. Jesus must have had this prophecy in mind when he made very clear to a woman of Samaria that the day had finally come when the true worshiper would worship God in spirit and truth (John 4:1–26). For the Christian, holiness of life and sincerity of worship must go together; they must be of one piece.

For the Reformed theologian the integrity of the service of God and the service of the neighbor is essential. Dr. Thomas Manton (1620–77), whom we might well reckon with the most brilliant of the Westminster Divines, tells us that when those who worship God live immoral lives the glory of God is obscured. On the other hand, when Christians reflect the holiness of God and are in fact the image of God, then God is glorified. When those who worship the holy God become through that worship holy themselves, they show forth the praises of him who has called them out of the darkness into his marvelous light (1 Pet. 2:9). This does not mean that holiness is a prerequisite to worship. If it were, none of us could worship. Holiness is rather the fruit of worship. Dr. Manton tells us that God is sanctified by his people when they discover him to be holy, the source of all holiness, and when God sanctifies us by working grace and holiness in us, then we declare him to be a holy God.[3] It is the Holy Spirit who purifies our worship by his continual work of sanctification. As the Spirit purifies the worshipers, the worship is made pure. When we worship, having our minds enlightened by the Spirit, our lives cleansed by the Spirit, our wills moved by the Spirit, and our hearts warmed by the Spirit, then our worship is transformed from being merely a human work into being a divine work.

But if worship is a divine work, it is God's saving work among us. It is God's work of building up the church. This point is made when the Westminster Shorter Catechism tells us that word, prayer, and sacraments are means of grace, "the outward and ordinary means whereby Christ communicateth to us the benefits of redemption."[4] From the very beginning Reformed theologians have been fond of speaking of worship as being edifying. Martin Bucer in particular liked to use this word to describe Christian worship. He had in mind that passage where the apostle Paul tells us that everything in the service of worship should edify the church (1 Cor. 14:1–6), that is, it should teach or build up the church. Worship that puts first the praise of God's glory, worship that is according to God's Word, worship that serves God and God alone does in fact edify the church. It edifies the church because it is the work of the Holy Spirit in the body of Christ. When in the worship of the church the word is truly preached and the sacraments rightly administered, then God calls, teaches, and leads his people into a new way of life. In coming together for worship we become the church (1 Cor. 10:16–17; 11:17–22). Here we are united together into one body by God's Spirit, are made participants in the coming kingdom. In worship we hear the good news of our salvation and are saved from our sins and transformed into the image of Christ. God has commanded us not to worship him by creating images of our own art and imagination because he wants us to be his image. Worship is the workshop where we are transformed into his image. When we are thus transformed into his image, we reflect his glory. Through the ministry of praise and prayer, the ministry of word and sacrament we are transformed to offer that spiritual worship that the apostle Paul tells us is acceptable to God (Rom. 12:1–2). This is what we mean when we say that worship is the work of the Holy Spirit in the body of Christ to the glory of the Father.

Chapter 2

Baptism

The Gospels tell us that God sent John the Baptist to prepare the way of the Lord. John prepared the way for the coming of Christ by calling the people of Israel to repentance and baptizing them in the Jordan River. It was significant that John carried out his ministry in the wilderness and that he baptized in the Jordan. The wilderness had always been a place of repentance, a place of preparation, a place of beginning anew. It was in the wilderness that God had for forty years prepared the children of Israel to enter the promised land. When the people had been prepared by learning the discipline of the law and by all the trials, wanderings, and testings that we read about in the story of the exodus, then they were led by Joshua across the Jordan River into the promised land. That John exercised his ministry in the wilderness and baptized in the Jordan implies a new entry into the promised land. It implied the reconstituting of Israel and the establishment of the long-promised kingdom of God.

Jesus, like many other Jews of his day, went out into the wilderness to hear John and accepted baptism at his hand. In doing this, Jesus became the new Joshua, leading the new Israel into the new kingdom of God. It was by God's specific direction that Jesus had been given the same name as Joshua. The name Jesus is but the Greek form of the name Joshua. Jesus was baptized not because he needed to have his sins washed away but because it was part of his ministry to lead the new Israel into the new kingdom of God. Through baptism Jesus entered into the kingdom of God, and through baptism the disciples followed Jesus into the kingdom. Even today, in baptism we too enter into the kingdom of God. Baptism is a prophetic sign at the beginning of our Christian life that we belong to the people of God. It is our entrance into the church.

Entering the kingdom of God was an act of repentance, and John made this clear in his preaching. When the Jews who went out to hear John were baptized, they were baptized "confessing their sins" (Matt. 3:6). John called on them to bear fruit that befitted repentance, to share their goods with one another, and to carry out their business and professions with honesty and fairness (Luke 3:14–17). Baptism is a call to make the crooked straight, but it is also a witness to Christ, the Lamb of God who takes away the sin of the world. The washing of water does not bear away the sin of the world but rather is a witness that in Christ there is the cleansing of sin. John the Baptist was very clear about how our sins are taken away. He told those whom he baptized, "Behold, the Lamb of God, who takes away the sin of the world!" (John 1:29). Christ is the Lamb of God. He by his sacrifice cleanses us from sin. The baptism that the disciples received from John pointed them to Christ. When we are baptized, the same thing happens to us. Our baptism points us to Christ.

When Jesus was baptized, the Holy Spirit descended upon him and the voice of the Father from heaven identified Jesus, "This is my beloved Son" (Matt. 3:17; Mark 1:11; Luke 3:22). So our baptism is a sign to us that we, too, are sons and daughters of our heavenly Father. We become sons and daughters of our heavenly Father by receiving his Spirit. We know that we are his children because his Spirit dwells within us. In baptism the promise of the prophets is fulfilled: "I will sprinkle clean water upon you, and you shall be clean. . . . A new heart I will give you, and a new spirit I will put within you; . . . and you shall be my people, and I will be your God" (Ezek. 36:25–28). With this, the New Covenant, which Jeremiah too had promised, had come into being (Jer. 31:31–34). As Joel had promised, God had indeed poured out his Spirit upon all flesh (Joel 2:28–32; Acts 2:17–21). In the baptism of Jesus the pouring out of God's Spirit became clearly visible, but in our baptisms the same thing happens. The giving of the Spirit is the invisible spiritual reality to which the sprinkling, pouring out, or washing of water gives witness. Baptism with water is the sign and promise of the giving of the Holy Spirit.

At the end of his ministry, our Lord sent out the apostles to make disciples of all nations by baptizing them and teaching them. When Jesus commissioned his disciples to baptize, he transformed the baptism administered by John in two very significant ways. First, he directed the apostles to baptize in the name of the Father and of the Son and of the Holy Spirit. By baptizing in the name of the Father, the apostles made it clear that those baptized have been adopted as children of the Father. By baptizing in the name of the Son, the apostles made it clear that those baptized were to be joined to Christ in his death and in his resurrection. By baptizing in the name of the Holy Spirit, they made it clear that baptism in water is a prophetic sign of being baptized in the Holy Spirit. Second, Jesus directed that they were to baptize not only the children of Israel but all nations. In doing this, Jesus opened up the kingdom of God to all peoples. John the Baptist had been sent to Israel; the apostles were sent to the whole world. Here is one of the most essential differences between the old kingdom of Israel and the new kingdom of God; the new kingdom of God was open to all the peoples of the earth. This was something very new, yet it was also something very old. When God first gave the Covenant to Abraham, he provided that in the seed of Abraham all the nations of the earth should be blessed. The New Covenant had been promised in the Old Covenant.

On the day of Pentecost, the apostles began to carry out the commission which Jesus had given them. Peter preached to the people of Jerusalem that God had raised up the Jesus who so recently had been crucified. God had appointed him the Lord of the kingdom the prophets had so long promised. With the proclamation of the new kingdom came the proclamation of a New Covenant, "Repent, and be baptized every one of you in the name of Jesus Christ for the forgiveness of your sins; and you shall receive the gift of the Holy Spirit. For the promise is to you and to your children and to all that are far off" (Acts 2:38–39). In this sermon Peter proclaimed the New Covenant. This New Covenant was like the Old Covenant in that God promised himself to his people, "I will walk among you, . . . and you shall be my people" (Lev. 26:12). Even in the form that the Covenant was given to Abraham and sealed by circumcision, it was a Covenant of grace. The Old Covenant promised the gift of the land and the establishment of descendants as numerous as the stars of the sky. The New Covenant, on the other hand, promised the pouring out of God's Spirit, salvation by grace, the putting away of sins, and everlasting life. Baptism was a sign of this New Covenant just as circumcision had been a sign of the Old Covenant. On the day of Pentecost three thousand people were baptized into the church. By receiving the covenant sign of baptism, they became participants in the New Covenant, children of the kingdom, and members of the church.

As the story of the earliest church unfolds through the book of Acts, we read of a number of different baptisms. The baptisms are at first baptisms of Jews in Jerusalem. Then we hear of the baptism of an Ethiopian, the baptism of a Greek woman, Lydia, and the baptism of the Philippian jailer and his whole house. In these baptisms the apostles were doing just what Jesus had directed them to do; they were making disciples of all nations. The New Covenant was being opened up to the Gentiles. We notice that the apostles baptized very quickly. Three thousand were baptized on the very day of Pentecost, the Ethiopian eunuch was baptized on the same day he heard the gospel, and the Philippian jailer and his family were baptized as soon as they cared for Paul's wounds. In the earliest Christian church baptism stood at the beginning of the Christian life.

The apostle Paul tells us that in baptism we are joined to Christ in his death and resurrection (Rom. 6:1–11; Col. 2:11–13). There are two possible ways of understanding this. First, one could understand this from the standpoint of the ancient Greek mystery religions. Understood as a Greek mystery, baptism would be a dramatic rite portraying the death and resurrection of Christ. When one went through such a rite, it was believed, that which had been dramatized would become a reality in the life of the one going through the rite. Paul probably did not understand baptism in terms of the Greek mystery religions. He was far too Jewish for that. A second explanation of these words of the apostle reaches back to the Hebrew concept of covenant. It understands baptism as a covenant sign given by Christ to his disciples. This covenant sign promises to us that our Lord will share with us the spiritual benefits, or consequences, of his death and resurrection. A covenant is an alliance or a bond that joins a community together. Once that community has been banded together, the members have a share in the spiritual endowments of the community. The church is a covenant community whose greatest endowments or treasures are freedom from sin, victory over death, and eternal life. Entering Christ's church by baptism, we share in his death to sin and his resurrection to new and eternal life. The fact that our union with Christ is to be understood as a covenantal union is made particularly clear by the strong emphasis the passage puts on the effects of receiving the covenant sign. The sign of baptism is not magic; it is a means of grace. God uses the sign to strengthen our faith, that we might "believe that we shall also live with him" (Rom. 6:8). God uses the sign to produce in us holiness of life, that "we too might walk in newness of life" (Rom. 6:4).

The New Testament tells us very little about how baptism was administered. We are often told that baptism was given by someone in the name of Jesus to someone else. We never hear of one baptizing oneself. Sometimes we hear of sermons preceding a baptism or of prayers following a baptism. We are not told what method of baptism was used, whether it was by total immersion, or by some form of pouring or sprinkling. Probably each of these was used at one time or another depending on the circumstances. Sometimes we hear of manifestations of the presence of the Holy Spirit, but not always (Matt. 3:16; Acts 2:3; 8:39; 9:17–18; 10:47–48). One thing is clear from numerous passages of the New Testament: baptism was understood primarily as a sign of washing (Acts 22:16; 1 Cor. 6:11; Eph. 5:26; Titus 3:5; Heb. 10:22). There are, of course, a number of other things that *baptism* means—for example, that we are joined to Christ in his death and resurrection, that we are born again from above, and that our hearts have been illumined by the word of truth—but the primary import of the sign of baptism is not these things. Baptism signifies above all the washing away of sin. This is the reason the word *baptism* was used. While in classical Greek baptism may have originally meant "to submerge or sink," in the popular Greek of New Testament times it meant "to wash" (Mark 7:4; Luke 11:38). One gets the impression that this baptismal washing was carried out in a very simple and straightforward manner. That, at least, is the case with the New Testament and with such very early Christian documents as the *Didache* and the *Apology* of Justin Martyr (ca.100–ca.165), which reflect the practice of the late first century and early second century.

It is another matter when one gets to the last half of the fourth century. By then the Christian sacrament of baptism had become an elaborate liturgical drama rivaling the initiation rites of the Greek mystery religions. The convert to Christianity was no longer baptized immediately, as had been the case in the New Testament, but was expected to go through as much as three years of preparation, instruction, and scrutiny before receiving baptism. We have several documents that tell us in considerable detail how baptism was celebrated at the end of the fourth century. First, there is a series of sermons *On the Sacraments* by Ambrose of Milan (ca. 339–97). Then there are a number of sermons by Augustine of Hippo that give us glimpses of how baptism was celebrated in North Africa. Most interesting of all is the *Mystagogical Catechism* of Cyril of Jerusalem (ca. 315–386). From these documents we find that several weeks before Easter those who were ready for baptism were solemnly enrolled. Each day they went to the church for special prayers, for instruction in the basic Christian beliefs, and for exorcism. A few days before Easter they were given the creed to be learned by heart, and probably the Lord's Prayer as well. On Saturday before Easter they returned to the church to make their profession of faith. Later that evening they returned to the church for the Easter vigil, a service that lasted all night. The baptism itself took place in the baptistry, a special building reserved for that purpose. With elaborate ceremony the baptismal font was blessed. In the baptistry those to be baptized removed their clothes. As a sort of final exorcism they were anointed with oil. Then they were immersed three times, in the name of the Father and of the Son and of the Holy Spirit. After this they were taken to the bishop, who laid hands on them and anointed them with chrism. Now they were dressed in white robes and led back into the church. All this had been timed in such a way that as the newly baptized reentered the church to receive their first Communion the light of Easter day was beginning to break.

Surely one would easily admit that this was all quite splendid as liturgical drama, but then one also has to admit that it was far removed from the sort of baptismal services held by the apostles. It no longer stood at the beginning of the Christian life. In fact we frequently hear that baptism was delayed until such a time late in life when one could be sure one could successfully lead a completely Christian life. Essentially, in that day one had to have already become Christian before one could qualify for baptism. Baptism had become a sign of salvation by works rather than salvation by grace.

By the beginning of the fifth century things began to change. Such church leaders as Augustine of Hippo (354–430) in the West and John Chrysostom (ca. 347–407) in the East began to urge Christians not to delay their baptism. Augustine, involved in a controversy with a very moralistic British monk named Pelagius (died after 418), argued that because baptism was a sacrament of grace it should be received at the beginning of the Christian life. Augustine claimed that ever since the days of the apostles it had been the practice to baptize the infant children of Christians. The baptism of infants, Augustine felt, demonstrated that salvation is a gracious gift of God. Furthermore Augustine pointed to the fact that baptism was a divine work and without that divine work no human work would avail for our salvation. In baptism, as Augustine understood it, the Christian is consecrated to serve God and equipped to do good works. From the time of Augustine on, the church began to emphasize the absolute necessity of baptism for salvation. Under the influence of Augustine, instead of delaying baptism to the end of life, it became increasingly frequent for the children of Christians to be baptized shortly after birth.

In the next thousand years baptism lost its importance in the worship of the church. More and more it became a semiprivate religious rite that celebrated the birth of children. The rite became overburdened with exorcisms and anointings, as though the main point of baptism were to chase out the devil. It became almost an act of magic by which one was automatically saved, rather than a sacrament or covenant sign. The absolute necessity of baptism for salvation had been so strongly insisted upon that the midwife often baptized a child immediately after birth, rather than risk the possibility that the child die unbaptized. Baptism was no longer preceded or followed with any kind of introductory instruction. The whole teaching ministry of the church declined seriously. By the time of the Protestant Reformation the rite of baptism was in serious need of reform.

In 1523 Martin Luther (1483–1546) published his *German Baptismal Book*. This was the first attempt to translate a liturgical form. It was primarily a German translation of the old Latin rite, yet several steps were taken to reform that rite. Within the next few months several Reformers published baptismal rites. In Zurich, Leo Jud (1482–1542) published a much more radical attempt at reforming the rite. In Nuremberg, Andreas Osiander (1498–1552) took another approach to the reform of the baptismal rite. He translated the text, but otherwise stuck closely to the old Latin rite. The Reformers of Strasbourg published a German baptismal service early in 1524 that might best be regarded as a rather timid attempt at reform, but within a year their reforms had become much bolder. The baptismal rite found in the *Strasbourg Psalter* of 1525 represents a thoroughgoing attempt to reform the rite.

In December 1524 the Reformers of Strasbourg published one of the most significant documents in the history of Reformed worship, *Grund und Ursach der Erneuerung*. We might freely translate the title of this work as "Fundamental Principles for the Reform of Worship." As the Reformers of Strasbourg saw it, the first thing necessary was to clear away from the rite of baptism all the extraneous exorcisms, anointings, consecrations, and other ceremonies that obscured the basic sign of washing. The Reformers were well aware that many of these ceremonies were very old, even if they did not go back to the days of the apostles. The problem was that these auxiliary rites, particularly exorcisms and anointings, confused the basic meaning of baptism. One did not need to assume that the children of Christians were demon-possessed. Likewise, the anointing with chrism after the baptism tended to imply that while baptism with water was a sign of the washing away of sins, something else was needed before the baptized receive the gift of the Holy Spirit. For the Reformers, baptism was a sign of both the washing away of sins and the pouring out of the Holy Spirit. They insisted that there was but one baptism and that the outward washing of water was a sign of the inward work of the Holy Spirit. Because the Reformers saw in the simple sign of washing such rich biblical meaning, they wanted to make this basic sign a prominent part of their worship.

Let us take a brief look at the way baptism was celebrated in the Reformed Church of Strasbourg at the end of the 1520s. Baptism was to be celebrated at the regular service of worship on the Lord's Day. After the sermon the parents and the child to be baptized met the minister at the baptismal font. There was first the Baptismal Exhortation. Here the minister set forth the promises of Scripture that are sealed in baptism, in the form of short commentary on one of the classic baptismal texts. A list of about a dozen is given. This was followed by the Baptismal Invocation, in which God was asked to send forth the Holy Spirit so that what is signified in the sign might become an inward reality in the life of the one baptized. The parents were admonished to bring up the child in the nurture and admonition of the Lord. An important part of this admonition dealt with the child receiving catechetical instruction when he or she came to the appropriate age. The child was then baptized by pouring water on the head three times, "in the name of the Father and of the Son and of the Holy Spirit." The impressive thing about this rite is the way the baptismal washing itself is emphasized. The use of trine pouring rather than a single immersion underlines the fact that it is washing which is primarily signified. One is struck by the fact that this rite includes no catechetical instruction, no confession of sin or act of repentance, and no profession of faith. Nevertheless, we can be quite certain that the Reformers considered all of these essential to baptism. These parts of the rite have been postponed. When the child gets to be ten or twelve years old, the child will be expected to learn the catechism and, having learned the catechism, to make a profession of faith. When one looks at the catechism that was used, it becomes particularly clear. It is indeed an elaborate confession of faith in which the Apostles' Creed is learned, explained, and confessed. Quite clearly those baptized are baptized unto repentance, unto the learning of all that Christ commanded, unto faith and the profession of faith; clearly baptism stands at the beginning of the Christian life as a sign of what the Christian life is to be.

Martin Bucer (1491–1551), the leading reformer of Strasbourg, was particularly concerned that baptism be performed as part of the regular worship of the Christian congregation, rather than as a private service conducted for the family. Bucer understood baptism as the sacrament of our incorporation into the church, the body of Christ. If indeed this was the case, then the church should be assembled when baptism was celebrated. Bucer and other Reformers tried to get parents to wait until the Sunday service to have their children baptized so that the sacrament of baptism might be a "Word made visible," to use the phrase of Augustine, reminding those present of the meaning of their own baptism. The logic of Bucer's teaching was quickly received by the other Reformers and the early Reformed church quickly restored baptism to the regular worship of the church.

Ulrich Zwingli (1484–1531), one of the most nimble-witted young scholars of his day, wrote a series of works on baptism in which he began to develop a very new approach to the understanding of baptism. Zwingli found it hard to believe that by sprinkling a few drops of water on the head of an infant, that child was automatically assured of eternal salvation. Zwingli reached back behind the theology of the Schoolmen and drew on the ideas of Tertullian (ca. 160–ca. 225), a North African theologian who wrote in about the year 200. It was Tertullian who really coined the word *sacrament*. In the Latin language the word *sacramentum* was used to speak of the oath of allegiance given by a soldier on entering military service. Zwingli, well trained by some of the outstanding literary scholars of the Renaissance, knew a great deal about how the earliest Christians used language. He could see how over the centuries the meaning of the word *sacrament* had changed. Zwingli began to understand that a sacrament was not a ritual that conferred salvation upon someone, but rather a sign or emblem that distinguished the members of a community. For Zwingli the ecclesial aspect of baptism was of greatest importance. Zwingli's successors would deepen his insights considerably, but Zwingli's basic insight is important. Baptism is a sign of our entrance into the church.

Certainly one of the Reformers' cardinal concerns in the reform of the sacrament of baptism was to find a way of understanding baptism that did not make it seem like a magical way of saving people by putting them through some sort of religious rite. For the Reformation it was very clear, "by grace you have been saved through faith" (Eph. 2:8). The ancient Greek and Roman mystery religions had taught that one would achieve salvation by going through their initiation rites, and it was natural and easy for the Christians of the third and fourth centuries to try to explain baptism in terms of these pagan mysteries or liturgical dramas. The Reformers soon found a much more biblical way of explaining baptism. The South German Reformers, particularly, were accomplished Old Testament scholars, and they soon discovered in the Old Testament concept of covenant a much better way of explaining the sacraments. They found that the New Testament used the language of Covenant theology to speak of the sacraments. They found evidences that the church fathers had also used covenant terms to speak of baptism and the Lord's Supper. It is probably to Zwingli, the reformer of Zurich, that credit should go for first developing this line of thought. (Quite possibly equal credit should go to John Oecolampadius [1482–1531], the reformer of the Swiss city of Basel.) Zwingli, very unhappy with the attempt of scholastic theology to explain baptism in terms of form and matter, suggested that baptism, like circumcision, should be understood as a sign of the Covenant (Gen. 17:11). From this point on, Covenant theology became the Reformed sacramental theology.

Both Zwingli and Oecolampadius died in 1531, early in the Reformation, and so it was left to Zwingli's successor, Henry Bullinger, to develop what today we call Covenant theology. Bullinger (1504–75), an excellent biblical philologist with a remarkable mastery of the ancient languages, carefully studied the biblical concepts of sign, symbol, and mystery, and particularly how these concepts are related to the concept of covenant. Bullinger showed that all the way through the Bible God made known his will through prophetic signs. These signs were visual evidences of God's promises. For example, after the great flood God promised never again to destroy the earth by a flood; seedtime and harvest, summer and winter, day and night would never again disappear. Then God gave a rainbow as a sign of that covenant promise (Gen. 9:13). The story of Gideon's fleece is an example of how God gave a sign to strengthen and confirm the faith of his people. God had promised Gideon victory. The sign of the fleece gave Gideon confidence that God would fulfill his promise (Judg. 6:36–40). The signs of the covenant in Scripture were God's way of making very clear to his people what he was about to do in their lives and thereby inspiring in them faith in himself. In the same way the signs Jesus performed announced and demonstrated the kingdom that was at hand. This particularly was the case with the signs reported in the Gospel of John. When Jesus turned the water into wine at the wedding of Cana, he demonstrated that he was the true bridegroom who had come to claim the bride. We read, "This, the first of his signs, Jesus did at Cana in Galilee, and manifested his glory; and his disciples believed in him" (John 2:11). The sign inspired the faith of the disciples. By explaining the sacraments in terms of the biblical concept of covenant signs, the Reformers were able to show how the sacraments were means of grace, that is, they were able to show the importance of the sacraments to saving faith. The function of the sacrament is to inspire, strengthen, and confirm faith.

For the Reformed understanding of baptism, the doctrine of the Holy Spirit is fundamental. In the fifth or sixth century, the sacrament of baptism began to be split into two sacraments. Baptism proper was understood as the washing away of sins, while the sacrament of confirmation was understood to confer the gift of the Holy Spirit. The Reformers were very much opposed to any understanding of baptism in which baptism with water was one thing and baptism of the Holy Spirit was something else. Using Augustinian terms, they saw baptism with water as the outward sign of baptism with the Holy Spirit, which was the inward grace. The physical washing with water did not save those who were baptized; rather the Holy Spirit in the hearts of the baptized gave them faith and thereby cleansed them from their sins. For the Reformers it became very important, then, that at the time of baptism the church should pray that the Holy Spirit accomplish inwardly the purification and sanctification that the outward sign of baptismal washing promised.

In 1523, when Martin Luther published his first German baptismal service, he had put a great emphasis on the prayers that accompanied the rite of baptism. As Luther saw it, these baptismal prayers should set the example of the prayer of the church. When someone is received into the church by baptism, it is the responsibility of the church continually to support that one in prayer. Bucer took up Luther's teaching that baptismal prayer is a type of prayer which is a contin- ual experience of the Christian throughout life. The Christian should continu- ally pray to be cleansed from sin and filled with the new life of the Holy Spirit. From Luther on, the Baptismal Epiclesis[1] or Baptismal Invocation has been an important part of the rite. In fact, without understanding the epicletic nature of baptism, one would miss one of the major facets of the Protestant understand- ing of the sacrament. It is the epicletic nature of the sacraments which distin- guishes them from magic.

Still another reform that the earliest Protestants were intent on making in the church's practice of baptism was the revival of some sort of catechetical instruc- tion. They remembered that Jesus had sent out the apostles to make disciples by baptizing them and by teaching them. Baptism, they believed, entailed teaching. The Reformers very much admired the institution of the catechumenate, which had so flourished in the fourth century. They tried to find some way of recover- ing something like the catechetical instruction of that period, taking into account the fact they were baptizing infants. The Reformers were amazingly successful in establishing regular catechetical instruction for children. By 1525, a few short years after the beginning of the Reformation, the churches of Zurich and Basel had regular religious instruction for children. In Strasbourg the pastors con- ducted weekly catechetical services for children in each parish. In 1527 Stras- bourg's Wolfgang Capito (1478–1541) published a catechism. About the same time, Oecolampadius published his first catechism in Basel. In 1528 Konrad Sam (fl. 1520–40) in Ulm published a catechism as well. *Luther's Shorter Catechism* of 1529 was the classic Protestant catechism. In fact, with the Reformation the min- istry of Christian teaching prospered generally. At the time children were pre- sented for baptism, their parents were asked to promise that their children would receive the regular catechetical instruction that all the early Reformed churches instituted for that purpose. After the children had received this instruction, they were asked to make a profession of faith before the whole congregation and then were admitted to Communion.

By 1525 the Reformed churches of the Upper Rhineland were just beginning to bring into effect their reforms of the rite of baptism. At this point they became aware of the position of the Anabaptists. The Anabaptists had a very different approach to the reform of the rite of baptism. They urged that only those be bap- tized who had undergone a conversion experience, had a conscious faith, and led a truly Christian life. They understood baptism primarily as a symbolic confes- sion of faith on the part of one who was already a Christian. To be baptized was a visual confession of faith that one had already been cleansed from sin. The Anabaptists claimed that in New Testament times the apostles had not baptized children and that it was only in later centuries that infants began to be baptized.

At first several of the Reformers of classical Protestantism were somewhat swayed by the position of the Anabaptists, but within a short time they began to see that the Anabaptist position was inconsistent with the Reformers' theology of grace. The Reformers were not convinced that the apostles had not baptized children, pointing to several passages of the New Testament that indicated whole families had been baptized (Acts 16:25–34; 18:8; 1 Cor. 1:16). John Oecolampadius, who had a profound knowledge of the literature of the early church, pointed to passages in the writings of Tertullian, Origen (ca. 185–ca. 254), and Cyprian (ca. 200–258) which indicated that the church had baptized the infant children of Christians from earliest times. These documents taken as a whole indicate that at the beginning of the second century it was taken for granted that the practice of baptizing the infant children of Christians went back to apostolic times. In defending infant baptism, once again the Reformers turned to the Bible, where children participated with their parents in the covenant. Children belonged to the people of God just as surely as their parents. It was Henry Bullinger who most fully worked out the ideas first developed by Zwingli and Oecolampadius. Bullinger pointed to the continuity between the Old Covenant and the New Covenant. As Bullinger put it, in the end there is but one covenant, the eternal covenant. The New Covenant is a fulfilling and opening up of the Old Covenant. If the Old Covenant included children, how much more should the New Covenant include children.

One of the strengths of Covenant theology is that it does full justice to the biblical concept of the unity of the family. Just as it was possible for Joshua to say, "As for me and my house, we will serve the LORD" (Josh. 24:15), so it was possible that Paul could say to the Philippian jailer, "Believe in the Lord Jesus, and you will be saved, you and your household" (Acts 16:31). It was very important for biblical peoples not only that God bless them but that the divine blessing be passed on to their children and grandchildren. When God first gave the covenant to Abraham, an essential aspect of that covenant was the blessing of the future generation of Abraham's seed. This is no less true in the New Testament than in the Old. When Peter proclaimed the New Covenant in his sermon on the day of Pentecost he made it clear that "the promise is to you and to your children" (Acts 2:38–39).

Equally important in Covenant theology is its recognition of the importance of baptismal typology. For the theologians of the New Testament church, typology was a significant way of understanding spiritual truths. While typology may not be in vogue today, one needs only to read the epistle to the Hebrews to see how important typology was to the earliest Christians. In 1 Peter baptism is understood in terms of the story of Noah and the flood (1 Pet. 3:20–21). The apostle Paul sees in the passage through the Red Sea a type of baptism and in circumcision a shadow of things to come (1 Cor. 10:1–2; Col. 2:11–12, 17). During the patristic period the explanation of the sacraments by means of the Old Testament types was exceedingly popular. Tertullian, Ambrose of Milan, Hilary of Poitiers (ca. 315–367), and Cyril of Alexandria (ca. 375–444) have left us elaborate explanations of the baptismal typology. In fact, one could say that the classic way of explaining baptism is by recounting the Old Testament types of baptism. As early as the beginning of the third century, we know that it was customary to read the Old Testament types of baptism at the baptismal service. Even the baptismal prayers drew heavily on the imagery of Noah and the flood, the crossing of the Red Sea, going over the Jordan, Jonah and the whale, and the three young men in the fiery furnace. Martin Luther in writing prayers for his first German baptismal rite did full justice to the baptismal types. Luther's lead in this matter was followed by both Leo Jud and Ulrich Zwingli.

Among the most important types of baptism should be reckoned circumcision. In Genesis 17, which tells us of the institution of circumcision, we read that circumcision is a sign of the covenant God made to Abraham. For the South German reformers the type of circumcision was of particular value in understanding baptism. The Scriptures are very clear that Abraham was justified by faith: "Abraham believed God, and it was reckoned to him as righteousness" (Gen. 15:6; Rom. 4:1–6). Further, the apostle Paul tells us that Abraham "received circumcision as a sign or seal of the righteousness which he had by faith while he was still uncircumcised" (Rom. 4:11). The Reformers saw the possibility of explaining baptism the same way, namely, that while we are justified by faith, the sacrament is given as a sign or seal of a righteousness that is to be had by faith alone. This cleared up for the Reformers the problem of the relation of faith and sacrament, but it did more. It also showed the Reformers how they could understand the baptism of infants. God had specifically directed Abraham to circumcise his male descendants as infants. That is, while Abraham received circumcision as a seal of a faith he already had, his descendants were to receive that same sign as a sign of a faith and a righteousness they were yet to have. For Abraham and his descendants, that rite of circumcision became the divinely given sign and seal of the covenant promises.

More and more the Reformers came to understand baptism in terms not only of the covenant signs found in Scripture but also in terms of the prophetic signs of Scripture. They identified a whole series of prophetic signs that they found in both the Old and New Testaments. When Jacob laid hands on the two sons of Joseph, it was clearly a prophetic act. Jeremiah took the potter's vessel and broke it as a prophetic act signaling the destruction of Jerusalem. Jesus' act of cleansing the Temple was a prophetic sign. Perhaps the prophetic sign most clearly analogous to the baptism of children is the story of Samuel anointing David to be king while David was still a shepherd boy. It would be many years before that prophetic act would be fulfilled. Surely David understood very little of what Samuel did to him. It was only as the years went by that the meaning of that act unfolded. Yet that act was there; it was there quite indelibly nurturing the faith of David. David believed God would be faithful to the promise, and indeed God was. The sign was given to awaken faith and nurture faith.

The question of infant baptism had been debated for more than ten years before John Calvin began to exercise theological leadership in the Reformed churches. He too gave great attention to the question of the baptism of infants. It cannot be said, as some have recently tried to say, that the Reformers baptized infants only because it was the common custom of the time and the Reformers never got around to thinking through the question. In the chapter of his *Insti-*

tutes of the Christian Religion that he devotes to the question of infant baptism, Calvin summarizes the argument from Covenant theology. Baptism when it is administered to children is a particularly clear sign that God out of his grace has taken the initiative for our salvation. If the classical Reformers of sixteenth-century Protestantism continued the practice of administering baptism to infants, it was because they had a very strong theology of grace. While the Reformers were strongly Augustinian, their opponents were openly Pelagian! The Anabaptists believed in decisional regeneration. That is, they believed one is saved by making a decision for Christ. There is a big difference between decisional regeneration and justification by faith. While the baptism of infants was perfectly consistent with a strong doctrine of grace and with the doctrine of justification by faith, it was not consistent with any kind of theology that makes salvation a matter of human decisions.

When Calvin published the *Genevan Psalter* of 1545, the Reformers of classical Protestantism had thought over the Anabaptist challenge very carefully for almost twenty years. The Reformers had thought out their baptismal rite both over against the old Latin rites and over against the Anabaptist teaching. This had the effect of making the rite very well balanced. Let us look at this Genevan baptismal rite.

The rubrics at the beginning of the rite specify that children are to be presented for baptism at a regular service of worship, for baptism is a solemn reception into the church and therefore should be celebrated in the presence of the congregation. After the sermon the children are to be presented, and the minister is to begin the service, "Our help is in the name of the Lord, who made heaven and earth. Amen." Then the minister is to ask, "Do you present this child to be baptized?" The parents answer that they do. The minister gives the Baptismal Exhortation much in the same way as at Strasbourg. Next follows the Baptismal Invocation. The prayer begins with an anamnesis of God's covenant with Abraham, "Lord God, Father eternal and almighty, since by your infinite mercy, you have promised to be not only our God, but the God and Father of our children as well . . ."[2] The prayer continues asking for the forgiveness of sins, the gift of faith, the sanctification of God's Spirit. It concludes with the saying of the Lord's Prayer. The prayers being finished, the parents are asked to promise that the child will receive catechetical instruction and be brought up in the nurture and admonition of the Lord. Notice that these promises are made by the parents not the godparents. The reason is to be found in Covenant theology. The children are baptized because of the faith of their parents, not because godparents have vicariously confessed faith for them. Such promises having been made, the parents are asked to name the child. It is quite clear that in the Genevan baptismal rite the child is given a Christian name. This was not done in the German-speaking Reformed churches of the Rhineland. Even before the Reformation it seems to have been a peculiarly French custom. Nevertheless the Reformers had noted that according to the Gospel of Luke it was at circumcision that names were given to children (Luke 1:59–60; 2:21). When one sees how important the Reformers considered the relationship between circumcision and baptism, one is not at all surprised to discover that the Reformers encouraged the practice of giving Christian names at baptism. The parents give the name to the child and the minister baptizes the child, "in the name of the Father, and of the Son, and of the Holy Spirit." The baptism is performed by a single sprinkling. This done, the minister gives a benediction to the child as well as to the parents.

Like the Reformed baptismal rite of Strasbourg, the rite contains neither catechetical instruction nor a profession of faith. Catechetical instruction was postponed until later years. The church of Geneva provided very thorough catechetical instruction for children from ten to twelve years old. Having received that instruction, the children made their profession of faith and were admitted to Communion. There was no thought that the baptism was incomplete until the catechetical instruction had been received and the profession of faith made. Rather, the Reformers understood that baptism entailed these things. The sign of washing was complete in itself, but its meaning would be unfolded through the whole of life.

In the Reformed understanding of baptism, baptism is a prophetic sign at the beginning of the Christian life, which continues to unfold throughout the whole of life. The sign of baptism claims for us the washing away of sins and calls us to newness of life. The sign of baptism calls us to repentance and to the profession of Christian faith. Whenever we confess our sins in prayers of confession or profess our faith by saying the Apostles' Creed, we are living out our baptism. Baptism is not something that is done once and then is finished and over. It is something that shapes the whole of the Christian life, from the very beginning to the very end. Baptism is a means of grace. It is the work of the Holy Spirit in our lives that brings about and fulfills what the sign of baptism had promised. That inward working of the Holy Spirit takes place through the whole of life until at last we die in Christ and are raised in Christ.

In the seventeenth century the Puritans developed this theme at considerable length. The Westminster Larger Catechism taught the importance of "improving our baptism." By this the Westminster Divines meant that Christians should "make good use of" their baptisms. This was to be done all through life, especially in times of trial and temptation. By a serious and thankful consideration of the divine promises made to us in our baptism, our faith is strengthened. Our assurance of God's grace and favor is refreshed. Matthew Henry (1662–1714), the great Bible commentator, wrote a treatise on baptism about the year 1700. Henry had been brought up and nourished by the practical Puritan piety of the Westminster Assembly. His writings are a good reflection of Reformed spirituality at the beginning of the eighteenth century. How much of this work is devoted to the question of "improving one's baptism"! For Matthew Henry the fact of his baptism as an infant determined the whole course of his life. He understood by this that from earliest childhood he had been called to the service of God and empowered by the gifts of God's Spirit to carry out that service. Baptism was the sign under which the whole of his life was lived.

The eighteenth century brought a radical change. It was an age of social revolution and religious revival, the time of both the American Revolution and the French Revolution, both the Methodist Revival and the Great Awakening. Count Nicholas von Zinzendorf (1700–1760), George Whitefield (1714–70), and Gilbert Tennent (1703–64) were as revolutionary in the church as Patrick Henry (1736–99) and John Adams (1735–1826) were in politics. Many Christians began to put the emphasis on conversion rather than on baptism as the way to salvation. This is not at all surprising. What could be more natural than that a century of revolution should understand the Christian faith in terms of conversion! In America the Great Awakening emphasized a very intense personal religious experience and presented the conversion experience as the means of entering this deeper kind of personal life. The preachers of the Great Awakening claimed that one's baptism in early childhood did not assure one of salvation. Baptism was no guarantee of eternal life. Much more important was a conversion experience. In fact, many preachers of the Great Awakening saw no real significance to baptism at all. Congregationalists, Methodists, and Presbyterians continued to baptize infants, but covenantal theology was largely forgotten.

Against this background Horace Bushnell (1802–76) wrote his famous *Christian Nurture*. Bushnell, who was pastor of North Congregational Church in Hartford, Connecticut, had himself, while he was a student at Yale, gone through the sort of conversion experience that the Great Awakening had fostered. His first ten years in the pastorate had been very uneventful. No revival came to his congregation, even though he prayed fervently and worked very hard. He began to question the idea that one had to go through a conversion experience to become a Christian. Why could not someone who was born and nurtured in a Christian family simply grow up a Christian? Had not the apostle Paul advocated that Christian parents bring up their children in the nurture and admonition of the Lord (Eph. 6:4)? Through a study of Richard Baxter (1615–91) and John Calvin (1509–64) he began to rediscover the covenantal understanding of baptism. He came to have a new appreciation of the significance of the covenant given to Abraham and his descendants (Gen. 17:7). On the basis of this passage he decided that Christian faith was not only an individual experience but a family experience as well. The Christian life had a community dimension as well as an individual dimension. If this is the case, the maintaining of a Christian family life was of the utmost importance. There was no reason, Bushnell taught, that a child receiving Christian nurture should not from earliest childhood have a consciousness of being a Christian so that, as he or she grew older, a profession of Christian faith would come of itself. Just as in the parable of Jesus, the seed of the Word striking root in good soil grows of itself. The Word of God has its own power within it. It grows slowly, to be sure, but it grows, first the blade, then the ear, then the grain in the ear (Mark 4:28). Bushnell's thought led to a new appreciation of the sacrament of baptism and gave a renewed emphasis to Christian education.

In the twentieth century the whole concept of sacrament went through a radical reinvestigation. Richard Reitzenstein (1861–1931), Franz Joseph Dölger

(1879–1940), Odo Casel (1886–1948), and others with a strong interest in the study of comparative religions suggested that sacraments came not from biblical or Hebrew origins but from Greek sources. Indeed, they claimed, the Christian sacraments and particularly baptism are the heritage of the Greek mystery religions rather than the Jewish Scriptures. Ideas like this were very popular in Germany during the first half of the twentieth century. The effect was to encourage the revival of a lush ceremonial around the sacraments. The liturgical renewal movement, made popular by the Second Vatican Council, tried to bring back many of the rites that the Reformers had so carefully removed. Particularly notable was the addition of various forms of exorcism, the renunciation of the devil, baptismal anointing, and the sign of the cross. Efforts were made to revive the rites of the Easter vigils of the fourth and fifth centuries, which had dramatized the death and resurrection of Christ. It took a generation, but gradually younger scholars were able to show the fallacy of this interpretation. With the studies of such scholars as Rudolf Schnackenburg (1914–), André Benoît (1919–), and Joachim Jeremias (1900–1979) it became more and more obvious that the Christian sacraments do, in fact, come to us from biblical sources. The sacraments are not to be understood in terms of the mystery religions of Hellenistic paganism. The basis for reviving the ceremonial of late antiquity has become increasingly questionable.

Baptism is the presupposition and basis of all Christian worship. Not only does baptism call us to holiness of life, it consecrates us to the priestly service of prayer and praise (1 Pet. 2:4–10; Rev. 1:5–6). In baptism we are set apart for God's service. At the center of that service is the service of worship. Baptism is a sign at the beginning of the Christian life that to serve God we must turn away from all other forms of service to the gods of this world. It is a sign that to serve God in truth we must be anointed by God's Spirit. It is God's Spirit who fits us and empowers us for his service. True worship is God's work within us, and we serve him best when we give ourselves to him and allow ourselves to become the members of his body. When our hands and our tongues are moved by the Spirit of Christ, we do the work of Christ in this world to the glory of the Father who is in heaven.

Chapter 3

The Lord's Day

Concern for the observance of the Lord's Day has always been a strong feature of Reformed worship. One notices that the Westminster Directory for Worship devotes a whole chapter to the observance or sanctification of the Lord' s Day. Let us look carefully at the commandment to remember the Sabbath and its Christian interpretation.

The Sabbath Day was, first of all, a day in which God commanded his people to remember. This word, *remember,* is a very rich word in the biblical vocabulary. The commandment means much more than "Don't forget today is the Sabbath." The commandment has in mind far more than a mere mental noting of the fact that it is the Sabbath Day when it rolls around each week. It has much more the meaning of, "Hold a service of memorial on the Sabbath." This becomes very clear when one compares the version of the Ten Commandments found in Exodus with the version in Deuteronomy. In Deuteronomy we find that the fourth commandment begins, "Observe the sabbath day" (Deut. 5:12). To remember the Sabbath Day means to observe the day, to celebrate the religious rites appropriate to the day.

What then was to be celebrated on this day? The Sabbath was a day in which a memorial was held celebrating God's works of creation and redemption. The celebrating of this memorial had the function of transmitting the witness to God's mighty acts, the creation of light out of darkness, the creation of heaven and earth, Adam and Eve, the call of Abraham, the deliverance of the children of Israel from Egypt, and the gift of the law and the promised land. When Jesus at the Passover shared the bread and the cup with his disciples, he told them that from now on they were to do this in remembrance of him. The sharing of bread and wine together with the recounting of God's mighty acts of salvation in Christ, his birth, ministry, suffering, death and resurrection, was the new memorial. To be sure, it was a memorial of the first creation, just as the old Sabbath had been, but it was more; it was a memorial of the new creation in Christ. It was a memorial of the new creation of which the first creation was a type and a promise. To be sure, the sharing of bread and wine was a memorial of the deliverance from Egypt, just as the old Passover had been, but even more, it was a memorial of the deliverance from sin and death accomplished in the fulfillment of the paschal mystery by Jesus. The new memorial celebrated Christ's passage from death to life, "out of this world to the Father" (John 13:1).

The Old Testament Sabbath was not only a day of remembrance; it was also a day of rest. "Remember the sabbath day, to keep it holy; . . . in it you shall not do any work" (Exod. 20:8–10). The two are intimately related to each other. In order to celebrate God's work, we refrain from our human works. John Calvin (1509–64) in his passage in the *Institutes* on the fourth commandment makes a great point of this: "[U]nder the repose of the seventh day the heavenly Lawgiver meant to represent to the people of Israel spiritual rest, in which believers ought to lay aside their own works to allow God to work in them."[1]

Let us look for a moment at the divine works of which the Old Testament Sabbath was a memorial. The creation story at the very beginning of Genesis explains the creation in terms of the six days of creation and the seventh day of rest: here we see very clearly that the Sabbath Day is a memorial of creation. The Scriptures are no less clear that the Sabbath was a memorial of deliverance from Egypt. In the version of the Ten Commandments found in Deuteronomy we read, "Observe the sabbath day; . . . in it you shall not do any work, you, or your son, or your daughter, or your manservant, or your maidservant. . . . You shall remember that you were a servant in the land of Egypt, and the LORD your God brought you out thence with a mighty hand and an outstretched arm; therefore the LORD your God commanded you to keep the sabbath day" (Deut. 5:12–15). Here the diaconal aspect of worship is clearly underlined. By releasing laborers and servants from servile work on the Sabbath, one celebrated release from slavery in Egypt.

The memorial, however, is not only a celebration of the past but a promise of the future as well. The consummation of history was understood as a Sabbath rest (Ps. 95:11). Jewish thinkers in ancient times often explained that just as there were seven days of creation, so there would be seven ages of history and finally seven ages of consummation. Particularly the Jewish apocalyptic writers of the two centuries immediately before Jesus developed these themes in a great variety of ways. During this time the Jewish messianic hopes and expectations became closely associated with speculations about the Sabbath and its implications for the future. We find some of this sabbatarian speculation concerning the ages to come in the book of Daniel. In the book of Revelation it is even more highly developed. The basic idea behind all this was that just as there were seven days of creation at the beginning, so there would be seven days of consummation at the end. The last day was thought of as a Sabbath of Sabbaths, a year of release, and this final Sabbath was to be brought in by the Messiah, who was the bringer of the new Sabbath. It is in the light of this Jewish eschatological sabbatarianism that many of the sayings of Jesus about the Sabbath are to be understood. Let us now turn to consider how Jesus understood the Sabbath and its observance.

First of all, we should notice how often the Gospels specifically tell us that Jesus healed people on the Sabbath (Mark 3:1ff.; Luke 13:10–13; 14:1–4; John 5:1–10; 9:1–8). The frequency of healings might even suggest that Jesus very purposely chose to heal on the Sabbath. He did this not to shock people, not to break the law, not to show that the law was worn out and old-fashioned, but rather as a sign that the day of release had come. When Jesus healed the woman with the crooked back, he explained, "And ought not this woman, a daughter of Abraham whom Satan bound for eighteen years, be loosed from this bond on the sabbath day?" (Luke 13:16). The Sabbath that the Messiah brought in was a day of release from the bondage of Satan. Healing is not a human work but a divine work. The work of Jesus in releasing the woman did not hinder the Sabbath rest but rather established a deeper quality of Sabbath rest. The old Sabbath rest was in fact a sign or type of the deeper Sabbath rest Jesus would bring. The Sabbath rest remembered the release from the bondage of Egypt but promised, as a sort of prophetic sign, release from the bondage of Satan.

The meaning of all this becomes even clearer, however, when we consider what great importance the New Testament gives to the fact that the resurrection took place on the first day of the week. All the Gospels are very clear and very explicit about this. The first day of the week was the day of the resurrection, the day when Jesus came to his disciples and broke bread with them. Jesus took the initiative of making this the day of Christian worship, the day of remembrance, the day on which, with the breaking of the bread and the sharing of the cup, the church celebrated the memorial of Christ's passage from death to life. On this day the risen Jesus again and again came to his disciples as they broke bread. The story of Jesus coming to two of his disciples on the road to Emmaus, on the first day of the week, first explaining to them the Scriptures and then breaking bread with them, is the prototype of the Christian Lord's Day service. The earliest Christians worshiped on the first day of the week because this was the day the risen Jesus came to them. This was the first day of a new age, the eighth day of the old age. This was the new Sabbath, brought in by the Messiah, the new Sabbath of release from the bondage of Satan, which Jesus fulfilled by appearing to his disciples and eating with them.

The question is, did Jesus or did someone else change the Sabbath from Saturday to Sunday and make of the first day of the week the Christian Sabbath? The New Testament gives us no clear statement as to what happened or how it happened. All we know is that already in New Testament times Christians celebrated worship on the first day of the week and that they called it "the Lord's Day" (Acts 20:7; 1 Cor. 16:2; Rev. 1:10). It is hard to imagine how any Jew would tamper with something so sacred as the Sabbath. Certainly the disciples would never have done it on their own. One can only imagine Jesus himself doing it, and then only if he had a profound sense of his having divine authority. Could we possibly imagine that Lord's Day worship was something that gradually evolved because someone thought it was a meaningful idea and after a while it gradually caught on? Never! The Sabbath had been established by divine authority, and only by divine authority could it have been changed. The old Sabbath would only come to an end when the anointed Son of God brought in the final Sabbath of the last day, the day of the Lord. If the first Christians worshiped on the Lord's Day, it was because they believed that Jesus, by his resurrection, had brought in the final age. The Lord's Day took the place of the old Sabbath because it was on that day when Jesus came to his disciples and celebrated with them the memorial of his entry into the new age, his passage from death to life. This was the mighty act of redemption toward which all the others had pointed, and this was what the first Christians celebrated when they broke bread and shared the cup in remembrance of Jesus. It is in a very real sense Jesus himself who, fulfilling the old Sabbath, established the Lord's Day. But did Jesus give us a specific word or a concrete act by which he instituted the Lord's Day? This he did when he commanded his disciples to "Do this in remembrance of me," when he rose on the first day of the week, and when he came to his disciples and ate with them on that day, which was from then on his day.

Let us look a bit more closely at some examples of Lord's Day worship in the primitive Christian church. On the day of Pentecost, the fiftieth day, the first day of the week after seven weeks, the Holy Spirit descended upon the church, and the first believers were baptized. Had it already, after only a few weeks, become customary for all the Christians to gather together on the morning of the first day of the week? Notice that it was on the Lord's Day that our Lord poured out his Holy Spirit. The first day of the week was not only the day of resurrection but the day of giving the Spirit as well. Later on we read that in Ephesus the Christians were gathered together to break bread on the first day of the week (Acts 20:7–11). Here the text seems to imply that it was the regular procedure to meet on the first day of the week and break bread. Again, it was probably because the first day of the week was already the day of Christian worship that Paul tells the Corinthians to make their collection for the saints of Jerusalem on that day (1 Cor. 16:2).

In the book of Revelation, however, we find the most elaborate development of the theme of the Lord's Day of which all Sabbaths and Sabbaths of Sabbaths are the prophetic type. It is the day of rest, the day of consummation, the day of never-ceasing praise and glory. The book of Revelation makes abundant use of the sabbatarian speculations of the Jewish apocalyptic writers. From the book of Revelation we discover what a rich theology of the Lord's Day the New Testament church had developed.

Following the history of Christian worship down through the centuries, we discover that the earliest documents make a considerable point of the fact that Christian worship is held on the first day of the week. In the description of Christian worship given by the Roman writer Pliny the Younger (61–ca. 113) in A.D. 110, it is specifically noted that it takes place on the first day of the week. Justin Martyr (ca. 100–ca. 165), writing about A.D. 160 in his *Apology*, says, "On the day which is called Sunday, all who live in the cities or in the countryside gather together in one place." In another one of Justin's works, *Dialogue with Trypho*, we find a roughly developed theology of Lord's Day observance. It was not, however, until the first Christian emperors, in the fourth century, that Sunday became a public holiday and a day of rest for pagan and Christian alike. There was nothing illegitimate about this development. It was only natural and proper that the day of worship should be the day of rest. Only with the Christian emperors was it possible for the day of worship to become a public day of rest.

Starting in the third and fourth centuries, the church developed an elaborate liturgical calendar of annual feasts and fast days. While the Christian observance of Easter and Pentecost may well have gone back to the first century, Christmas and Epiphany developed much later. Christmas we know to have been the remodeling of the pagan celebration of the sun god. Lent started out not as a time of remembering our Lord's passion but as a time of penitential preparation for baptism at the Easter vigil. Advent and Lent became increasingly important as the whole of Christian devotion became obsessed with penance. Especially in the middle of the fifth century, when the barbarian invasions had engulfed the civilized world, penance became the prevailing temper of much Christian devotion. Christians were in almost continual lamentation.

It was in this period that the liturgical calendar began to become so elaborate. Asceticism set the foundation of much in the liturgical calendar. Advent and Lent were, above all, seasons of fasting. During the Middle Ages the season of Advent was carefully cultivated, but the twelve days of Christmas were of considerably less concern. Particularly in the West, the penitential season of Lent called forth the most lush devotional practices, while the joyful seven weeks of Easter remained secondary. Advent and Lent, rather than the feasts of Christmas and Easter, became the religious seasons of the year. The development of the calendar of the saints goes back quite far in the history of the church, but during the Middle Ages it became increasingly elaborate. On the other hand, it was only toward the beginning of the fifth century that the Marian feasts took on their importance.

In the course of the Middle Ages, the liturgical calendar showed great vitality and developed with flamboyant complexity. The multiplication of feasts and saints' days tended to obscure the celebration of the Lord's Day. Penitential purple was even allowed to veil the Easter glory of Sunday. By the beginning of the sixteenth century, the trimming of the calendar had an obvious place on the agenda of church reform. Different Reformers had different approaches to calendar reforms. The Lutherans emphasized the liturgical seasons, giving great importance to the penitential seasons of Advent and Lent. The Lutherans also celebrated most of the major feasts of the Christian year: Christmas, Circumcision, Epiphany, Good Friday, Easter, Ascension, and Pentecost. They also observed those saints' days that commemorated saints mentioned in the New Testament. The Lutheran calendar represented a moderate reform. Its strong point was that it provided a christocentric celebration of the calendar that emphasized the central acts of redemption: the incarnation, the passion, the resurrection and the glorification of Christ.

The South German churches took a much more incisive look at the problem and began to delve into the deeper meaning of the biblical sign of the Sabbath. They had no more begun their reform than some of the Anabaptists proposed going back to observing the Jewish Sabbath, claiming that Sunday worship was the invention of the Emperor Constantine. The Strasbourg reformer Wolfgang Capito (1478–1541), a colleague of Martin Bucer (1491–1551), studied the matter very carefully, and his work had great influence on the practice of Reformed churches. Capito was uniquely qualified to study this matter. Not only was he one of the pioneering Old Testament scholars of the day, he was trained in the history of the law, having a doctorate in law as well as in theology. Not only did he study the Old Testament concept of Sabbath, but he was able to study the development of the Lord's Day observance in Roman law during the period of the Christian emperors. As Capito and the Strasbourg reformers understood it, the question was basically one of the relation of the Old Testament to the New Testament. Capito in a typically Augustinian manner found a strong continuity between the two Testaments. He stressed the position that the Old Testament prefigured and promised the New. With an appeal to Hebrews 4, Capito claimed that the old Sabbath was a sign of the rest and salvation that would begin with the resurrection of Christ. The old Sabbath was a promise of a day of rest that the Jews under the law had not yet experienced (Heb. 4:8). While that day of rest was the final day of consummation at the end of history, it is, even in this life, already experienced in the Lord's Day, the day of resurrection, which clearly, according to the Gospels, is the first day of the week. Ever since this basic study of Wolfgang Capito, Reformed churches have given special attention to the liturgical implications of the Lord's Day.

In the early 1530s there was considerable discussion in the Reformed church of Strasbourg as to whether other feast days should be observed in addition to the Lord's Day. Capito, good patristic scholar that he was, turned his attention to the quartodeciman controversy in the second century, because much of the earliest thinking of Christians regarding the calendar came to light in the course of that discussion. The church of Strasbourg observed Easter and Pentecost from the beginning of the Reformation. About the celebration of Christmas there was considerable reservation, because the Reformers knew from patristic sources that it had not been observed until the fourth century. Within a few years the Reformed church calendar was fairly well established. The heart of it was the weekly observance of the resurrection on the Lord's Day. Instead of liturgical seasons being observed, "the five evangelical feast days" were observed: Christmas, Good Friday, Easter, Ascension, and Pentecost. These were chosen because they were understood to mark the essential stages in the history of salvation. Lent and Advent were not observed because of their basically ascetic and penitential orientation. Saints' days were not observed at all except insofar as it seemed appropriate on weekdays to mention the witness of the martyrs and the example of holy men and women who had gone before. John Oecolampadius (1482–1531), the reformer of Basel and one of the leading patristic scholars of his day, was concerned that the church should maintain a remembrance of the great Christians of the past, particularly the martyrs. He recommended that this be done during the weekday services through sermon illustrations. We find much the same sentiments echoed by the English Puritan Richard Baxter (1615–91). Although the Reformed church did not want a calendar of saints, it had no intention of forgetting about great Christians of the past.

In England, the Anglican party pressed for a more elaborate observance of feasts, penitential seasons, and saints' days. The calendar reform became a major point of tension between the Anglican party and the Puritan party. The so-called "High Churchmen" put a greater and greater emphasis on the feasts and the liturgical seasons while the more radical Puritans underlined Sabbath observance to the point of tedium. When under Cromwell the more radical Puritans gained control of Parliament, they tried to suppress all the feasts and even the observance of Christmas. Sunday alone, as they saw it, was to be observed. In those Anglo-Saxon churches that to one degree or another share the Reformed tradition, whether Congregational, Methodist, Disciples, Baptist, or Presbyterian, there runs a strong current of Puritanism. This is particularly to be seen in the calendar. Even a hundred years ago, few Presbyterian, Congregational, or Disciples congregations held a service on Christmas Eve or even noted that Pentecost Sunday had rolled around again. In regard to the calendar, the Anglo-Saxon Puritan tradition was definitely different from the Continental Reformed usage.

Among the more moderate Puritans, a very rich theology of the Lord's Day was developed. A good example of this is found in a work by Thomas Shepard (1605–49), one of the first American Reformed theologians. He was the first pastor of the Church of Christ in Cambridge, Massachusetts, and one of the founders of Harvard University. In a manner typical of Reformed theology, Shepard finds the worship of the church already instituted in the law. Christians are to observe the Sabbath, according to Shepard, on the first day of the week, because that is the day on which Jesus rose from the dead. Jesus taught his disciples to worship on the first day of the week. Although this is not recorded in the Bible, we can be sure that it took place, because we find in the Bible that the primitive Christian church did this. Shepard presents the Sabbath as a sign of our eternal rest, "that so his perfect blessedness to come might be foretasted every Sabbath day, and so has begun here."

Any attempt at recovering a Reformed spirituality would do well carefully to study the best of the Puritan literature on the observance of the Lord's Day.

In addition to the weekly celebration of the Lord's Day, the Puritans in both England and America observed special days of humiliation and fasting as well as days of special thanksgiving. The Westminster Directory for Worship speaks at length of how these days were to be observed. When there was a threat of war, when there was drought or plague, the church was to be called together to pray for God's mercy and protection. At such times it was appropriate to sing psalms of lamentation and offer prayers of confession and repentance. Such days were primarily days of public and personal prayer. They were not days for the celebration of the sacrament, and they never rivaled the importance of the Lord's Day. They did not have a regular place on the calendar but were called only as occasion suggested. Sermons were preached appropriate to the occasion, and, particularly on days of thanksgiving, alms were given to the poor. Thanksgiving Day, which has now become a particularly American institution, originated in Puritan New England as this kind of feast day. It was originally called by the Pilgrim Fathers to give thanks for the blessings of the first year of the new colony.

In Scotland down through the centuries, the Lord's Day has been observed with deep reverence. One of the most beautiful works to come out of Scotland on this subject is John Willison's *Treatise Concerning the Sanctification of the Lord's Day*. Pastor in Dundee on the shores of the North Sea from 1720 to 1747, Willison (1680–1750) was well known for his careful attention to every aspect of Christian worship. His *Treatise Concerning the Sanctification of the Lord's Day*, in fact a work on the whole subject of worship, is unique among works on worship in that it treats worship from the standpoint of the worshiping members of the congregation. Today we might say that it is a work on the spirituality of worship. It tells us how we are to prepare for worship, how family prayers are to be conducted, how we are to receive the preaching and enter into the prayers and the celebration of the sacraments, and how we are to approach the giving of alms. He treats such themes as appropriate meditations while walking to church, doing our necessary chores, and before going to sleep at night. It is clear that, as John Willison understands it, the Lord's Day is, above all, a day of worship. It is a day when we rest from our worldly labors so that we might give the whole day to glorifying and enjoying God in the public and private exercising of God's worship.

Willison's work is filled not only with instructions in Christian piety but with marvelous insights into the theology of worship and brilliant interpretations of Scripture as well. One of his most interesting points is that the commandment to keep the Sabbath is part of the moral law rather than the ceremonial law. It was instituted and blessed by God in creation itself and therefore transcends the law of Moses. Another significant teaching of Willison's is that the Sabbath need not be on the seventh day of the week. The word *Sabbath* means "rest"; it means "to cease from work." A sabbath day can be made of the first day of the week as well as the seventh day, particularly if the change is made at God's command. Willison teaches that the purpose of the Sabbath is, first of all, the manifestation of God's glory, but the commandment is also given out of compassion for fallen humanity. The philanthropic dimension of giving rest to laborers, Willison tells us, is clearly in the fourth commandment as we find it in Deuteronomy (Deut. 5:12–15). Another purpose of the Sabbath was to keep before us a lively impression of the essential truths of the Christian faith, such as the creation of the world, Christ's incarnation, death, and resurrection, and the Christian hope of eternal rest above. Very interestingly Willison recounts to us a teaching of the Talmud. God created Adam and Eve on the day before the Sabbath that they might immediately begin to observe it and forthwith to fulfill their eternal destiny. This was to show that the Sabbath existence is the end of our creation. The work as a whole, with its careful, biblical interpretations, its learned air, its sense of tradition, and its lyrical illustration, gives us a sense of that dignified, simple, and sacred joy that has always been so characteristic of Scottish Protestantism. Here one sees so clearly that the Sabbath calm is a witness to the eternal glory.

It was in the 1830s that the High Church Movement first began to challenge the traditional worship of English-speaking Protestantism. It was the aim of this movement to make the Church of England a Catholic church, but, with some notable exceptions, such as John Henry Newman, who eventually became a Roman Catholic cardinal, they wanted to be Anglo-Catholic rather than Roman Catholic. As the High Church Movement saw it, Protestantism was the result of German radicals, who, having no sense of tradition, grabbed hold of a few good ideas and demanded a few legitimate reforms, but ended up "throwing the baby out with the bath," as they liked to put it. The High Church Movement was determined to bring back the ritual and ceremonies of the Middle Ages. They revived monasticism and a great number of ascetic devotional practices.

Consistent with their goal of recovering a medieval piety, they emphasized the observance of the liturgical calendar. The penitential seasons of the liturgical calendar, as well as fasting every Friday, were crucial to their objectives. Lenten devotions were a perfect symbol of the Pelagian theology of the High Church party. Lent made clear that the salvation proclaimed at Easter must be earned by acts of self-denial. Above all, Lent became the religious season of the year, the time when Christians were to make their greatest efforts at being devout. The feasts of Christmas, Epiphany, Easter, Ascension, Pentecost, Trinity Sunday, and All Saints were decked with all the ceremonial the Reformation had removed. To add solemnity to saints' days and the Marian feasts, the ritual books of the Middle Ages were searched for every conceivable liturgical ornament. In fact, the feasts and fasts of the liturgical calendar became the basis on which the Anglo-Catholics reorganized the liturgy. A conscientious observance of the Lord's Day slipped from sight.

The emphasis on the liturgical calendar did much to weaken the devotional significance of the Lord's Day. To be sure, the spiritual vigor of Sabbath observance had in many quarters shriveled into a brittle legalism of what could be done and what could not be done on Sunday. But instead of trying to recover the true meaning of the Lord's Day, the High Church Movement replaced it with medieval ascetic practices that soon become legalistic themselves. They may have had the appearance of devotion, but in the end they have little spiritual value (cf. Col. 2:23). It was easy to see good reasons to observe the major Christian feasts, and certainly the rigors of the penitential seasons had the appearance of devotion. It is easy to see why many Protestants were attracted to the celebration of the Christian year. Unfortunately this new emphasis on liturgical feasts and fasts seemed to go hand in hand with a neglect of the Lord's Day. Sabbatarian legalism was abandoned, but the deeper significance of the Lord's Day was forgotten as well.

With the new theological scholarship of the twentieth century, Protestant theologians have begun once more to appreciate the importance of the Lord's Day. Willy Rordorf (b.1933), a contemporary Swiss Reformed patristic scholar, published a study of the observance of the Lord's Day in the New Testament and other documents of the early church. This work has done much to show the christological significance of the celebration of the Lord's Day. Worship on the Lord's Day was to Christians of earliest times a witness to their faith that Christ is Lord of the Sabbath and that it is he who will lead to the final Sabbath rest when we will all rejoice in the consummation of God's work.

Chapter 4

The Ministry of Praise

The beginnings of Christian praise go back at least as far as King David and the worship of Solomon's Temple. Let us look then at the Temple praises to discover what they really were. There were two major places in the Temple worship where hymns of praise were sung: on entering the Temple and during the immolation of the sacrifice.

When pilgrims went up to Jerusalem, they sang as they went. Psalms 121 and 122 were probably first written for pilgrims going off to the Temple:

> I was glad when they said to me,
>   "Let us go to the house of the LORD!"
> . . . .
> Jerusalem, built as a city
>   which is bound firmly together,
> to which the tribes go up,
>   the tribes of the LORD,
> as was decreed for Israel,
>   to give thanks to the name of the LORD.
>   (Ps. 122:1–4)

In Psalm 84 we get a vivid picture of the pilgrims going up to Jerusalem.

> How lovely is thy dwelling place,
>   O LORD of hosts!
> My soul longs, yea, faints
>   for the courts of the LORD;
>
> . . . .
>
> Blessed are the men whose strength is in thee,
>   in whose heart are the highways to Zion.
> As they go through the valley of Baca
>   they make it a place of springs;
>
> . . . .
>
> They go from strength to strength;
>   the God of gods will be seen in Zion.
>   (Ps. 84:1–7)

When David brought the ark of the covenant to Jerusalem, the ark was accompanied by hymns of praise (2 Sam. 6:1–15; Ps. 131). In fact the usual way to approach Zion was with hymns of praise. Psalm 100 tells us,

> Make a joyful noise to the LORD, all the lands!
>   Serve the LORD with gladness!
>   Come into his presence with singing!
>
> . . . .
>
> Enter his gates with thanksgiving,
>   and his courts with praise!
>   Give thanks to him, bless his name!
>   (Ps. 100:1–4)

Praise can be defined as the sense of awe and wonder that we have when we enter the presence of God. That is why the entering of the Temple is with hymns of praise.

When the pilgrims approached the gates of the Temple, there were evidently particular rites for opening the gates. At least two psalms come from these rites, Psalms 15 and 24. When we add these psalms to the seventh chapter of Jeremiah, we get a fairly clear picture of what happened during the ceremonial opening of the gates at a great feast. The people approached the gates singing a hymn of praise, "This is the temple of the Lord, the temple of the Lord" or, as we have it in Psalm 24:1, "The earth is the LORD's and the fulness thereof, the world and those who dwell therein." This opening hymn of praise might chant God's glory and power, or it might greet or acclaim Mount Zion or the Temple itself. Having arrived at the Temple gates, one of the Temple prophets, Jeremiah, for example, preached a penitential sermon designed to lead the people to examine their lives, confess their sin, and so to enter the Temple.

> Who shall ascend the hill of the LORD?
>   And who shall stand in his holy place?
> He who has clean hands and a pure heart,

> who does not lift up his soul to what is false,
> and does not swear deceitfully.
>
> (Ps. 24:3–4)

After the people had confessed their sin, the prophet was supposed to intercede for the people (cf. Jer. 7:16; 14:7–9). Then the prophet bestowed on them a benediction or assurance of pardon. At last the people cry out, "Lift up your heads, O gates! and be lifted up, O ancient doors!" (Ps. 24:7). The gates were opened, the hymns began again, and the people entered the Temple.

Notice here, first, that the beginning of worship is always praise, and, second, that praise and the confession of sin go hand in hand. Just as Isaiah, when he was confronted by the presence of God in the Temple, was first caught up by the seraphic song (Isa. 6:3), "Holy, holy, holy is the LORD of hosts," and then prostrated himself on the ground with his humble confession, "Woe is me! . . . for I am a man of unclean lips, and I dwell in the midst of a people of unclean lips" (Isa. 6:5), so we approach God in both praise and confession.

It was during the actual immolation or burning of the sacrifice that the singing of the psalms played its primary role. While the sacrifice was being burned on the altar, a psalm of praise and thanksgiving was sung by the Levites as the one who offered the sacrifice circumambulated the altar (Pss. 25–26). That is, the worshipers walked around the altar, usually seven times, by which rite they "owned" the sacrifice, identifying it with themselves as the smoke of the sacrifice ascended to heaven. Worshipers praised and thanked God for the works of creation and providence and recounted the story of God's saving acts toward Israel. Often the story of the election of the patriarchs, the deliverance of the children of Israel from Egypt, their trials in the wilderness, and their possession of the promised land was recounted. At other times more personal acts of deliverance were described. In such cases the psalm was the personal witness of the worshiper. The psalm told what God had done in the worshiper's life. Such a psalm was a confession of faith, but it was also a confession in the sense that it admitted to the obligation the worshiper now bore by virtue of having received the deliverance and gracious bounty of God.

In later times, that is, in the days of the Second Temple, a psalm was sung at the very end of the service. Seven particular psalms were used at that point, one for each day of the week. Starting with Sunday, these psalms were 24, 48, 82, 94, 81, 93, and 92 for the Sabbath. The Temple worship was understood to end with praise just as it had begun with praise.

When the Temple of Solomon was destroyed and the Jews were deported to Babylon, the normal place of worship came to be the synagogue. This involved far more than just a change in architectural setting. It involved two very different liturgies and two very different approaches to worship. While the Temple service centered on the sacrifices, the synagogue service centered on the study of the law and on the saying of the daily prayers. The synagogue service never took over the sacrifices. They were performed exclusively in the Temple, but the synagogue did take over from the Temple the psalms that had accompanied the sacrifices. Just when these psalms began to be used in the synagogue service and just which psalms were used is not clear. When the psalms were used in the synagogue, however, they were sung without the elaborate instrumental accompaniment used in the Temple.

From Psalm 137 we perhaps find a hint that the first Babylonian exiles did in fact sing the psalms, the songs of Zion, when they gathered together for worship, even though it was with heavy hearts.

> By the waters of Babylon,
>   there we sat down and wept,
>   when we remembered Zion.
> On the willows there
>   we hung up our lyres.
> For there our captors
>   required of us songs,
> and our tormentors, mirth, saying,
>   "Sing us one of the songs of Zion!"
>   (Ps. 137:1–3)

At least by the time of Jesus the synagogue service included the singing of psalms. Rabbinical sources from that time indicate that the synagogue worship began with psalmody. On weekdays Psalms 145–150 were sung and on the Sabbath Psalms 95–100. Again, although the sources are rather late, we learn that the seven psalms that were sung at the end of the Temple service were also sung at the end of the synagogue service. It is quite possible, nevertheless, that this usage went back long before the first Christian century. To begin and end the service of worship with psalms of praise was a very natural thing to do in synagogue worship, just as it had been very natural in the Temple.

The first Christians took over many of the worship traditions of the synagogue. They did not take over the rich and sumptuous ceremonial of the Temple, but rather the simpler synagogue service, with its Scripture reading, its sermon, its prayers, and its psalmody. We find many evidences of this in the New Testament. In Acts 4:23–31 we read of Christians gathering for prayer. Their prayer service began with the whole congregation singing psalms. Several times the apostle Paul tells Christians to sing psalms. In 1 Corinthians 14:26 Paul tells the church that when they are gathered together for worship, among other things they are to sing psalms. The text actually reads, "When you come together, each one has a hymn, . . . a revelation." This probably means that the whole congregation is to sing a psalm, but it may indicate that the first Christians had cantors like the synagogue. The cantor would sing the text while the congregation answered by singing "Hallelujah" after each verse. It surely did not mean that everyone was supposed to get up and sing a solo.

In Paul's letters to the Ephesians and to the Colossians we read of singing, "psalms and hymns and spiritual songs." The psalms of the Old Testament were considered perfectly acceptable for Christian worship. They were the songs of the

Holy Spirit. The first Christians were particularly conscious of the presence of the Holy Spirit in their worship. It was the Spirit who inspired their worship. Their preaching and their interpretation of the Scriptures was the work of God's Spirit crying out within them. The Spirit within them bore witness that Jesus was the Christ, the Lord's anointed. The same Holy Spirit moved them to praise. Often the mention of singing psalms and hymns in the New Testament is accompanied by references to the Holy Spirit. For example, Paul admonishes the Ephesians to be filled with the Holy Spirit, to sing psalms and spiritual songs, making melody in their hearts (Eph. 5:18–20). In Acts 4 we find another example. We read that the congregation, "lifted their voices together." Then a line from Psalm 146 is quoted and after that several lines from Psalm 2. What is of particular interest is that Psalm 2 is introduced by a benediction very similar in literary form to the benediction used to introduce the psalmody in the synagogue, "[T]he mouth of our father David, thy servant, didst say by the Holy Spirit . . ." (Acts 4:25). Quite obviously for the first Christians this was an important consideration. When they sang the Psalms, the Holy Spirit was praising the Father within their hearts.

The Psalms formed the core of the praises of the New Testament church; nevertheless the earliest Christians sang praises other than the one hundred fifty canonical psalms and the occasional psalms or canticles found elsewhere in Scripture. In the first place we find a number of Christian psalms such as the Song of Mary (Luke 1:46–55), the Song of Zechariah (Luke 1:68–79), and the Song of Simeon (Luke 2:29–32). These are clearly Christian psalms written in the literary genre of the Hebrew votive thanksgiving psalms. In a sense these Christian psalms complete the Old Testament Psalms. So many of the Psalms contained prophetic oracles that intimated the reign of the Christ. Now that the Christ had indeed come, surely the people of God should sing the votive thanksgiving psalms. In Covenant theology the thanksgiving hymn filled a most significant role. It confessed the obligation God's people owed to their Redeemer. They had cried to God; God had heard their cry and saved them; now they owed to God their lives in obedient service. Even more than that, the thanksgiving hymn was a thankful confession before the world of the covenant faithfulness of God to his people. The Old Testament Psalms had for generations cried out for the Lord's anointed; now the New Testament psalms confessed that the cry had been heard and the promise fulfilled.

The canticles in the Gospel of Luke are the core of Christian praise. From these Christian psalms, Christian hymns rapidly developed. Yet these Christian hymns went beyond the Hebrew literary forms and took on Greek poetic features more familiar to the new Gentile congregations that were springing up over the whole Mediterranean world. In the epistles of Paul we find two hymns to Christ that many scholars feel reflect the hymnody of the Greek-speaking congregations. The so-called christological hymn of Philippians is the leading example:

> Christ Jesus, who, though he was in the form of God, did not count equality with God a thing to be grasped, but emptied himself, taking the form of

a servant, being born in the likeness of men. And being found in human form he humbled himself and became obedient unto death, even death on a cross. Therefore God has highly exalted him and bestowed on him the name which is above every name, that at the name of Jesus every knee should bow, in heaven and on earth and under the earth, and every tongue confess that Jesus Christ is Lord, to the glory of God the Father. (Phil. 2:5–11)

A similar hymnlike passage is found in Colossians:

He is the image of the invisible God, the first-born of all creation; for in him all things were created, in heaven and on earth, visible and invisible, whether thrones or dominions or principalities or authorities—all things were created through him and for him. He is before all things, and in him all things hold together. He is the head of the body, the church; he is the beginning, the first-born from the dead, that in everything he might be pre-eminent. For in him all the fulness of God was pleased to dwell, and through him to reconcile to himself all things, whether on earth or in heaven, making peace by the blood of his cross. (Col. 1:15–20)

There is little question that the first Christians wrote hymns to Christ and sang them in their worship side by side with the psalms they sang as fulfilled prophecies of the coming messiah. In fact, very shortly after New Testament times, we read in one of the letters of the Roman governor Pliny the Younger (61–ca. 113) to the Emperor Trajan (53–117) a short description of a Christian worship service. It clearly says that the Christians sang hymns to Christ.

There is another kind of singing that we find in the New Testament, the worship of heaven. In the Gospel of Luke we hear the song of the angels, "Glory to God in the highest, and on earth peace, good will toward men" (Luke 2:14 KJV). In the Revelation we hear the angels worshiping God, "Holy, holy, holy, is the Lord God Almighty" (Rev. 4:8). It is said that the angels never cease to sing this hymn. They sing it over and over again as they sing "Hallelujah" again and again. But perhaps the most interesting thing we read about this heavenly hymnody is that the saints sing the song of Moses and the Lamb (Rev. 15:3). The song of Moses is the hymn we find in Exodus 15:

"I will sing to the LORD, for he has triumphed gloriously;
the horse and his rider he has thrown into the sea."
(Exod. 15:1)

This song of Moses was regularly sung in the Temple in New Testament times. Was the song of Moses and the Lamb a Christian version of Exodus 15, or was it an entirely new composition based on the song of Moses? Perhaps it is a hymn like the one John hears?

"To him who sits upon the throne and to the Lamb be blessing and honor and glory and might for ever and ever!" (Rev. 5:13)

We cannot say exactly. The hymns of the book of Revelation surely reflect the praises of the earliest Christians. Scholars have often said this, and it is no doubt true. Scholars have also pointed to the fact that the hymns of Revelation are very closely patterned on the Temple hymnody. They are a Christian reworking of the seraphic hymn of Isaiah, the song of Moses, and the Psalms. That, at any rate, is the way some scholars would put it. The way the early church understood it, however, would have been more like this: just as the architectural structure of the Temple followed the patterns of the heavenly sanctuary, so the hymns of the Temple followed the pattern of the angelic worship. The hymns of Revelation are more nearly like the heavenly worship. John heard the heavenly worship more clearly than either David or Isaiah. He understood that the song of Moses was in reality the song of the Lamb. For this reason the canticles, reworked in a Christian manner, became increasingly important in the worship of the church.

But now the question is, did the first Christians understand their hymns, the hymns they wrote, to be the hymns of the Holy Spirit in the same way they understood the Psalms to be the hymns of the Holy Spirit or the canticles to be the reflection of the heavenly worship? When Paul spoke of "spiritual songs" did he mean songs inspired by the Holy Spirit, which were a Christian counterpart of the Old Testament Psalms? Probably not. The reason is that all these early Christian hymns disappeared. The New Testament never included a collection of Christian psalms to go with the Gospels and Epistles. In the course of the second century the gnostics wrote lots of "spirit-inspired hymns." But the orthodox became more and more of the opinion that there was something much more inspired in the psalms and canticles than in the "spiritual hymns" that appeared in the worship of the early church. It seems much more likely that the earliest Christians understood their hymnody as a sort of elaboration, a sort of drawing out, a commentary, or perhaps a sort of meditation on the canonical psalms and canticles traditionally used in the worship of the Temple and the synagogue.

The *Odes of Solomon* is the only sizable collection of Christian hymns which has come down to us from the earliest centuries of the church. They seem to have been composed at the close of the first Christian century. Originally they were composed in Syriac. They are the praises, not of the Western church, but the Eastern church, a church still very close to the Semitic roots of Christianity. The *Odes of Solomon* are Christian psalms in a way very similar to the canticles in the Gospel of Luke. That, of course, is implied by the title of the work. Just as Solomon, the son of David, continued the doxological service of his father by writing the Song of Solomon, so Christians continue the doxological service of the Son of David, anointed by the Spirit, by singing Christian psalms. The title is a sort of apologetic for Christian hymnody. There are more than forty of these odes, each a Christian elaboration of one of the canonical psalms. Although sometimes the imagery is a bit strange to our modern Western ears, these ancient hymns are great Christian poetry. It probably gives us about as clear a picture of the worship of the early church as any document that has come down to us. The spirit of New Testament worship is found in these hymns with an amazing freshness and vitality. And even if their language comes from the ancient Orient, they seem to have a classic evangelical quality about them. They are as eloquent about

Christian love as ever the Franciscans, about grace as the Calvinists, about holiness as the Wesleyans, and they are as filled with the Spirit as ever any charismatic could wish.

Not too long after the close of the New Testament period the church began to cultivate psalmody as the preferred expression of Christian praise. More and more the orthodox became weary of new hymns supposedly inspired by the Holy Spirit. In the Eastern churches the writing of Christian hymns enjoyed some popularity in orthodox circles, but it was more characteristic of various gnostic sects. In the West the church sang psalms and canticles almost exclusively until the time of Ambrose of Milan (ca. 339–97) toward the end of the fourth century. The hymns of Ambrose were so popular that other Christian poets began to try their hand at writing hymns. We find hymns by Prudentius (348–410), Venantius Fortunatus (530–610), and Gregory the Great (540–604). Prudentius, born and raised in Roman Spain, was a lawyer by profession. He was surely the most prolific of the Latin hymnodists of the patristic age. His hymns were widely used in the Spanish church until the Muslim conquest in the eighth century. These Latin hymns, however, never replaced the psalms during the patristic period either in cathedral churches or in monasteries. Both hymnody and psalmody continued to be cultivated. Gregory the Great did much to develop both hymnody and psalmody with the music that today we call Gregorian chant.

The Syriac church had a much stronger tradition of hymnody. Ephrem the Syrian (ca. 306–73) was the Shakespeare of the Syriac language. He produced an amazing amount of hymnody. In fact he preached in poetry as well as producing hymns. This tradition continued for some time. It even began to spill over into the Greek church. Romanos the Melode (ca. 510–ca. 560) took up the practice and preached long metrical sermons. They were dramatic ballads that told the sacred story and admonished the faithful to Christian faith and a devout life. Some of these *kontakia* are still in liturgical use today.

With Gregory the Great we begin to enter the Middle Ages. More and more it was the monks who were charged with the praise of the church, particularly in the monasteries, but also it was the monks who as members of the *schola cantorum* provided music for the cathedrals. It was only at the beginning of the ninth century that the church began to use organs. Up until that time, there was no instrumental music in Christian worship. As the Middle Ages progressed, church music became more and more elaborate. The monks did much to develop Christian praise during the period. They had both the leisure and the culture, and they used them well. It is really the church of the Middle Ages that developed the choral and instrumental music of the church that today we take so much for granted.

The grandeurs of medieval church music were largely inspired and generously supported by the Carolingian dynasty. At the end of the eighth century, Charlemagne (742–814), the king of the Franks, did much to pull Europe out of the Dark Ages. It was his dream to reestablish a new, holy Roman Empire and to recover the Christian culture of late antiquity. Eager to ensure the *romanitas* of his empire, he insisted that the Roman church music, that is, Gregorian chant, be used in the cathedral churches and monasteries of his realm. To this end he had the musical books used in Rome brought north. He established musical schools throughout his empire. Charlemagne was a patron of Benedictine monasticism, and the Benedictine monasteries north of the Alps cultivated Gregorian chant with enthusiasm. In the hands of these devoted monks church music soon became one of the greatest glories of the Carolingian renaissance. It was during this period that Theodulf of Orleans (ca. 750–821) wrote his Palm Sunday processional "All Glory, Laud, and Honor." The Latin hymn "Veni Creator Spiritus," one of the most enduring of Latin hymns, was written by Rhabanus Maurus (780–856). Rhabanus, abbot of Fulda and archbishop of Mainz, was a universal man. One of the best scholars of the age, he was also an effective ecclesiastical statesman, and yet now, a thousand years later, it is his hymns that still remain, sung not only in Latin but in many translations as well.

Up to this point medieval hymnody was largely confined to the daily office, that is, to the daily prayer services held in monasteries. There were exceptions such as the processional hymns sung in cathedrals and introit and gradual psalms sung at the celebration of the Mass, but still it was for the monastic daily office that medieval hymnody was intended. This is not surprising. Ambrose had written his first hymns for the daily office. This began to change toward the end of the Carolingian Renaissance, when the singing of sequences began to develop in the celebration of the Mass. The sequence was a hymn that elaborated the theme of a feast or saint's day. The sequence followed the reading of the Scripture lessons and originally was a development of the more traditional "alleluia." Notker of St. Gallen (ca. 840–912) is supposed to have brought the sequence to its fullest expression. Notker was born in Switzerland not too far from the great Benedictine monastery of St. Gallen. Here he lived his whole life. The great accomplishment of Notker is that he provided the medieval church with hymns that could be sung at Mass on all the feasts of the liturgical calendar. Scholars are not unanimous on whether Notker was primarily the author and composer of these hymns or their collector and popularizer. Quite in the spirit of monasticism, much medieval hymnody is anonymous. However this may be decided, the Notkerian sequences brought to the celebration of the Mass much very sophisticated liturgical poetry.

The most famous composer of sequences was Adam of St. Victor (ca. 1110–ca. 1190). Almost nothing is known of Adam. It is not clear whether he was from Brittany or from Britain. We know that he entered St. Victor, the renowned Augustinian monastery in the suburbs of Paris, about the year 1130, when Hugh of St. Victor (ca. 1096–1141) and Richard of St. Victor (d. 1173) had brought the monastery to the zenith of its theological culture. The Victorines were characterized by their absorption in the mystical interpretation of Scripture. Adam produced a very large collection of sequences for the feast days, but, even more importantly, for the saints' days. His sequences for the feasts of the Virgin Mary were particularly prized, so that he was styled the hymnodist of the Virgin.

About the same time Abelard (1079–1142) lived in Paris. It may come as something as a surprise, but he too was a hymnodist. He wrote a complete hymnary for the Convent of the Paraclete, of which his beloved Heloise (1101–64) was the abbess. Among the noteworthy pieces in this collection is the beautiful "O quanta qualia." The same century also produced those two classics of Bernard of Cluny (1090/91–1153), "Jerusalem the Golden" and "Jesus, the Very Thought of Thee," which in the translations of John Mason Neale are found in most Protestant hymnals.

With the thirteenth and fourteenth centuries medieval hymnody continued to flower. Among the many hymn writers of this period are Thomas Aquinas (1225–74) and Bonaventure (ca. 1217–74). The Franciscan Thomas of Celano (ca. 1190–ca. 1260) is supposed to have written the "Dies irae," often considered the masterpiece of medieval sacred poetry. Hymnologists today are inclined to think the work is anonymous, like that other masterpiece, the "Stabat mater." The hymnody of the late Middle Ages became increasingly subjective, and yet that hymnody became an ever more important part of sacred worship. Medieval hymnody was essentially meditative, leading the worshiper to meditate on the mysteries that the liturgy celebrated and supporting the highly contemplative piety of the age. It was beautifully otherworldly and mysterious. Set apart from the sounds and rhythms of this world, it aimed at discovering the melodies of heaven. Nevertheless, it has to be admitted that the very fact that the great bulk of this hymnody was in Latin kept much of its glory within the confines of religious communities. The common people could neither sing it nor understand it. It was by and large, although not completely, the treasure of the cathedral and the monastery rather than the town church or the village chapel.

With the Reformation the praises of the church took a very different direction. The Reformers wanted the whole congregation to sing the praises of the church. They wanted the people to sing in their own language and in music simple enough for the people to learn. This meant, quite practically speaking, the production of a wholly new church music. One could not really expect the whole congregation to sing what the trained monastic choirs had been singing, nor could one simply translate the Latin texts into German or French and sing the new text to the old music. Besides that, taste in music was changing rapidly. The average Renaissance musician regarded the liturgical music of the late Middle Ages with disdain. Even the sophisticated Erasmus would rather hear no music in church than hear the music of the monks. This often happens to even the best of music; people simply get tired of it. Those who sing it get tired of it, and those who hear it get tired of it. The music was not bad as much as it was stale. The Reformation was amazingly successful in refreshing the praises of the church.

The contribution of Martin Luther (1483–1546) to the history of Christian praise and even to the history of music in general is enormous. He wrote music himself and wrote hymns that are still immensely popular. Of the more than thirty hymns of Luther's that have come down to us, we have German versions of Psalms 12, 14, 46, 67, 124, 128, and 130. Luther did as much as anyone to revive and popularize psalm singing in the sixteenth century. Luther also produced a number of festal hymns, that is, hymns for the feasts of Christmas, Easter, and Pentecost. Luther's contributions to church music are well known, but Luther was only one reformer among many, particularly in this respect. Because there was a whole host of hymn writers traveling the same road as Luther, within a generation the churches that received the reform had developed a rich tradition of doxology.

We first turn to the Reformed church of Strasbourg. The city was well known for its poets and musicians, and with the reform of worship they quickly set to work producing psalms and hymns in the German language. In the early days the Psalms received the greatest attention. Just a few years before the beginning of the Reformation, Johann Reuchlin (1455–1522), the great Christian humanist who did so much to revive the study of biblical Hebrew, published a Latin translation of a little book by Athanasius on the praying of the Psalms. Athanasius (ca. 296–373), one of the greatest of the church fathers, had been patriarch of Alexandria at the beginning of the fourth century. This little book gives us a good idea of how important the Psalms were to the prayer life of the early church. From Athanasius the reformers of Strasbourg got the inspiration of developing a popular psalmody for the church of their own day. Originally the developing of a popular psalmody was thought of in terms of the singing of the daily office, the daily prayer services, which with the coming of the Reformation were held each morning and evening in the cathedral and in the neighborhood churches of the city of Strasbourg.

The *Strasbourg German Service Book* of 1525, the first attempt at a Reformed service of worship, appeared with a number of metrical psalms to be sung by the congregation. Metrical psalmody was part of Reformed worship from the very beginning. Two psalms of Luther's are included; there are several psalm versions by Matthew Greiter, the director of music at the cathedral, and Wolfgang Dachstein, one of the most renowned organists of the day. Ludwig Oehler began a systematic translation of the Psalter, and his versions of the first eight psalms are included. With each succeeding edition of the *Strasbourg Psalter* the number of psalms has augmented.

As these psalm versions were being produced, Martin Bucer (1491–1551) was busy producing his remarkable commentary on the Hebrew text of the Psalms. For a thousand years Christian biblical scholars had neglected the original Hebrew text of the Psalms. Bucer returned to the original text. The Strasbourg reformer made himself thoroughly familiar not only with the commentaries of the church fathers but with the standard rabbinical commentaries as well. In this commentary Bucer took pains to make the original meaning of the Hebrew text quite clear, but he also recognized the legitimacy of the Christian interpretation of the Psalms. The New Testament itself, Bucer recognized, again and again gives us the Christian interpretation of the Psalms. For Bucer, just as for the New Testament church, the Psalms were the songs of the Holy Spirit and were therefore most appropriate for Christian prayer. The biblical research of Bucer gave theological substance to the revival of psalmody in the church of Strasbourg.

In the meantime another notable collection of praises was being developed by the Reformed church of Constance. Constance, famous as the seat of an ecumenical council a century before the Reformation, had been led into the Reformation by Johannes Zwick (1496–1542) and the brothers, Ambrosius and Thomas Blarer (1492–1564 and 1499–1570). All three of these men wrote hymns that even today are included in the standard Swiss and German hymnals. They produced festal hymns for the feasts of Christmas, Easter, Ascension, and Pentecost. They left us hymns for both morning and evening prayer, and of particular interest they provided a collection of catechetical hymns for children. These included versions of the Lord's Prayer, the Creed, the Ten Commandments, and the Beatitudes. Johannes Zwick, a man of diverse talents, was particularly dedicated to the Christian education of children. Having studied law in Italy, he became professor of jurisprudence in Basel. He had already won a good reputation in the legal profession when he was called into the ministry of his native city. There he distinguished himself as a preacher, but even more as a teacher of children. His catechism is regarded as one of the best produced in the sixteenth century. He wrote these catechetical hymns for the Sunday afternoon children's services in order that praise and prayer might be an integral part of catechetical instruction.

The *Constance Hymn Book* of 1540 deserves to be recognized as one of the most significant monuments in the history of Reformed worship. There must have been an edition of the *Constance Hymn Book* at least as early as 1533, but the oldest edition that has come down to us is the edition of 1540. The preface written by Johannes Zwick is a notable defense of the new Protestant approach to the use of popular psalmody and hymnody. The volume contains more than 150 pieces, half of which are metrical psalms. While a good portion of the hymns were produced by local authors and composers, we also find hymns by the reformers of Wittenberg, Johann Agricola, Justus Jonas, and, of course, Luther. The psalmodists of Strasbourg—Ludwig Oehler, Johannes Englisch, Heinrich Vogtherr, Matthew Greiter, and Wolfgang Dachstein—are represented by a significant number of works. We also find works by Hans Sachs, the almost legendary meistersinger of Nuremberg, and by Augsburg's Jakob Dachser and Zurich's Leo Jud. This hymnbook testifies to the vitality of Protestant hymnody in the early sixteenth century.

In the meantime the *Strasbourg Psalter* had been growing rapidly. Each new edition increased the number of psalms and canticles available. With the *Strasbourg Psalter* of 1537 there was a major revision of the liturgy of the Reformed church of Strasbourg. This revision was the result of discussions with other Reformed churches in the Upper Rhineland. In regard to the ministry of praise the Strasbourgers had initially been inclined toward the singing of the biblical psalms and canticles alone, but with the *Strasbourg Psalter* of 1537 they have obviously yielded to the lead of their colleagues in Constance. The new edition of the Psalter added the festal hymns of Johannes Zwick and the Blarer brothers, as well as their morning and evening hymns and even their catechetical hymns. The 1537 edition of the *Strasbourg Psalter* is a magnificent liturgical book, containing the standard liturgical texts for the Lord's Day, matins, vespers, baptism, and the marriage service. But one thing this psalter makes very clear is that the psalms and hymns themselves are to be counted among the basic liturgical texts of Protestantism. These texts are the prayers of the people. From now on, it is the Psalter which is the fundamental liturgical book of Reformed Protestantism.

The year following the publication of this epoch-making edition of the Psalter, John Calvin (1509–64) became pastor of the congregation of French exiles who had taken refuge in Strasbourg. Calvin set about developing a similar collection of psalms and prayers in the French language. The collection included thirteen psalms by Clément Marot. Calvin tried his hand at five psalms, but withdrew them in succeeding editions. Marot's metrical psalms were magnificent! Clément Marot (ca. 1497–1544) was the leading French lyric poet of the sixteenth century. The metrical psalms of Marot represent French lyrical poetry at its best. He used a great variety of meters and rhythm structures. We are not too sure how Calvin and Marot first got together, but in 1542 Calvin was able to publish another Psalter with additional psalm versions by Marot. In addition to the new psalms, the *Genevan Psalter* of 1542 contained some canticles and catechetical hymns. As the years went by, Calvin was able to secure the service of some very fine poets and musicians. Louis Bourgeois and Claude Goudimel provided excellent music, and Theodore Beza provided some fine texts. When the *Genevan Psalter*, or as it is more popularly called, the *Huguenot Psalter*, was finally finished, it was a classic, providing the prototype of Reformed psalmody for generations to come.

Unfortunately Calvin did not follow the lead of Strasbourg and Constance in maintaining a balance between psalmody and hymnody. The *Genevan Psalter*, while it contained a few gospel canticles and catechetical pieces, settled almost exclusively for psalmody. In the preface to the *Genevan Psalter* Calvin gives us his reasons for this: "The psalms incite us to praise God, to pray to Him, to meditate on His works to the end that we love Him, fear, honor and glorify Him. What St. Augustine says is quite true, one can not sing anything more worthy of God than that which we have received from Him." For this reason, Calvin continues, no matter where we search, we will not find better or more appropriate songs for our worship than the Psalms of David. For after all, these songs come from the Holy Spirit. When we sing them, God himself is putting the words in our mouths so that he himself sings within us, exalting his glory. For this reason, Calvin tells us, Chrysostom exhorts men, women, and children regularly to sing the psalms so that in this way they might join themselves to the company of the angels. One notices that Calvin does not appeal to the authority of Scripture in this matter. In defending his preference for psalmody, Calvin appeals not to Scripture but to John Chrysostom (ca. 347–407) and Augustine (354–430). This being the case, one can be sure that Calvin had no objection if in other churches hymns other than Psalms were sung. His use of exclusive psalmody was a matter of preference. He did not consider it the rule of Scripture.

Like Bucer before him, Calvin began work on a commentary on the Hebrew text of the Psalms. Today this four-volume work is considered by some Calvin's greatest biblical commentary. The commentary gives considerable attention to the nature of prayer as revealed in the Psalms. Calvin begins his commentary by developing one of the themes set forth by Athanasius in his essay on the devotional use of the Psalms. The book of Psalms is an anatomy of all the parts of the soul. Every emotion that we experience is reflected in the book of Psalms as in a mirror. Here the Holy Spirit has revealed all the griefs, sorrows, fears, doubts, hopes, and confusions with which our minds are apt to be disturbed. The Spirit has uttered these prayers in our own utterance that we might the better grasp them. In the psalms we are drawn to examine ourselves and discover our true need; for, as Calvin never tires of saying, true prayer proceeds first from a sense of our need and next from faith in the promises of God. Calvin sees the use of psalms in meditation and self-examination as an important function of the psalms in worship. He has in mind particularly the many psalms of lamentation found in the Psalter.

Psalmody also has a didactic function for Calvin. We use the psalms in worship because in the psalms we learn God's Word. In the psalms we meditate on the law. Calvin is fond of the text from Psalm 1 that tells of the delight of the righteous in meditating on the law day and night. That the study of the law should be something of such joy may be difficult for us to fathom, but surely this is one of the clearest characteristics of a Calvinist spirituality. There is a joy in learning the law of the Lord!

For Calvin the chief function of psalmody in the worship of the church is doxological. The psalms lead us in the right manner of offering the sacrifice of praise to God. Calvin is fond of saying that in praying the psalms we are exercised in praise. When the whole congregation sings a psalm of praise together, then all are stirred up to more and more genuine devotion to God. In this sense Calvin speaks of the praying of the psalms as an exercise. In the psalms we hear of God's mighty acts of creation, providence, and redemption. We hear of one deliverance after another, and, hearing all this, we are encouraged to direct our hopes to this same almighty God. When the church thus grows in its praise, God is magnified.

Even with Wittenberg, Constance, and Strasbourg taking the lead for a generous supplementing of the Psalms with Christian hymnody, the preference of Geneva for exclusive psalmody prevailed in Reformed churches for the next two hundred years. In England a Psalter was gotten together as early as 1547 by Thomas Sternhold. Before his death in 1549 he was able to compose thirty-seven psalms. The work was taken over successively by John Hopkins (d.1570) and John Day (1566–1628). The complete edition, printed in 1562, is commonly known as the *Sternhold and Hopkins Psalter.* The *Sternhold and Hopkins Psalter* enjoyed tremendous popularity for the remainder of the sixteenth century, although it drew criticism from many quarters. The High Church party disdained the metrical psalms because they lacked the artistic finesse of monastic psalmody. With a sneer Queen Elizabeth I dismissed them as "Geneva jigs." On the other side, they were criticized because they did not stick closely enough to the original text of the Hebrew Psalms. A certain legalism set in at this point.

More and more, the work of the poet was hampered by the demand for very literal translations. This literalism tended to ossify the tradition.

A number of other attempts were made to come up with better psalters. The most memorable of these were the *Scottish Psalter* (1635), the *Bay Psalter* (1640), and Nahum Tate and Nicholas Brady's *New Version of the Psalms* (1696). The *Bay Psalter* had the distinction of being the first book printed in America. The Psalms were put into meter by Richard Mather (1596–1669), Nathaniel Ward (1578–1652), and Thomas Shepard (1605–49), leading ministers of the Massachusetts Bay colony. To accompany this Psalter Thomas Shepard wrote a work on psalmody, *Singing of Psalms, a Gospel Ordinance,* which gives us a good insight into the liturgical theology of early New England. In 1643, Francis Rous (1579–1659) published *Psalms Translated into English Meter.* Rous had studied at both Oxford and Leyden. For more than thirty years, from the reign of Charles I (1600–1649) through the great days of the Commonwealth, Rous sat in Parliament. He never took ordination but was a respected amateur theologian. His version of the Psalms was approved by the Westminster Assembly and authorized by Parliament. Many of his psalms found their way, in revised form, into the *Scottish Psalter* and are still in use today. Unfortunately none of the versions ever attained anything like the poetic or musical quality of the *Huguenot Psalter.*

At the beginning of the eighteenth century, the psalmody and hymnody of the English-speaking Reformed churches experienced a substantial revival under the leadership of Isaac Watts (1674–1748). Isaac Watts was an English Congregational minister who because of ill health had had to retire from his London pastorate. Watts wrote both Christian hymns and metrical psalms. He translated the psalms into English meter with a free hand never shrinking from finding Christ in the Psalter. For example, his version of Psalm 72 begins,

> Jesus shall reign where'er the sun
>   Does his successive journeys run;
> His kingdom stretch from shore to shore,
>   Till moons shall wax and wane no more.

In fact, some complained that his versions were not metrical psalms so much as psalm paraphrases. Nevertheless the Watts psalms were extremely popular, and surely one of the reasons for this is that he allowed himself such a free hand in rendering the psalms into metrical versions. Isaac Watts's version of Psalm 90,

> O God, our help in ages past,
>   Our hope for years to come,
> Our shelter from the stormy blast,
>   And our eternal home.

is surely one of the most beloved hymns in the English language. Again Watts's version of Psalm 98, "Joy to the World!" is indeed a very free rendering, yet it is a very fine and sensitive Christian interpretation.

The remarkable thing about Isaac Watts's hymns and spiritual songs is the way they take on the character of Christian psalms. In a way not unlike the Christian psalms of the New Testament, the hymns Watts wrote were elaborations and meditations on the canonical psalms. One of Watts's hymns gives the impression of being an imitation of a psalm:

> I sing the mighty power of God,
>   That made the mountains rise;
> That spread the flowing seas abroad,
>   And built the lofty skies.
> I sing the wisdom that ordained
>   The sun to rule the day;
> The moon shines full at his command,
>   And all the stars obey.

The devotional quality of Watts's hymns is unsurpassed. Perhaps his best remembered hymn is "When I Survey the Wondrous Cross," a meditation on Christ's passion. Such hymns paved the way for a far greater acceptance of Christian hymnody. Watts was followed by a whole host of hymn writers, such as Philip Doddridge (1702–51), Charles Wesley (1707–88), John Newton (1725–1807), and William Cowper (1731–1800).

The work of Isaac Watts exemplifies the Reformed doxological tradition at its best. We find in his work a balance between psalmody and hymnody. The hymnody springs from the psalmody; it is inspired by the psalmody. Watts's hymnody comments on, interprets, and continues the psalmody. While one would not want to return to a legalistic insistence on exclusive psalmody, one can certainly see great benefit in an attempt to recover psalm prayer for our day. The church has not always through its long history kept a balance between psalmody and hymnody. Pendulumlike the Christian devotional tradition has regularly swung from one extreme to another. For a while we seem to rely on psalms alone and then for a while "hymns of human composure" seem to monopolize our liturgical life. Christian doxology is best served when there is a dynamic relation between the two.

With the coming of Pietism, hymnody came to a new flowering. In fact, it is in the field of hymnody that Pietism has made one of its most lasting contributions to Christian worship. In Germany toward the close of the seventeenth century Pietism came to its classic expression in the ministry of Philipp Spener (1635–1705) and August Hermann Francke (1663–1727). Putting an emphasis on religion as an inward personal experience, Pietism preached and practiced holiness of life, simple devotional disciplines, and practical charity. The backbone of the Pietist movement was the small group fellowship where faith was nurtured by an intimate sharing of one's religious experiences, Bible study, extemporaneous prayer, and, as the movement developed, the singing of hymns.

Joachim Neander (1650–80) was one of the first Pietists to express his faith in the writing of hymns. Headed toward the ministry, Neander served as director of a high school maintained by the Reformed church of Dusseldorf. In 1680 he published a collection of hymns that have remained classics down to this day. Neander's hymn

> Praise ye the Lord, the Almighty, the King of creation!
> O my soul, praise him, for he is thy health and salvation!
> All ye who hear,
> Now to his temple draw near;
> Join me in glad adoration!

is very close in its style and its content to the psalmody traditional in Reformed churches. The same is true of his famous morning hymn:

> Heaven and earth, and sea and air,
> All their Maker's praise declare;
> Wake, my soul, awake and sing:
> Now thy grateful praises bring.

In fact, one quite easily recognizes this hymn as a paraphrase of Psalm 19. With the renewed devotion that Pietism brought, it became the regular practice among German-speaking Protestants to begin each day with the singing of a morning hymn such as this.

When the king of Prussia established the University of Halle and appointed August Hermann Francke as professor, Halle became the center of the Pietist movement. Pietism had a tendency to soften divisions between the Lutheran and the Reformed. This was especially the case when it came to the ministry of praise. The Prussian royal house was very favorable to Pietism because of its more ecumenical spirit and supported Halle generously. Here Francke not only taught but established a host of benevolent institutions. There was an orphanage, a teacher training school, a dispensary, and a publishing house. To his assistant and son-in-law, Johann Freylinghausen (1670–1739), Francke gave the responsibility of gathering together the hymnbook of the Pietist movement, the immensely popular *Geistreiches Gesangbuch* of 1704. This hymnbook provided German Pietists, both Lutheran and Reformed, with a heartfelt, popular hymnody that has inspired the rich musical culture of Germany ever since. Perhaps the most characteristic piece in the collection is the hymn "Jesu meine Freude," which, if we do not sing as a hymn, we know in Johann Sebastian Bach's choral prelude.

The musical contribution of the Moravians has long been recognized. Even before the Reformation the Czech Brethren had developed a sizable collection of hymns, but when Count Nicholas von Zinzendorf (1700–1760) gathered a group of Moravian refugees at Herrnhut on his estate in Saxony, Moravian hymnody once more blossomed forth. Herrnhut became a Christian utopian community with a vigorous devotional life that inspired the whole of Protestantism for many generations. The Moravians not only wrote a considerable number of new hymns, but they also accompanied their hymns with instrumental music. The use of brass choirs was a significant feature of Moravian church music. The unquestioned piety of the Moravians gave an important sanction to the use of musical instruments in Protestant worship. The praise of the Moravians was fervent and lively, and the music of brass instruments accentuated these vivacious praises. When the Moravians came to America, they brought their musical instruments with them, making their communities in Bethlehem, Pennsylvania, and Winston-Salem, North Carolina, seedbeds of our musical culture.

The Wesleys may not have been Calvinists, but their theology of worship was thoroughly Reformed, albeit in a thoroughly Pietist mode. John Wesley (1703–91) was among those whose faith was inspired by the Moravians. The story is often told of how Wesley marveled at the faith of a group of Moravians who were fellow passengers with him during his voyage to Georgia in 1736. During a storm at sea they strengthened their confidence in God by singing hymns, and Wesley realized they had a much stronger and deeper faith than he. Later Wesley was to translate Count Zinzendorf's hymn

> Jesus, thy blood and righteousness
> My beauty is, my glorious dress;
> Midst flaming worlds, in these arrayed,
> With joy shall I lift up my head.

In fact Wesley has left us a number of English translations of the hymns from Freylinghausen's *Gesangbuch*. German Pietism continued to have a strong influence on Wesley. A Moravian missionary, Peter Böhler, was "doctor in attendance," so to speak, at his conversion experience. A few months later Wesley was on his way to Germany, where he visited both Halle and Herrnhut.

Charles Wesley (1707–88), John Wesley's brother, was, to be sure, the classic hymnodist of the Wesleyan revival. Even more, he and Isaac Watts share the honors of being the greatest hymnodists of English-speaking Christendom. For devotional intensity, mystical fervor, and theological insight, the hymns of Charles Wesley are unexcelled. A hymn such as

> Love divine, all loves excelling,
>   Joy of heaven, to earth come down,
> Fix in us thy humble dwelling,
>   All thy faithful mercies crown!
> Jesus, thou art all compassion,
>   Pure, unbounded love thou art;
> Visit us with thy salvation,
>   Enter every trembling heart.

fairly radiates the personal faith of evangelical Protestantism. It is a faith so intimately experienced that one cannot help but sing about it. One cannot help but be moved with the delight that Wesley's hymns take in the things of God. But to understand the hymnody of the Wesleys one has to understand how closely connected it was to the evangelistic preaching which it accompanied. This preaching proclaimed Christ as Lord and Savior, and the hymns that followed affirmed and confirmed this proclamation:

> Ye servants of God, your Master proclaim,
> And publish abroad his wonderful name;
> The name, all-victorious, of Jesus extol;
> His kingdom is glorious and rules over all.

Many of the earliest Wesleyan hymns were written to follow the preaching of a particular sermon. After the preaching of the sermon, the newly written hymn would be lined out so that the congregation could affirm the Word that had been preached. It belongs to a covenantal theology of worship that God is worshiped when his people, having experienced his grace, confess and bear witness to that grace. This is what the typical Wesley hymn does. It is thanksgiving in its most biblical form, a witness to God's saving power and a confession of the obligation we therefore have to God of living out that salvation. The Wesleyan hymn—and in fact this is true of the hymnody of Pietism in general—is a confession of faith. It is a creed sung by the congregation in thanksgiving to God and in witness to the world.

Charles Wesley was a very versatile hymnodist. He composed a good number of the more traditional metrical psalms. In fact, if I have been correctly informed, he put all the one hundred fifty canonical psalms in metrical form, as well as a large selection of canticles. In addition to his metrical psalms and canticles, he wrote several hymns for morning and evening prayer. His morning hymn

> Christ, whose glory fills the skies,
> Christ the true, the only light,
> Sun of Righteousness, arise,
> Triumph o'er the shades of night;
> Dayspring from on high, be near;
> DayStar, in my heart appear.

is a classic. Besides that he wrote several hymns for each of the major Christian feasts, Christmas, Easter, and Pentecost. His Easter hymn

> Jesus Christ is risen today, Alleluia!
> Our triumphant holy day, Alleluia!
> Who did once upon the cross, Alleluia!
> Suffer to redeem our loss. Alleluia!

is perhaps the favorite Easter hymn of American Protestantism, and certainly his Christmas hymn

> Hark! the herald angels sing,
>   "Glory to the newborn King;
> Peace on earth, and mercy mild,
>   God and sinners reconciled!"

> Joyful, all ye nations, rise,
>   Join the triumph of the skies;
> With th'angelic host proclaim,
>   "Christ is born in Bethlehem!"
> Hark! The herald angels sing,
>   "Glory to the newborn King!"

is among the best known even in our own day.

Pietism had its effect on the whole of Protestantism. In America it was an important factor in producing the Great Awakening. A disciple of the Wesleys, George Whitefield (1714–70), made several preaching tours of the colonies that brought to a climax a number of local revivals which had developed under the ministry of such men as Jonathan Edwards (1703–58) in New England and Gilbert Tennent (1703–64) in the middle colonies. Samuel Davies (1723–61), later president of the College of New Jersey at Princeton and perhaps the best preacher the American colonies produced, took the Great Awakening to Virginia. In fact it was he who organized the Presbyterian church in Virginia. The greater part of his ministry he served the Presbyterian churches of Virginia's Hanover County. Samuel Davies, like the Wesleys and many other Pietists, wrote hymns to follow his sermons and then lined them out for his congregation to sing. Such a novelty would hardly have been allowed in the Old School Presbyterian churches further north, but the newly established Presbyterian churches in Virginia had no long-standing tradition of exclusive psalmody to hold them back.

In New England the Great Awakening introduced the psalms and hymns of Isaac Watts (1674–1748). Everywhere the *Psalms and Hymns* of Isaac Watts replaced the more traditional psalm versions. The door had clearly been opened to hymns "of human composure." A Christian Indian from Connecticut, Samson Occom (1723–92), wrote the first hymns to come out of New England. He published the first Native American hymnbook. Occom, a fervent disciple of the Great Awakening, had studied for the ministry at Yale and for a number of years pastored various Native American congregations throughout New York and New England. George Duffield (1732–90), pastor of Philadelphia's Old Pine Street Presbyterian Church during the American Revolution and a great supporter of the American cause, wrote his famous "Stand Up, Stand Up for Jesus, Ye Soldiers of the Cross."

In old England the new hymnody was flourishing. The Evangelical Revival was gathering momentum; as it grew, it praised God with a veritable symphony of hymns. Among the most notable books of this flood tide of praise was John Newton's *The Olney Hymns*. In this hymnbook one finds not only Newton's ever popular "Amazing Grace" and "Glorious Things of Thee Are Spoken," but also William Cowper's "God Moves in a Mysterious Way," a paraphrase of the canticle found in Job 28. Cowper was one of the more accomplished poets of his day and one of the few poets who was equally gifted in hymnody. Hymnody has its own distinct genius, and few poets seem to be able to manage it.

Augustus Toplady (1740–78), one of the stauncher Calvinists of the Evangelical Revival, produced an important hymnal, the best known hymn of which is

"Rock of Ages, Cleft for Me." Like many of the masterpieces of eighteenth-century hymnody, his hymn draws on a wealth of biblical imagery and typology that was understood very well by those who had been nurtured by the richly biblical preaching of the period. Watts, Doddridge, the Wesleys, Newton, Cowper, and Toplady brought in a golden age of Christian doxology that the Christian church would do well to cultivate even today.

In Wales a very distinct hymnody developed. It came to flower during the Welsh Revival, which started in the eighteenth century, recurred frequently in the nineteenth century, and continued well into the twentieth century. The Welsh Revival had a unique character. It was a staunchly Calvinistic revival, even if it had been largely inspired by disciples of the Wesleys, such as George Whitefield and especially Daniel Rowland (1713–90). Rowland wrote many Welsh hymns, some of which he translated into English. With the strongly Calvinistic flavor of Welsh piety, it is not surprising that Welsh hymnody is characterized by a wondrous sense of awe before the majesty of God. The coal miners and cotters of Wales are a profound people, and their deep Celtic seriousness is immediately evident when they sing their hymns at church, at work, or even at football games. Hymnbooks are hardly needed in Wales; everyone knows the words by heart. Hymns are sung everywhere by all kinds of people! It is a folk hymnody. "Guide Me, O Thou Great Jehovah" may be attributed to William Williams (1717–91), the most popular of all Welsh hymn writers, but many of the favorite Welsh hymns are anonymous, as true folk songs usually are. What makes Welsh hymnody so remarkable is the music. One hears in it the Celtic modes of centuries past. The music impresses one as sacred music, eminently appropriate to the expression of our deepest thoughts and most serious devotion in the service of God.

With the coming of nineteenth-century romanticism, a reaction against the Evangelical Revival began to develop. More and more Anglicans began to despise anything Calvinistic or Methodistical. As they saw it, the very popular hymnody of the Evangelical Revival lacked cultural refinement. The High Church Movement despised the hymnody of Watts and the Wesleys, of Newton and Cowper, and tried to return to the hymnody of the Middle Ages. It is not surprising that the Gothic Revival should bring with it an attempt to revive medieval hymnody. Some Anglicans wanted to discontinue hymnody altogether and return to chanting the psalms alone and that in Anglican plain chant. Others, such as John Mason Neale (1818–66), favored translating medieval Latin hymns and patristic Greek hymns into English. Neale provided us with a number of excellent translations of hymns that have survived. "O Come, O Come, Emmanuel," "Let All Mortal Flesh Keep Silence," and "Of the Father's Love Begotten" are a few of his better known translations. There were also some, such as Bishop Christopher Wordsworth (1807–85), who wrote original hymns. They were particularly concerned about producing a "churchly" hymnody that emphasized the themes of the liturgy, the saints' days and the Christian calendar. The exemplar of High Church hymnody was *Hymns Ancient and Modern*, first published in 1861. In spite of its pretentiousness, and, one has to admit, its sentimentality, it has provided several hymns that even thoroughly Protestant churches have found quite serviceable, such as "Onward, Christian Soldiers," "The Church's One Foundation," and "For All the Saints."

In both Great Britain and America the High Church Movement had a limited appeal. The Evangelical Movement, on the other hand, continued to appeal to a much broader spectrum of the population. Among the Blacks of the American South the spiritual began to develop. Closely related to the psalms of lamentation in the Bible, the spirituals became a means of pouring out one's sorrows before God and lifting one's hopes toward heaven. It was a deeply meditative kind of praise that worshiped God in the darkest of days and the most troubled of times. "Nobody Knows the Trouble I've Seen" typifies these lamentations, and yet suddenly one finds among the spirituals brilliant bursts of holy joy such as "Glory, Glory, Hallelujah."

Of a very different sort were the gospel songs produced by the revival meetings of the frontier. These songs had as their purpose the stimulation of religious spirit. As the spiritual was a type of folk music, so was the gospel song. The charm of these gospel songs is the charm of folk music. While they lack the poetry of the hymns of Isaac Watts and Charles Wesley, they have a color and vitality all their own. Fanny Crosby (1820–1915) has proven to be one of the most enduring of the gospel-song writers. Her "Blessed Assurance, Jesus Is Mine" and "Praise Him, Praise Him, Jesus Our Blessed Redeemer" express a simple joy in the Savior that is truly doxological. Ira Sankey (1840–1908) and Homer Rodeheaver produced gospel songs that appealed to the millions of Americans who flocked to the revivals of Dwight L. Moody (1837–99) and Billy Sunday (1862–1935). Unlike the songs of Fanny Crosby, few of the works of Sankey and Rodeheaver have found entry into the hymnbooks of "mainline denominations," and yet they are a distinct part of the prayer life of American Christianity. Even though they often express the weaknesses as well as the strengths of revivalism, they occupy an important place in the popular religion of our nation.

With the beginning of the twentieth century Americans became more and more conscious that they had achieved a place of importance in this world. They were aware they had a distinct culture and began to prize that culture, and they also realized they were beginning to have a place in the world of art, music, and literature. This had a tremendous effect on the hymnody of the church. Nothing expressed the optimism of American Christian culture more perfectly than Henry van Dyke's hymn

> Joyful, joyful, we adore thee,
>   God of glory, Lord of love;
> Hearts unfold like flowers before thee,
>   Opening to the sun above.
> Melt the clouds of sin and sadness,
>   Drive the dark of doubt away;
> Giver of immortal gladness,
>   Fill us with the light of day.

To make even clearer the claim to culture, the hymn is sung to Beethoven's *Hymn to Joy*. Henry van Dyke (1852–1933), a Presbyterian minister, was professor of English literature at Princeton University and an accomplished author in his time. He was dedicated to making worship more literate, and indeed his great contribution was the *Book of Common Worship*, which for several generations pointed Presbyterians to a more thoughtful, more orderly worship.

With a very similar approach Louis F. Benson (1855–1930) labored to produce a hymnody of truly poetic character. Benson was convinced that good hymnody must be good poetry, and he appealed to John Calvin, Clément Marot, and the Wesleys to make his point. Benson was a true scholar. Having a considerable fortune at his disposal, he gathered an extraordinary collection of psalters, hymn books, and other liturgical documents that made it possible for him to study the hymnody of the Christian church in a way that few had studied it before. This collection, now housed in the library of Princeton Theological Seminary, is a monument to American liturgical scholarship. In 1933, when the Presbyterian Church published *The Hymnal,* Benson had provided its editors with a tremendous amount of historical information that made it possible to produce a hymnal of excellent literary quality. Before congratulating ourselves too fervently at this point, caution might be in order. All too often something begins to go awry when one begins to put too much emphasis on the cultural value of hymnody. Somehow the liturgy of culture has a way of getting misdirected.

Quite recently a revival of psalmody has begun in American churches. The pendulum is beginning to swing back. For over a century even Presbyterians gave only a minor place in their hymn books to the metrical psalms. By way of compensation the responsive reading of the Psalter became popular in some circles. This practice sometimes degenerated into a mere splicing together of Bible verses on some subject appropriate to the theme of the day. Even the best responsive Psalters had a way of heavily editing the canonical psalms in such a way that disturbing passages were eliminated. Sometimes the selections are too short, offering no more than six or a dozen verses. From my own pastoral experience I would say that nothing could improve the worship of the average American congregation more than a regular responsive reading of the Psalter. *The Hymnal* published in 1933 by the Presbyterian Church contained one of the best collections of responsive readings from the Psalms. For those of us who were brought up on that Psalter, the responsive readings of the Psalms gave worship an air of solemnity and majesty. They lifted up our thoughts to eternal things. The Psalms have a way of emphasizing the sacredness of worhsip.

One advantage of a systematic responsive reading of the whole Psalter is that it exercises the congregation in the full diet of prayer. It teaches the congregation the language of prayer, the vocabulary, the similes, and the metaphors of the life of prayer. Each Lord's Day, at the dominical service, there should be a regular responsive reading of at least twenty verses, even if this means doing two or three psalms together. Clearly some psalms ought to be used more than others, such as Psalms 96, 97, and 98 or Psalms 103, 104, 105, 136, and 145. These psalms are especially helpful as expressions of wonder and adoration. There are a few psalms one should use only on the rarest occasions. Then, there are some shorter psalms that would be better used as choral anthems, such as Psalms 8, 19, 84, 100, 113, 117, and 133.

One practice my pastoral experience leads me to recommend is the regular use of psalms of lamentation. Psalms 22, 27, 42–43, 51, 80, 90, and 91 are good examples. These psalms might be used most often at Sunday evening vespers. Over the years I have given special attention to the value of crying before God when we are in pain. The Psalms help us to do this. It may not pass the muster of those who insist on positive thinking, but it helps us to minister to those who need our prayer support. The psalms of lamentation give us a way of praying both for and with those who suffer. They give us an opportunity to put our arms around those who are in pain. Nothing makes more clear the fellowship of corporate prayer.

Another very clear sign of a revival of psalmody in the Reformed tradition is the *Trinity Psalter*, published by the historic Independent Presbyterian Church of Savannah, Georgia. The church was founded by Scottish settlers in 1755. Architecturally, this church is the crown jewel of Savannah's historic district. Its attempt to recover the Scottish metrical psalms fits in so beautifully with that church's witness to the continuity of the faith over the centuries. In much the same spirit is a recent recording of a selection of psalms from the *Genevan Psalter* by the Meeter Center at Calvin College. There is nothing more characteristic of Reformed worship than the praying of the psalms.

At the bottom of this recovery of the Psalms as Christian prayer is the work of modern biblical scholars, who have begun to discover the original liturgical origins of the psalms as well as their history in the worship of the church down through the centuries. The result of modern psalm study has been a new understanding of the psalms as Christian prayer. A number of poets and composers have attempted modern psalm settings. Arlo Duba (b. 1929) and Fred Anderson (b. 1941) have produced numerous new psalm versions that promise to spearhead a revival of Christian psalmody.

Of a very different character, however, are the psalms and psalm paraphrases that have been produced by the Jesus People movement at the end of the twentieth century. Starting in the late '60s the youth revival began to discover that the biblical psalms could be sung to the accompaniment of guitars. This gave a very different character to psalm prayer. One thinks of Mary Rice Hopkins's version of Psalm 51, "Create in Me," Rob Mathes's version of Psalm 124, "If the Lord Had Not Been on Our Side," and Dave Doherty's version of Psalm 95, "Come, Let Us Worship and Bow Down." Another important development was the collection of psalm versions produced by Bill Batstone for Maranatha! Music. In Great Britain Michael Perry and David Peacock have published a large collection, *Jubilate, Songs from the Psalms.*

In the last few years the contemporary Christian music movement has introduced us to a very different approach to Christian music. It is hardly limited to psalmody. In fact its variety is astounding. This should not surprise us. We have often seen this happen before. The ministry of praise wells up from the grass roots of Christian faith. It is a folk art that, inspired by the Holy Spirit, comes naturally in its own time. It is of the very nature of American Protestantism that the ministry of praise is so central to its worship and flows forth so abundantly and in such rich variety.

Chapter 5

The Ministry of the Word

In the Scriptures one often reads of preaching, but not often of preaching in a service of worship, or at least not in such a way that we can determine much about how it was done. There are a few exceptions. One of these is the sermon Jeremiah preached at the Feast of Tabernacles (Jer. 7:1–15). From the rather brief report we have of that sermon, it would appear that it was a sermon on the Ten Commandments. The prophet goes over the commandments one by one and then exhorts the people to live by them. The giving of such a penitential sermon surely belonged to the liturgy of the Feast of Tabernacles. We have evidence of this in Psalm 24 as well as other entrance psalms. Perhaps sermons of other prophets had their liturgical setting in the Feast of Tabernacles.

Surely preaching and teaching were an integral part of the worship of the Temple. We know, for example, that the regular reading through of the Book of the Covenant was an essential part of the rites of the renewal of the covenant (Deut. 31:10–13). It was no doubt the Temple ministry of the prophets to proclaim the Word of God when the people gathered as a holy assembly. That Jeremiah preached in the Temple was surely nothing exceptional. That Amos preached in the king's sanctuary was extraordinary only because he was neither a prophet nor a prophet's son. Ordinarily one expected prophets to preach in the Temple. In the days of Jesus the great rabbis and teachers of the law taught daily in the courts of the Temple. One might even say that it was in the courts of the Temple that the classes of the theological seminary of Jerusalem were held. This custom must have stemmed from much older traditions of sacred learning that went far back into history. Even from earliest times the priests also must have had a ministry of the Word. They were ministers of the Word as well as ministers of the altar.

PREACHING IN THE SYNAGOGUE

In Nehemiah 8 we read of a solemn reading of Scripture that tells us much about the origins of liturgical Scripture reading in both synagogue and church. About 445 B.C. the Persian emperor, Artaxerxes sent Ezra to reestablish the Jerusalem Temple and its customary services. Ezra initiated the newly regularized worship by calling a solemn assembly. At this solemn assembly he had read the entire book of the law. A special wooden platform was built for the occasion. Ezra, escorted by the leading elders of the nation, ascended the pulpit. They lifted up the scroll of the law so that it could be seen by all, then unrolled it over the wooden pulpit. As a mark of respect the whole assembly rose to its feet, a prayer was said before beginning the reading, and the people concluded the prayer by saying, "Amen, Amen." Ezra began to read, and after he had read a section, one of the Levites stepped forward and explained the passage that had just been read. Then another passage was read, and it too was explained. So, it continued all morning long each day for an entire week until the whole of the law of Moses had been read. Several particular points should be noticed.

First, it occurs on the first day of the seventh month. The usual day for the beginning of the Feast of Tabernacles was the fifteenth day of the seventh month. The tenth day was the Feast of the Atonement and the first day a solemn assembly, according to Numbers 29. The reading was a sort of preface to the solemnities of the seventh month. That this should be done is already mentioned in Deuteronomy, but Deuteronomy sees it taking place only in the year of Jubilee. How the Scripture reading changed from the Sabbath month of the Sabbath year to each weekly Sabbath is not at all clear. It may well have been one of Ezra's reforms.

Second, Ezra is described as a scribe, although Ezra was himself of priestly lineage. He had been sent by Artaxerxes to supervise the restoration of the Temple and its worship; he was not acting primarily as a royal official but as a scribe, as the text tells us. The ministry of Ezra is conceived of primarily as a ministry of the Word. Ezra was a scholar, devoted to the study of Scripture. What seems to be behind this is that during the exile the study of Scripture had become increasingly important. Because of the neglect of the law and an overemphasis on the sacrificial ceremonial, God had turned the Israelites over to the rod of their enemies. The prophets had warned that this would happen, and so under the chastening of captivity the Jews turned to an intense study of the law. The reading and preaching of the Scriptures became a primary element in their worship. The member of the house of Aaron became a scribe; the performer of sacrifices became a student of the Scriptures; the priest became a preacher.

Third, it was an act of public worship. It was done with great solemnity and reverence. It was a public event, not merely the private teaching of a particular rabbi. The presence on the platform of the leading elders of the religious community gave it an official character. It was an act of the whole religious community.

Fourth, it was this rite that was taken over by the synagogue when each Sabbath the Scriptures were publicly read and explained in the synagogue service. All the elements of the synagogue service are clearly recognizable: the lifting up of the scroll of the law, the introductory prayer, the pulpit, the standing of the people, the presence of a number of readers, and the explaining of the passage that was read.

Fifth, the whole book of the law was read during the seven-day feast. This public reading of the whole of the law in the course of seven full mornings was not taken over by the synagogue but rather rearranged so that a portion of the law was read each Sabbath. In the course of a year, or perhaps three years, the whole of the law was read. It was read in what today is called a *lectio continua,* that is, the reading took up each Sabbath where it had left off the Sabbath before.

Sixth, before the Scriptures were read, there was a prayer or benediction accompanied by the usual gestures of prayer. After the benediction the people said, "Amen." That the reading of the Scripture was already prefaced at this time by a prayer is significant. The fact shows clearly that the reading was considered an act of worship.

Finally, the passage was explained. This is the origin of our sermon. From the very beginning the sermon was supposed to be an explanation of the Scripture reading. To what extent this was necessary because the congregation found it hard to understand the more classical Hebrew is not clear. At any rate, one point is quite clear: a sermon is not just a lecture on some religious subject; it is rather an explanation of a passage of Scripture.

A second passage of Scripture that tells us how the Scriptures were read and preached in the synagogue is found in the Gospel of Luke. It is the familiar story of Jesus preaching in the synagogue of Nazareth. We can assume that the service began with the traditional psalmody and the traditional prayers. We can also assume that the law was read in the manner that by then was traditional. Jesus was called to the platform. It was already an old custom that a visiting rabbi should be invited to read a passage of Scripture and then to comment on it. Jesus was handed the book of the prophet Isaiah, and he opened it to the place he had in mind. He stood at the pulpit and read the passage. The book was closed and handed to an attendant, who replaced it in the ark, a great cupboardlike chest where the copies of sacred Scriptures were kept. While this was being done, a psalm may well have been sung, and Jesus sat down in the seat of Moses, a great thronelike chair behind the pulpit, and began to preach.

In this passage from the Gospel of Luke we have the oldest historical record of the second lesson. The synagogue service had first a lesson from the Law and a second lesson from the Prophets. Each Sabbath had its lesson from the Law. In Palestine the lessons were divided up so that in the course of three years the whole Law was read through. Eventually the beginning and ending were uniformly established so that every synagogue in Palestine had the same lesson from the Law on the same Sabbath. The second lesson, however, the lesson from the Prophets, was left to the discretion of the preacher, who chose a passage from the Prophets that would explain the passage from the Law. The sermon then showed how the one passage explained the other. Already the principle was at work that Scripture was to be explained by Scripture.

Luke tells us that it was the custom of Jesus to go to the synagogue on the Sabbath. It was the custom not only of Jesus but of his disciples as well, and they continued in their custom well after the day of Pentecost. With Paul and presumably other early Christian missionary preachers, the synagogue custom of inviting visitors who were well versed in the Scriptures to read a lesson and preach on it afforded an excellent missionary strategy (Acts 13:14–43). When Paul went to a new city, he started his work by going to the synagogue and claiming his right to preach. When controversy over Jesus began to divide the synagogues, Christians established their own synagogues (Jas. 2:2). In these Christian synagogues many of the traditional forms of worship were continued, much as they had been previously observed in the Jewish synagogues. Certainly one of these traditions was the reading of the Old Testament Scriptures. Paul tells Timothy to see to the public reading of the Scriptures in the same way that he instructs him in conducting public prayers (1 Tim. 4:13). Paul's admonition obviously concerns the reading of the Law and the Prophets, not the New Testament books, which were probably not yet considered Holy Scripture.

There is another passage of Scripture that reports for us even more clearly the homiletical methods of Jesus. It is the sermon on the bread of life in the sixth chapter of the Gospel of John. John presents the material in the form of a discourse; nevertheless the material he gives us perfectly fulfills the form of the synagogue sermon. Indeed, at the end of the discourse we read, "This he said in the synagogue, as he taught at Capernaum" (John 6:59). Surely this statement encourages us to find here a fully liturgical sermon.

The text from the Law is quoted: "He gave them bread from heaven to eat" (John 6:31). This text comes from the story of the manna in the book of Exodus (Exod. 16:4ff.). Since John specifically tells us that "[t]he Feast of Passover was at hand" (John 6:4), we have every reason to believe that we are dealing with the lesson normally read on the Sabbath before Passover. The sermon has a second lesson, a lesson from the Prophets, "And they shall all be taught by God" (John 6:45; Isa. 54:13). With the aid of the text from Isaiah, Jesus interprets the text from Exodus. Scripture is to be interpreted by Scripture. This homiletical maxim Jesus himself honored. More importantly, however, Jesus demonstrates for us in this sermon the dynamic relation of the two lessons. This liturgical form flowered in the time of Jesus, and the sermon in John 6 proves Jesus to be a master craftsman of this liturgical form.

As we study this sermon, we find that Jesus takes four phrases from the text and explains each phrase in turn. First he takes the phrase "He gave" and explains that it was not Moses who gave the manna, but "[m]y Father gives you the true bread from heaven" (John 6:32). Next Jesus explains what is meant by bread. He tells them, "I am the bread of life" (John 6:35). Then Jesus explains what is meant by the bread being from heaven. He tells them that he is the living bread that comes down from heaven. Here he applies the text from Isaiah, "And they shall all be taught by God." Jesus presents himself as fulfilling this prophecy. In Jesus' teaching God himself is teaching his people. Finally Jesus explains the word *to eat* by telling his listeners, "He who eats my flesh and drinks my blood has eternal life" (John 6:54). From the text Jesus took from the Law he developed a four-point sermon. From the standpoint of homiletical method it is a good rabbinical sermon conforming perfectly to the liturgical forms of the synagogue, but even more it is the prototype of the Christian sermon because it announces that the Law and the Prophets are now fulfilled. In this sermon Jesus moves from the promises of the Old Testament to their fulfillment in himself.

PREACHING IN THE EARLY CHURCH

Let us now turn our attention to the historical development of Christian worship from the end of the New Testament period. The earliest source documents for the history of Christian worship indicate that in the worship of the church, just as in the worship of the synagogue, the reading and preaching of the Scriptures was an essential element. Justin Martyr (ca. 100–ca. 165), writing in the middle of the second century, tells us that at the ordinary Sunday service there were readings from the "Memoirs of the Apostles or the Writings of the Prophets." Then when the reader was finished, the one presiding gave a discourse encouraging the people to practice these examples of virtue. From this it is clear that by this time there were Old Testament readings, as there had been in the synagogue, and New Testament readings as well. Already the writings of the apostles, both Gospels and Epistles, were being read as New Testament Scripture. There was as yet no fixed lectionary, for Justin tells us that these writings were read, "as long as there is time." Unlike the synagogue there seems to be a single reader and a single preacher. The preacher was the one who presided over the service.

The first Christian preacher from whom we have any sizable collection of sermons is Origen (ca. 185–ca. 254), the genius of the early church. Raised in Alexandria, the cultural capital of Egypt, he was well trained in the literary and philosophical disciplines of Hellenistic antiquity. As a young man he was appointed leader of the catechetical school of Alexandria, a position that in those days implied an apologetic ministry; that is, it was his job to explain the Christian faith to those coming to Christianity from other religions. Falling out of favor with the bishop of Alexandria, he traveled widely and finally settled at the city of Caesarea in Palestine. Origen always was very controversial. Even today some think of him more as a heretic than as a saint; nevertheless, he does give us a very clear picture of the preaching of the earliest Christians. On weekday mornings Origen preached through the books of the Old Testament one by one. Today we have some twenty of his sermons on Genesis, about fifteen on Exodus, and a similar number on the other historical books. We have these sermons because Rufinus of Aquileia visited Caesarea in the fourth century and translated a selection of Origen's sermons into Latin. Rufinus seems to have translated only the more remarkable sermons. Until the sixth century the library at Caesarea had preserved Origen's series of sermons on most of the books of the Old Testament and many of the books of the New Testament. Sad to say, the Emperor Justinian (483–565) had the works of Origen destroyed, but over the centuries copyists and translators had visited Caesarea and copied out or translated selections of his sermons. For example, a series of Origen's sermons on the first four chapters of the Gospel of Luke, apparently preached on Sundays, was translated by Jerome (ca. 347–419/20) into Latin about the year 400. Jerome translated the sermons on the first four chapters into Latin. What has come down to us is of the highest quality. In Caesarea, the ministry of Origen was to preach through the whole of the Bible, book by book, chapter by chapter—a ministry that few other ministers of the Gospel have performed with such singular brilliance.

Origen was the first great Christian biblical scholar, and that, of course, is why his sermons have been preserved. This is well recognized, but what is not as well recognized is that he was an accomplished evangelist. Both in Alexandria and in Caesarea a large part of the population was Jewish. Origen's evangelistic efforts were directed to the Jewish population of those two cities. His evangelistic message was that Christ is the fulfillment of the Scriptures. In Jesus all the promises of God found in the Old Testament are fulfilled, all the intimations of eternity fully realized, all the mysteries of the universe finally made clear. In the pulpit of Origen the exposition of the Bible, day by day, chapter by chapter, was an effective evangelistic technique.

In the fourth century we begin to find a liturgy that is considerably more fixed. The *Apostolic Constitutions,* which represents the worship customs of Antioch, shows us that there were at each service four Scripture lessons, a reading from the Law followed by a reading from the Prophets, just as there had been in the synagogue, and then a reading from the Epistles and a reading from the Gospels, as a sort of New Testament counterpart to the double lesson from the Old Testament. This usage may well go back much further into history. Between the lessons, psalms or parts of psalms might be sung. Following the lessons there was a sermon.

Christian preaching flourished from the middle of the fourth century until well into the fifth century. Let us look at a few of the greatest preachers of the patristic period.

John Chrysostom (ca. 347–407) crowns his age. While still a presbyter of his native Antioch, he preached daily at the patriarchal cathedral for some twelve years from 385 to 397, winning a great reputation as a preacher. John Chrysostom mastered classical rhetoric and perfected the art of public speaking. This he combined with great skill as an interpreter of Scripture. Even today he instructs us with his sober Antiochene exegesis, always respecting the simple grammatical sense of the text. John Chrysostom was a great ethical preacher who sharpened the text so as to thrust it deeply into the heart of a moral issue. His excellence we appreciate today from an exegetical point of view, from an ethical point of view, and from a literary point of view.

The preaching of this master centers in his series of exegetical sermons on individual books of the Bible. John Chrysostom preached through most of the books of the New Testament. We have eighty-nine sermons on the Gospel of Matthew. When we look at these sermons, we discover that he proceeds through the whole of the Gospel explaining the text verse by verse. He begins his sermon with exegetical remarks on the text, and having done this at some length, he then makes his application. He applies the text to the practical problems of the Christian life and in moving oratory urges the Christian to live according to the Word of God. He preached through the Gospel of John in the same way, leaving us ninety sermons. His series on the Acts of the Apostles counts some forty-four sermons, and his series on the Pauline epistles more than two hundred fifty sermons. He has also left us several series on the books of the Old Testament: sixty-seven sermons on Genesis, a long series on the Psalms, and another on Isaiah. Few preachers in the history of the church have piled up such a treasury of expository sermons.

While John Chrysostom's expository preaching forms the center of his ministry, we also have hagiographical sermons on the martyrs of the church of Antioch, preached at services remembering the anniversary of their witness. For the feast days of Christmas, Epiphany, Easter, and Ascension, he composed special sermons. Both in Antioch and Constantinople this fearless preacher regularly addressed the issues of the day. Intrigues at court he exposed, members of the imperial household he called to repentance, and the conscience of the general populace he rallied in times of civil emergency. While the heart of his preaching was expository, he was perfectly capable of using other homiletical forms. Nevertheless his great authority as a preacher rested in his faithfulness to Scripture. When he preached, there was never any question but that it was the Word of God which he preached.

In the West, Ambrose of Milan (ca. 339–97) was a renowned preacher. He preached in Milan, the capital of the Western empire, at the same time John Chrysostom filled the pulpit in Antioch. Ambrose fascinated his congregation with his expositions of the Old Testament. Unfortunately Ambrose reworked these expository sermons as treatises before publishing them, so that we no longer have his actual sermons. Nevertheless we can deduce a great deal about his work as a biblical preacher. He was greatly influenced by Alexandrian exegesis. Alexandrian exegesis, unlike the Antiochene exegesis championed by John Chrysostom, quickly left the literal meaning of the text of Scripture, preferring allegory to the grammatical, historical method of understanding the text. His treatises on

Genesis draw much from Philo, an Alexandrian Jew who was a contemporary of Jesus; Ambrose's long series of sermons on the Gospel of Luke depends heavily on Origen. For us today this Alexandrian allegorizing of the text holds little interest, although it delighted his listeners at the time. Like John Chrysostom, Ambrose was a preacher to the court and exercised his Christian political responsibility well. His sermons, although remaining primarily expository sermons, frequently responded to the social and political issues of the day. Unlike John Chrysostom, Ambrose had led a very successful career as a high state official before being called into the ministry, and he knew well how to exercise his influence in civil affairs. He was more apt to exert his influence on the court through his letters and his pastoral work than through his actual preaching.

The catechetical sermons of Ambrose claim our particular attention. Each year before Easter he prepared those to be baptized by preaching to them daily, carefully explaining the basic teaching of the Christian faith. He would always treat in turn the Apostles' Creed, the Lord's Prayer, and the sacraments of baptism and Communion. This procedure remained the schema for classical catechetical preaching for generations. The Protestant Reformers of the sixteenth century revived this same design when they wrote their catechisms and preached their catechetical sermons. Indeed one might even regard Ambrose as one of the fathers of catechetical preaching.

Augustine of Hippo (354–430) might well be regarded as the disciple of Ambrose. He was the greatest Latin theologian of antiquity. After being baptized in Milan, he returned to his native North Africa and became a very popular preacher. He was a master of classical oratory. Like John Chrysostom and Ambrose of Milan, Augustine was a great expository preacher. Several of his courses of sermons on various books of the Bible have come down to us either in sermon form or slightly reworked into commentaries. We have a long series on the Sermon on the Mount. We have 124 sermons on the Gospel of John. His commentary on 1 John is really a course of sermons preached to the newly baptized just after Easter in the year 413. His very lengthy commentary on the Psalms is compiled from his sermons over a period of several years. Besides these longer series of sermons we have a collection of perhaps three hundred separate sermons of that most profound of thinkers.

Ordinarily Augustine preached a *lectio continua,* as did John Chrysostom and Ambrose, but in the preaching of Augustine we begin to find evidence for the evolution of a different principle of selecting the Scripture passages to be read during worship. This is the principle of the *lectio selecta.* According to this principle special lessons were selected for special days. Augustine tells us, for instance, that it was the custom to read the resurrection story from the Gospel of John on Easter Sunday morning. In Augustine's day the Christian year was developing rapidly, and so the custom proliferated of choosing appropriate lessons for the feast days and fast days of the newly evolving religious calendar. For Augustine, to be sure, only a small portion of the year was involved. At the beginning of the fifth century, only the feasts of Easter, Pentecost, and Christmas, a few fast days, especially those before Easter, and a limited number of saints' days would merit a special lesson. Things changed. Within a few centuries this principle of the *lectio selecta* would almost entirely supplant the *lectio continua*.

The sermons of Augustine are remarkable. Here we find one of the greatest intellects of history trying to make his profound teaching so clear and simple that the ordinary people of a small provincial city might hear with enjoyment and profit. Today we respect Augustine for his works on philosophy; we highly honor him as one of the four doctors of the Western church, a theologian without parallel. His reputation rests on the *City of God*, a profound work on the philosophy of history. It rests as well on his *Confessions*, a work that treats the deep themes of how the individual soul comes to faith and is a classic in the field of religious psychology and a turning point in the science of epistemology. The sermons are very different. They show how a lofty mind grasped as well the simple basics. If the biblical expositions of John Chrysostom most often instruct the faithful in matters of Christian conduct, the opening of the Scriptures was used by Augustine to teach Christian doctrine. Augustine was a great doctrinal preacher, and yet he simplified doctrine in his sermons. He used rhetoric to clothe the most complex philosophical ideas in similes and figures of speech. His artful allegorical interpretations delight, amuse, and cajole us into discovering the truth even today.

Augustine wrote a manual on preaching, *De doctrina christiana*, "On Christian Teaching," that is worthy of careful study by the preacher of our own day. Much of what the great rhetor has to say about method is still quite valid. He talks about the value of studying the text in the original languages, the great value of literary studies to preaching, and the importance of mastering the use of language. He gives us a classic statement on using Scripture to interpret Scripture and much else. However, the purest gold to be mined from this work is what he has to say about the spiritual tools of exegesis. For Augustine the understanding of Scripture is a spiritual discipline to be undertaken with prayer and carried out in faith, in hope, and in love.

Leo the Great was the bishop of Rome from 440 to 461. In these years, the eternal city suffered political collapse, and more than any other person he saved his people from utter destruction. Through his personal mediation he was able to win important concessions for the city, even to the point of persuading Attila the Hun to leave Italy. His preaching ministry comes clearly to light in ninety-six sermons that have come down to us. They are remarkable for their brevity, simplicity, and clarity of style. These sermons also interest us because they reflect the growth of the liturgical year. His preaching is not primarily a systematic attempt to interpret Scripture but rather a series of sermons based on the lectionary. The *lectio selecta* has developed rapidly since the days of Augustine, and Leo's sermons are based on the *lectio selecta*. His sermons are not intended to explain the Scripture lessons that have been read so much as to present the liturgical theme of the day. They are liturgical homilies rather than expositions of Scripture. The great majority of Leo's sermons were preached for one of the two great liturgical cycles of the year. First, attention is given to the paschal cycle that begins with Lent, Holy Week, and Easter and concludes with the feasts of Ascension and Pentecost. Second, there is the nativity cycle, which begins with Christmas and ends with Epiphany. Today liturgists study these sermons with great delight because they are the prototype of "preaching the lectionary."

The golden age of patristic preaching all too quickly ran to its end. With the barbarian invasions and the disruption of regular education, the study of Scripture and the cultivation of preaching began to be neglected. The great preachers of the fourth and fifth centuries, John Chrysostom, Theodore of Mopsuestia (ca. 350–428), Ambrose of Milan, Augustine, Basil of Caesarea (ca. 329–79), Gregory of Nazianzus (ca. 330–ca. 389), Cyril of Jerusalem (ca. 315–386), Leo the Great (d. 461), and finally Gregory the Great (540–604), all disappeared with the eventide of classical civilization.

PREACHING IN THE MIDDLE AGES

During the Dark Ages, the period roughly from the fall of the Roman Empire to the establishment of the Frankish Empire, Christian preaching receded in importance. More and more frequently public worship omitted even the simplest kind of sermon. Some of the missionary monks were effective preachers, but too often the ordinary parish priest lacked the education to do much more than read a sermon from a homiliary. Even that was all too frequently omitted simply because in those days it was so difficult to obtain a literary education. Charlemagne (742–814), the emperor who brought the Frankish Empire to its zenith, tried very hard to remedy the situation. It was his goal to have a sermon in every church on every Sunday and holiday of the year. To achieve this goal Charlemagne put a strong emphasis on preaching the lectionary. In this he was following the example of Gregory the Great. Charlemagne gave the English monk Alcuin (ca. 732–804) the responsibility of revising the Roman lectionary for use in his entire empire. Then he encouraged the development of a homiliary based on that lectionary. This homiliary contained several example sermons based on each selection found in the lectionary. With the aid of the lectionary and homiliary even the scantily educated priests of that day could construct a simple sermon. This did at least provide some teaching content for the ordinary church people of the day. Just as *lectio continua* preaching had been typical of the patristic age, so lectionary preaching became typical of medieval preaching. Sad to say, several centuries were yet to pass before the church was supplied with a more substantial ministry of the Word.

For the Western church, at least, Bernard of Clairvaux (1090–1153) was the herald of a rebirth of preaching. Bernard was best known for his powerful preaching of the Crusades. Through his prophetic sermons thousands of men were enlisted for the cause of liberating the Holy Land from the Muslim invaders. Bernard is also well known for his series of allegorical interpretations of the Song of Solomon. These sermons of spiritual catechism were addressed to his monks rather than to men and women living in the world. The same was true of Bernard's great series of lectionary sermons, probably the finest lectionary sermons produced by the Middle Ages.

For the average Christian in the early Middle Ages, that is, for those who did not live in monastic communities, there was very little preaching of the quality we find in the sermons of Bernard. However, by the beginning of the thirteenth century that began to change. This change was brought about largely by the two preaching orders, the Franciscans and the Dominicans. Francis of Assisi (1181/82–1226) founded the Franciscan order for the purpose of carrying on a preaching ministry especially to the poor. Francis was especially interested in the preaching of Scripture. With the help of Anthony of Padua (1195–1231) Francis and his followers did much to deepen the biblical content of medieval preaching. Anthony had received a thorough grounding in biblical studies from the Augustinians at the University of Coimbra in Portugal. The Augustinians at St. Victor in Paris were the best biblical scholars of that day. The Franciscans learned all they could from them and significantly raised the biblical content of medieval preaching.

Dominic (ca. 1170–1221), on the other hand, founded the Order of Preachers, commonly called the Dominicans. Dominic's vision was very similar to that of Francis except that Dominic was especially concerned with using preaching to guard the faithful against the false doctrines and heresies so rife in the Middle Ages. The Dominicans emphasized catechetical preaching rather than expository preaching.

Both the Franciscans and Dominicans had a real passion for preaching. They did an outstanding job of cultivating the art of public speaking and sharpening their tools of communication. One of the greatest preachers of the High Middle Ages was Bonaventure (ca. 1217–74), sometimes called the second founder of the Franciscan order. Especially to be remembered are Bonaventure's expository sermons on the Gospel of John and his remarkable spiritual exegesis of the creation story in Genesis, the *Hexaemeron*. Another typical Franciscan preacher was Bernardino da Siena (1380–1444). An outstanding evangelist, he preached against the sins of his age, gambling, usury, luxury, and vanity. He called for conversion and often brought whole cities to repentance. He might be called the Billy Graham of fifteenth-century Italy.

Although usually thought of as a systematic theologian, Thomas Aquinas (1225–74) was an outstanding preacher as well. Typical of his Dominican order, he is best known for his catechetical preaching. At the Church of San Domenico Majore in Naples he preached an outstanding series of sermons on the Apostles' Creed, the Ten Commandments, and the Lord's Prayer. Another great Dominican preacher was Girolamo Savonarola (1452–98), well known for his attempt to establish a Christian democratic commonwealth in the city of Florence. In Savonarola there was a remarkable rebirth of prophetic preaching. He took the Old Testament prophets for his examples, denouncing the tyranny of the house of Medici and the corruption of the papal court. Finally he won the martyr's crown a generation before the Reformation began.

There was much great preaching in the Middle Ages, but there was also plenty of bad preaching, preaching that had lost its focus, preaching that had become too theatrical and too melodramatic, preaching that had lost contact with the Word of God and aimed at worldly success and popularity. This can happen to preaching. Every so often it goes to seed. There was plenty of preaching at the end of the Middle Ages; it was just that Christian people yearned for a purer, more devout, and more enlightened preaching.

PREACHING AND THE REFORMATION

With the sixteenth-century Reformation, biblical preaching once again took a prominent place in the regular worship of the church. People were eager to learn and eagerly sat under the pulpits of preachers who could expound to them the Holy Scriptures.

Martin Luther (1483–1546), professor of Scripture at the University of Wittenberg, was one of those bright young men who took most seriously the job of explaining the Scriptures from his classroom lectern, but he also took just as seriously the ministry of preaching from the pulpit of the castle church in Wittenberg. For the most part Luther preached the Gospels and Epistles of the Roman lectionary. He had plenty of criticisms of the lectionary, but nevertheless he stuck to it whenever he preached on Sunday morning to the faithful who came to hear Mass. For him it was a sufficient reform to explain the text of the traditional pericopes of the lectionary. This he did with new insight and considerable fervor. While Luther was primarily a preacher of the lectionary, he did several series on individual books of the Bible or major portions of those books. We have series of sermons on the Gospels of Matthew and John, a series on the Psalms, and a series on both Genesis and Exodus. Apparently, however, these series were not given in the context of worship, even though they still maintained the form of the homily. Luther, whether preaching from the lectionary or preaching in course, normally went through the selected passage verse by verse, first explaining the text and then applying it. For Luther the essential matter was to present the clear message of the passage before him.

Ulrich Zwingli (1484–1531) blazed for preaching a much more thoroughgoing path of reform. After his studies at the University of Basel the young Christian humanist scholar hid himself away in a valley of the Swiss Alps as parish priest of the little town of Glarus. With an extraordinary personal library of biblical and patristic literature he worked away in his study for more than a dozen years. He mastered the literary disciplines of the Renaissance during those years and assiduously applied them to his study of the sacred writings. The Reformation had just begun when in 1519 he was called to Zurich to begin his ministry of preaching. He started out by taking the Gospel of Matthew and preaching through it verse by verse, day after day for a whole year. To use the technical term, he preached a *lectio continua* of the Gospel of Matthew. Every man, woman, and child who could possibly get there crammed into Zurich's Great Minster to hear him. Zwingli began his reform with a return to the classical practice of systematic expository preaching. One of his most important guides in this enterprise was the great preacher of the fourth century, John Chrysostom, the patriarch of Constantinople. Zwingli had in his library the recently published first edition of the sermons of John Chrysostom, from whom he learned how to preach the *lectio continua*. Zwingli, true to the ideals of the Christian humanism that had trained him, was interested not in religious revolution but rather in restoration. The motto of the Christian humanists was *ad fontes*, that is, "to the sources," or "Let us drink from the clear springs of classical Christianity." We should not be surprised that Zwingli studied the classical sermons of Christian antiquity. Like a Christian Ezra, he based his reform on preaching through the law of Christ. Like a Swiss John Chrysostom he preached through the Bible, verse by verse, one book at a time.

On the threshold of the age of reform the Upper Rhineland could boast a high level of the preaching art. Johannes Heynlin von Stein (1430–96), former rector of the University of Paris, had retired to Basel's Chartreusian Monastery. While there Heynlin became a regular preacher at the cathedral. The distinguished Johann Ulrich Surgant (1450–1503) was preaching at the Church of St. Theodore in one of the suburbs. Down the Rhine in Strasbourg, Johann Geiler von Kayserberg (1445–1510), who is reckoned as one of the outstanding preachers in Christian history, filled the cathedral pulpit. Most of the South German and Rhenish cities had one or more handsomely endowed pulpits. These endowed pulpits were a feature of the church life of the day. Monasteries, parish churches, or cathedrals might have such endowed pulpits. Learned preachers were in demand for these positions. Often these preachers were required to have a university doctorate. While their appointment sometimes rested with the bishop, abbot, or cathedral chapter, they were often appointed by the city council or even the syndics of a guild. The demand for learned and literary preaching was well supported, and good preachers were enthusiastically received.

In 1518 John Oecolampadius (1482–1531), a Christian humanist scholar who had mastered both Greek and Hebrew, was called to fill just such an endowed pulpit at the cathedral of Augsburg, only a few months after Luther had posted his ninety-five theses on the door of the Wittenberg church. With all the literary tools of the new learning he began his work. While in Augsburg, he carefully studied the classic sermons of Gregory of Nazianzus and Basil of Caesarea; then he discovered John Chrysostom. He began to translate the sermons of the great church father from Greek into Latin, making much of this treasury of expository preaching available to the Western world for the first time. Returning to Basel he became preacher at St. Mark's Church, where he set to work preaching, just as John Chrysostom had done, through one book of the Bible after another. From the very beginning of his ministry he gave special attention to the Old Testament prophets. In 1523 he was invited by the city council to preach to them on Isaiah. Preaching on the Hebrew text, as he did, was a startling innovation in that day.

Only very rarely in the Middle Ages had a theologian been able to study the Bible in Greek, let alone in Hebrew. The scholarly preaching of John Oecolampadius so completely won the city that a few years later in 1529 Basel officially embraced the Reformation.

Strasbourg, like Basel, fairly bubbled up and overflowed with excitement for the new learning of the Christian Renaissance. In that imperial free city lived many of the great thinkers of the day. One only need mention the names of Sebastian Brandt (1458–1521), the German folk poet, or Johann Gutenberg (ca. 1397–1468), who only a few years before had invented the printing press. At the beginning of the sixteenth century, Strasbourg, like Basel, was one of the centers of the printing industry. In 1518, Matthew Zell (1477–1548), the rector of the University of Freiburg, was called to fill the distinguished pulpit of Johann Geiler von Kayserberg. He began his ministry by preaching through the four Gospels in a popular manner designed to appeal to the burghers of that very free and independent city. His presentation of Jesus was fresh and human, very moral and practical. Although Zell was a scholar, he had an ability to speak to the guild members and artisans of the city. Early in his ministry he declared for Luther and the Reformation.

Zell was soon joined by Wolfgang Capito (1478–1541), a distinguished Renaissance scholar who had earned doctorates in law, medicine, and theology and who, like his friend Oecolampadius, was distinguished by a mastery of both Greek and Hebrew. When the Reformation broke loose, Capito held the endowed pulpit in the cathedral of Basel, where his preaching won for him the admiration and friendship of Erasmus (1469–1536), the prince of Renaissance scholars. In 1523 he was called to be probst of Strasbourg's famous Thomas Stift. The Thomas Stift was an endowed college of scholars. To be named "probst" made him dean. He was the paradigm of the gentleman scholar, devoting much time to his personal correspondence with Erasmus, Luther, and Zwingli. For Wolfgang Capito, who preached regularly at the Church of St. Peter the Younger, preaching went step by step with a careful exegesis of the text of Holy Scripture. Capito's remarkable study of the prophet Hosea gave an insight into the message of an Old Testament prophet who up to this time had been all but unknown to Christendom. Capito as a preacher was irenic and moderate, allowing the carefully explained biblical text to speak for itself. Having family connections with the flourishing printing industry of Strasbourg, Capito saw to the publishing of the commentaries of his good friend Oecolampadius. This scholarly work, to be sure, bore fruit in his pulpit as Capito preached through Isaiah, Jeremiah, and Ezekiel following the commentaries of his colleague in Basel. The gentle reasonableness and kindly intelligence of this man did much to win the leading thinkers of his day for the Reformation. His life and his teaching were of one piece. The preaching of such a man was true worship because it bore a sincere witness to the glory of God.

Martin Bucer (1491–1551), the best known of the Strasbourg reformers, arrived in the city in 1523 and was soon given charge of the Church of St. Aurelius, the most proletarian congregation in Strasbourg. There his preaching won a devoted following. He frequently preached in the cathedral, and was invited to lecture on the interpretation of Scripture in the home of Capito and then later in the Dominican priory. Unfortunately less than a dozen sermons of Bucer have come down to us, and all of these can be classified as occasional sermons. What we discover even in these occasional sermons is that Bucer chose a passage of the Bible appropriate to the occasion and carefully explained the text and then applied it to the matter at hand. Bucer's long series of expository sermons formed the heart of his preaching ministry. He did a long series of sermons on the Gospel of Matthew, the Gospel of John, the first epistle of Peter and the book of Psalms. Bucer wrote commentaries on the Pauline epistles of Romans and Ephesians, and we can assume that this exegetical work reflected his preaching.

From the early editions of the *Strasbourg Psalter* we learn much about the preaching ministry of Bucer and his colleagues. For the Sunday morning celebration of Communion the passage of Scripture selected was taken from one of the Gospels. This was done in such a way that each Gospel was preached through on the principle of the *lectio continua*. The Gospels and Epistles of the Roman calendar were set aside because they were considered inadequate for fully presenting the message of the biblical writers. The pericopes are disparagingly called "scraps and remnants" or "bits and pieces" of Scripture. If the Gospels were preached through in course on Sunday morning, then the New Testament Epistles were preached through either later on Sunday, at vespers perhaps, or else at the daily preaching services. It was the same with the Old Testament books. Strasbourg had a wealth of capable preachers and biblical scholars, and they were all involved in the work of daily expounding the word of truth. Even today one would be hard-pressed to find a theological seminary where more learned biblical exposition takes place in the course of a week than took place in the city of Strasbourg in the age of the Reformation.

Catechetical preaching was a major concern of the Strasbourg reformation. Each Sunday afternoon the catechism was preached. In Strasbourg this meant that each year the Creed, the Lord's Prayer, the Ten Commandments, and the sacraments of baptism and Communion were explained in detail. One immediately recognizes the schema of the catechetical sermons of the patristic age, especially those of Cyril of Jerusalem and Ambrose of Milan. Just as the Reformers had been inspired by the expository preaching of the patristic age, so they were inspired by the catechetical preaching of the patristic age. Although the catechetical preaching of Strasbourg was probably the most intensive of the early sixteenth century, much the same thing was being done in Wittenberg, Zurich, Basel, and, above all, in Constance, where the catechetical work of Johannes Zwick won great renown.

For his day, Bucer pioneered much that in our day seems more than obvious. He has left us a short work on his hermeneutical principles, originally written in a letter to the Waldensian pastor Fortunatus Andronicus. The Latin title might be translated, "An Instruction on How the Sacred Scriptures Are to Be Handled in Sermon." The work is rich in its insights and practical advice. Bucer defines the purpose of preaching as to offer to individuals the grace of Christ in such a way that it is laid hold of by faith and realized in a life of Christian love. He emphasizes that since all Christian teaching is in the end the work of the Holy Spirit the sermon must be prepared through prayer and that the preacher must pray that the Holy Spirit grant to the preacher the right words and to the hearers the right frame of mind to hear the Word of God. He gives great attention to the selection of the text, going into detail about how he understands the use of the *lectio continua*. First the Gospels and the Acts of the Apostles should be preached. This is because they are most easily understood. Then one should preach the easier Pauline Epistles, that is, the Pastorals, and the letters to the Colossians, Philippians, and Corinthians. Romans and Galatians are to be preached to a more mature congregation. Only when this foundation is well established should one proceed to the Law and the Prophets of the Old Testament. The parts of Exodus, Leviticus, and Numbers that regard the ceremonial law and such things can be left on the side, as well as the apocalyptic visions of Ezekiel and Zechariah.

One should above all have regard for the capacity of one's hearers. As Bucer saw it, it was one thing to preach on some of the more difficult Old Testament books to advanced theological students at the Thomas Stift on Sunday afternoon and something quite different to preach to the normal congregation at the cathedral on Sunday morning. For Bucer the sermon is not the place for the speculative, the controversial, and the obscure. He comes out strongly against the allegorical interpretation of Scripture. The sermon should not be used by the preacher to display his own cleverness and ingenuity. Elaborate attempts to harmonize the apparent contradictions of Scripture should be avoided. The sermon should be a witness to Christ as Lord and should make clear to Christians the path of life. The preacher should have uppermost in his mind that these things "are written that you may believe . . . and that believing you may have life" (John 20:31).

Zwingli, Oecolampadius, and Bucer did not rediscover preaching, as though it had been neglected for a thousand years. They were brought up under the pulpits of great preachers. It was far more that their reform of preaching consisted in establishing regular and systematic expository preaching. It was this approach to preaching that John Calvin (1509–64) introduced to Geneva and that those who were exiled during the reign of Queen Mary (1553–58) took with them when they returned to England and Scotland. The exposition of Scripture in course became one of the biggest planks in their platform of Christian revival. To them it was an essential component of a Christian worship that was according to Scripture and after the example of the early church. To these reformers the sermon was an act of worship, the fruit of prayer, a work of God's Spirit in the body of Christ; it was the doxological witness to the grace of God in Christ. Set in the praise and prayer of the worshiping congregation, it called Christians to communion with God and sent them out into a life of Christian service.

When Calvin began his ministry in Geneva, William Farel (1489–1565) had already established in that French-speaking city-republic many of the liturgical reforms that had by then become familiar in the Rhineland. The service book Farel published in 1533 had directed in regard to preaching that the minister should first read the Scriptures and then preach a sermon explaining the text that had been read. This, Farel reminds us, is what Jesus had done in Nazareth. In the same way, following the example of Ezra, the minister was to preface the preaching of the Scriptures with a prayer that the Holy Spirit would make clear the true meaning of the Word in such a way that it would bear fruit in the lives of the people. Calvin closely followed this pattern, with the same devotion to expository preaching and to preaching books of the Bible through in course that his Rhenish predecessors had. Calvin regarded the lectionary of the Christian year as cutting up the Bible into unrelated scraps. It imposed an arbitrary arrangement on Scripture. As Calvin saw it, the pericopes of the lectionary often separated a text from its natural context. The texts of Scripture should be heard within the total message of a particular biblical author. A lectionary could not help but encourage over the years a stereotyped interpretation. Part of the pastoral responsibility of the faithful minister of the Word was to select those passages of Scripture that were most needed for the nourishment and upbuilding of the church at any particular time.

Happily, a good many of Calvin's sermons have been preserved. For well over ten years (1549–60) at the height of Calvin's ministry, provision was made for a stenographer to record Calvin's sermons. More than two thousand sermons were taken down. From 1542, when he returned from his exile, Calvin was the ordinary preacher at the Cathedral of St. Pierre. Sunday morning Calvin normally preached through the Gospels or the Acts of the Apostles. At Sunday vespers he would preach through the Psalms or perhaps a New Testament epistle. On weekday mornings he preached through Old Testament books. Other preachers were responsible for weekday evening sermons, and they preached through New Testament books. The reformer has reserved the Gospels for Sunday morning when he could count on the greatest number of hearers.

Calvin preached through most of the books of the Bible, and he preached his way slowly through each book. Normally, he took three to six verses at a time. This system produced, for example, 123 sermons on Genesis, 200 sermons on Deuteronomy, 159 sermons on Job, 176 sermons on 1 and 2 Corinthians, and 43 sermons on Galatians. In more than twenty years as preacher at Geneva, Calvin must have preached through almost the entire Bible. He seems to have missed only a few books. He preached through most of the historical books. First and Second Chronicles, Ezra, Nehemiah, and Esther he never reached, having finished 2 Kings shortly before his death. He probably did not think it necessary to preach through those passages of Exodus, Leviticus, and Numbers that treated in detail the interpretation of the law. Calvin did, nevertheless, write a commentary on these passages. He preached on all of the prophets, both major and minor. He does not seem to have treated Proverbs, Ecclesiastes, or the Song of Solomon.

He did not preach on the Revelation. He did preach a long series on the Synoptic Gospels, on Acts, and the Pauline Epistles. Sermons have not come down to us on the Gospel of John or the Catholic Epistles, but we can assume that Calvin preached through these books early in his ministry before the stenographer was made available. In all probability he preached through the Gospels, certain Pauline epistles, and the Psalms more than once. Taken as a whole, however, his life's work was to preach through the whole Bible. What a life's work that was!

Calvin's purpose in preaching was to present the message of the text in a simple and straightforward manner and then to apply the text to the lives of his hearers. What surprises the modern reader of Calvin's sermons is the simplicity of his sermons. We find no engaging introductions, no illustrative stories nor anecdotes, no quotations from great authors, no stirring conclusions. Although Calvin was one of the most literate men of his age and a master in the use of language, his sermons depend not at all on literary elegance. The forcefulness of his sermons is to be found in the clarity of his analysis of the text. Calvin seems to have no fear that the Scriptures will be boring or irrelevant unless the preacher spices them up. In fact, Calvin seems to have a horror of decorating the Word of God. Scripture does not need to be painted with artists' colors! So confident is the reformer that God will make his Word alive in the hearts of his people, that Calvin simply explains the text and draws out its implication. The simplicity and directness of his style is based in his confidence that what he is preaching is indeed the Word of God. This simplicity is an expression of reverence.

This does not mean that Calvin was unaware of rhetoric. He was a master of it! He knew Aristotle (384 B.C.–322 B.C.), Cicero (106 B.C.–43 B.C.), and Quintilian (ca. 35–96) well. He had carefully schooled himself in John Chrysostom and Augustine, both accomplished in the art of rhetoric. As is often said of very great artists, he had mastered his art so completely he knew how to hide it. Calvin was well aware of all the classical rhetorical forms. As Professor Rodolphe Peter has recently shown, Calvin, in his commentaries on Scripture, never tires of pointing out the use of various rhetorical forms. He is forever admiring striking similes, effective metaphors, an audacious hyperbole, or a clever pun. His sermons often use similes, metaphors, epithets, synecdoche, and antithesis. One often finds the use of climax, apostrophe, prosopopoeia, epiphonema, and anaphora in his sermons. Yet when Calvin uses these rhetorical forms they are never studied, artificial, or contrived; they flow naturally.

The most important method Calvin used to explain a text was to bring to it a parallel text. A single sermon will often quote a dozen or more passages from other parts of the Bible. Like Augustine, he believed Scripture is best interpreted by Scripture. It is rather strange that Calvin did not use a second Scripture lesson, but then he probably figured that was best done in the course of the sermon. Another method Calvin frequently used was to paraphrase the text. Often he says something like, "It is as though Jeremiah had said . . ." Sometimes he engages the prophets or apostles in conversation. He frequently delves into the reasons behind the biblical characters' actions or thoughts, "Why then did the shepherds go to

Bethlehem?" All these methods Calvin found used in most exemplary fashion in the sermons of John Chrysostom.

According to T. H. L. Parker the primary characteristic of Calvin's style is his clarity. Compared to Luther, Calvin is bland and colorless. One has to say the reformer of Geneva lacks imagination, the flair for the dramatic, and the emotional appeal. He seems to be concerned about one thing alone, presenting the Word of God simply and directly. This he does with great ability.

In Scotland the Reformed tradition of preaching bloomed with vigor. The expository preaching of books of the Bible in course became a continuing feature of the Scottish pulpit. Early in the Reformation, George Wishart (1513–46) began a typical Reformed preaching ministry. After graduating from Kings College in Aberdeen, he traveled in Germany and Switzerland in 1539 and 1540. While on the Continent he fully informed himself of the Reformers' preaching method. Returning to Scotland in 1544, he began a remarkable preaching ministry. While in Dundee he preached through Paul's epistle to the Romans. In addition to this he is known to have preached in Montrose, Perth, Edinburgh, Leith, and Haddington. His ministry, though brilliant, was unfortunately short. In 1546 George Wishart was burned at the stake at St. Andrews.

John Knox (1513–72), won for the Reformation by Wishart, took up his master's torch almost, as it were, from the flames of his martyrdom. Right there in St. Andrews, Knox began to preach the Reformation. Soon Knox was arrested for his preaching and sentenced to the galley ships. Nevertheless during that short ministry he must have won a good reputation, for as soon as he was released he was called to England by Archbishop Cranmer (1489–1556), named chaplain to King Edward VI, and sent about England to preach the Reformation. In the course of the next five years he became one of the best known of English preachers. He was even offered a bishopric in the Church of England! With the accession of Queen Mary to the throne of England, Knox, like other leading Protestants, went into exile on the Continent. Knox settled in Geneva as pastor of the English-speaking congregation. He spent several peaceful years there. The peaceful years in Geneva gave him time to study Greek and Hebrew and the opportunity to sit under the pulpit of Calvin.

Soon the respite came to an end. The cause of the Reformation was gathering strength in his native Scotland, and Knox returned to lead the nation in those most critical years. With the official adoption of reform in 1560, Knox became preacher at St. Giles Cathedral in Edinburgh. There he exercised as dramatic and powerful a preaching ministry as any preacher in the history of Christendom. Concerning his preaching at St. Giles the English ambassador is supposed to have written to Lord Cecil, "I assure you the voice of one man is able, in an hour, to put more life in us, than six hundred trumpets." From the pulpit Knox exercised his tremendous influence on the history of Scotland. Fearlessly he attacked the easy morality of the court. With all the audacity of a John Chrysostom denouncing the Byzantine empress, Knox opposed the religious policies and politics of Mary, Queen of Scots. Even in the presence of the Queen's consort, Lord Darnley, he preached against his vacillating opportunism. And he did this in the course of expository preaching, never departing from the text of Scripture. His hearers knew he was preaching the Word of God. Fearing no one, he exhorted Scotland to be obedient to God and God alone. As John Knox understood it, even the queen had authority only insofar as she bowed to God's authority. The same principle was behind his own authority as a minister of the Word of God. As a minister he had authority only to the extent that he faithfully expounded Scripture. Amazingly, Scotland recognized the authority behind the preaching of Knox, and in a generation Scotland was a changed nation.

Knox had been influenced by John Calvin. But Knox had something as a preacher Calvin never had. One of Knox's greatest sermons was preached in St. Giles at the funeral of the Earl of Murray, the murdered regent of Scotland. He preached on the text "Blessed are the dead which die in the Lord." Thomas M'Crie tells us, "Three thousand persons were dissolved in tears before him, while he described the regent's virtues, and bewailed his loss."[1] The "Thundering Scot" could move the hearts of a congregation. While Calvin's appeal was to the mind, Knox's appeal was to the heart. That does not mean that Knox was simply an emotional rabble-rouser, as some people have presented him. Knox was far more. Like Calvin, Knox was a studying preacher. He knew how to search out the meaning of the text and make it speak to the problems of the day. For Knox a careful exposition of the text was essential to a sermon. For this reason Knox could awaken the conscience in a way that a simple emotional appeal could never do.

If Knox followed in a great tradition, he also founded a great tradition. Ever since Knox Scotland has abounded in great preachers. One of his successors in the pulpit of St. Giles was Robert Bruce. Born to one of Scotland's noble families, he attended St. Andrews University in the day George Buchanan and Andrew Melville had brought the university to its zenith. He mastered the new learning of the Renaissance, applying himself particularly to the study of Greek and Hebrew. He gave careful attention to the study of the Fathers, particularly Augustine and Irenaeus. Bruce is remembered especially for two series of sermons. The first series was preached during the threatened invasion of the Spanish Armada in 1588. Professor Thomas Torrance has called these sermons an outstanding example of how great preaching can strengthen a nation in time of crisis. The second, frequently reprinted even to this day, is his series of catechetical sermons on the sacraments.

THE PURITANS

In England during the reign of Queen Elizabeth I, William Perkins (1558–1602) was the most notable exponent of the Reformed approach to preaching. While today Perkins's fame has faded, he was one of the most notable English theologians of his day. His theological treatises were translated into numerous other languages, and in Germany, Holland, and Switzerland he was clearly the most widely read of

English theologians. He was particularly well known for his defense of Calvinism against the attacks of Arminianism. In England he was highly regarded as a preacher. He began his ministry as a preacher to prisoners in the Cambridge jail; nevertheless in 1585 he was appointed rector of St. Andrew's Church in Cambridge, giving him the opportunity to preach to one of the intellectual centers of the nation. Many of Perkins's publications were a reworking of his sermons. His commentaries on the Sermon on the Mount, Galatians, Hebrews, Jude, and Revelation reflect his ministry of expository preaching. In the same way, his catechetical preaching is reflected in his works on the Lord's Prayer, the Ten Commandments, and the Apostles' Creed. A good number of his other treatises reflect occasional sermons. For example, *The Calling of the Ministerie* was originally a series of sermons designed to encourage Cambridge students to enter the pastorate.

Perkins was particularly concerned with the cultivation of good preaching. In 1592 he published a short work on preaching, *The Art of Prophesying*. In this work he tells us that prophecy is a public and solemn speech of the prophet, pertaining to the worship of God and the salvation of our neighbor. He tells us there are two parts to prophecy, "preaching of the word and conceiving of prayers." According to Perkins the prophet is the voice of God when he preaches and the voice of the people when he prays. He goes on to define the preaching of the Word as "prophesying in the name and room of Christ, whereby men are called to the state of grace and conserved in it." What is fascinating about this essay on preaching is the way it reaches back to the Old Testament concept of prophet and defines the preacher in terms of the prophetic ministry. Nevertheless Perkins's concept is thoroughly Christian. He has obviously been influenced by what the apostle Paul has to say about preaching and the gift of prophecy in 1 Corinthians 14. When Perkins tells us that the Christian minister prophesies "in the name and room of Christ," he clearly means that the ministry of the Word continues the prophetic ministry of Christ.

Perkins underlines the importance of the minister being diligent in his private study. As preparation for his ministry the preacher needs a solid education in the liberal arts, in philosophy, and very particularly in literature. Then he needs to study the Scriptures using all the tools of grammatical, rhetorical, and logical analysis. He should study the great theologians both ancient and modern. Perkins, like the Puritans who followed him, gave a high value to a "learned ministry." It is most clear that by this is meant particularly a literate ministry. In order to understand the written word the minister must study great literature and pursue literary studies. After all, how can one be a minister of the Word without being skilled in the use of words?

True to the Reformed tradition, learning and godliness are understood to be equally necessary for the preacher. As Perkins understood it, speech is gracious when it comes from a grace-filled heart. The minister must have a good conscience, or else he would not dare to preach. Without integrity the minister cannot be a sound preacher. He must have "an inward feeling of the doctrine to be delivered. . . . [H]e must be godly affected himself who would stir up godly affections in other men." The preacher must have a sense of "the fear of God, whereby being thoroughly stricken with a reverent regard of God's majesty, he speaketh soberly and moderately." Again we recognize the influence of Augustine, who gave such great importance to faith, hope, and love as the spiritual tools of exegesis. A preacher must have a love of the people. That this might come about, Perkins admonishes the would-be preacher to be fervent in prayer for the people of God. What comes through with particular clarity in this work of Perkins is this balance between learning and piety. Nothing could be more characteristic of a truly Reformed spirituality.

With the seventeenth century the number of truly great preachers became astounding. Among the Puritans particularly the quality of preaching rose. One should mention among the leading preachers during the next two centuries at least the following: John Preston (1587–1628), the great preacher at Trinity Church in Cambridge; Stephen Charnock (1628–80), another one of the Cambridge Presbyterians, so distinguished for his works on systematic theology; and Dr. James Ussher (1581–1656), the Calvinist archbishop of Armagh, universally recognized for his learning. One should mention Edmund Calamy (1600–1666), one of the fathers of the Westminster Assembly. Dr. Calamy was commonly regarded as the greatest of the Puritan preachers. Thomas Watson (ca. 1620–90) was another Presbyterian highly regarded as a preacher. His 176 catechetical sermons based on the Westminster Shorter Catechism, as well as his catechetical sermons on the Lord's Prayer and the Ten Commandments, are particularly valued. Richard Baxter (1615–91) was surely one of the most able preachers of the century. In New England right from the beginning there were outstanding preachers: Richard Mather (1596–1669), Thomas Shepard (1605–49), and above all, Jonathan Edwards (1703–58).

By the middle of the seventeenth century when the Westminster Assembly produced its directory for worship there was considerable departure from the approach of the Continental Reformers. We notice, for instance, that the Westminster Directory for Worship has separate chapters for the "Publick Reading of the Holy Scriptures" and "The Preaching of the Word." It is obvious that the two are thought of as separate parts of the worship service. The public reading of the Scriptures in the congregation is one of the means that God has appointed for the edification of his people. Such reading is worship, the Directory tells us, because we thereby acknowledge our dependence on God. The Directory further teaches us that normally a whole chapter from the Old Testament and a whole chapter from the New Testament should be read at each service, but the exact length of the lesson is left to the wisdom of the minister. "All the canonical books are to be read over in order, that the people may be better acquainted with the whole body of the scriptures; and ordinarily, where the reading in either Testament endeth on one Lord's day, it is to begin the next."[2] On the other hand, we read that those portions of the Scriptures that the minister considers, "best for the edification of his hearers," are to be read more frequently. This reading is not necessarily the passage on which the sermon is to be preached, for we read,

"When the minister who readeth shall judge it necessary to expound any part of what is read, let it not be done until the whole chapter . . . be ended."[3] The sermon comes later in the service. Clearly the Westminster Divines saw a value in the public reading of the Scriptures aside from simply reading out the passage on which the sermon was based.

In its chapter on preaching the Westminster Directory weakened the stand of the Continental Reformers.

> Ordinarily, the subject of his sermon is to be some text of scripture, holding forth some principle or head of religion, or suitable to some special occasion emergent; or he may go on in some chapter, psalm, or book of the holy scripture, as he shall see fit.[4]

What the fathers of the Westminster Assembly obviously envision is primarily textual preaching on various topics or occasions and only secondarily the expository preaching of books of the Bible in course. Nevertheless, the Westminster Directory for Worship does have in mind that a sermon is to be a careful and learned interpretation of Scripture. One easily recognizes that the Westminster Directory for Worship was a compromise document. There was considerable variety in the way the members of the Assembly saw some of these things.

In time the Puritans became masters of the occasional sermon. They preached at all kinds of occasions, in addition to the usual Sunday morning and Sunday evening sermon. There were sermons for special days of fasting and repentance, for special days of rejoicing and thanksgiving. Sermons were preached at weddings and at funerals, or any other public occasion. In New England there were election day sermons. There is, however, a dark side to this growth of the occasional sermon. The occasional sermon tended to go adrift from the liturgy. It is unfortunate that the Puritans lost the unity between word, prayer, and sacrament that the Continental and Scottish Reformers had tried to recover. In England the old medieval separation between preaching and the Communion liturgy, on one hand, and between preaching and the order for morning and evening prayer, on the other hand, was not healed by the Reformation. It is therefore not at all surprising that in the Westminster Directory for Worship preaching has lost much of its liturgical character.

An outstanding example of the preaching ministry of a Puritan divine is found in the work of Dr. Thomas Manton (1620–77). More than many of the Puritans, Dr. Manton followed the tradition of the Continental Reformers. Manton was brought up in a devout family, having a minister for father and ministers for grandfathers on both sides of the family. After his studies in Oxford he quickly won a reputation as a learned preacher. Manton had read widely in the literature of the early church and in the Continental Reformers, and possessed a large private library that was greatly admired by his colleagues. He was particularly well known for his knowledge of the scholastic theologians. From 1653 until 1662 he was pastor of St. Paul's Covent Garden, the most prominent Puritan pulpit in London. Although not a member of the Westminster Assembly, he was chosen to write the preface to the Assembly's Confession of Faith. He was one of those Presbyterians who supported the restoration of Charles II but who refused to go along with episcopacy and was therefore under the Act of Uniformity denied the right to preach. Manton was a prolific writer. Twenty-two volumes of his works, a large part of which are sermons, have come down to us.

The bulk of Manton's sermons is made up of his *lectio continua* preaching. One notices, however, that with Manton the *lectio continua* has slowed down to such a pace that he is no longer preaching through individual books but rather through chapters. We find, for example:

27 sermons on Matthew 25

45 sermons on John 17

24 sermons on Romans 6

47 sermons on Romans 8

40 sermons on 2 Corinthians 5

65 sermons on Hebrews 11

32 sermons on Ephesians 5

16 sermons on 2 Thessalonians 1

18 sermons on 2 Thessalonians 2

190 sermons on Psalm 119

One can surely object that when the *lectio continua* is preached so slowly, one of the advantages of this approach to preaching is lost. One does not get the whole message of a particular biblical writer. This approach did nevertheless produce a remarkable faithfulness to Scripture, and in the pulpit of Thomas Manton it made for great preaching.

The series of sermons on Psalm 119 is indeed famous in the history of preaching. It is remarkable for the fact that Dr. Manton was able to go through the 176 verses of the psalm in 190 sermons without becoming tedious or repetitious. Only a man of tremendous intellectual vitality could have preached such a series and yet maintain the interest of his congregation. These sermons were delivered in the course of a bit more than a year. Each week he preached two sermons on the Lord's Day and one during the middle of the week.

In addition to these sermons we find a number of sermons for funerals and weddings. As England became better supplied with preachers, we find that funerals and weddings were more and more considered appropriate occasions for sermons. At one wedding service Manton chose a text from Genesis 2:22, "And [God] brought her to the man." Dr. Manton develops the text in such a way that the providence of God in choosing a husband or wife is recognized. Christians should receive their life partner from the hand of God. He reminds us of the story of Isaac and Rebecca. He quotes from Proverbs 19:14, "Riches and honours are an inheritance from our fathers: but a good wife is from the Lord." Manton tells us that when the Christian sees God's hand in this relationship he will be more diligent and patient in seeking God's blessing in it. The Westminster Directory for Worship in its chapter "The Solemnization of Marriage" had explicitly taught that an exhortation from the Word of God was a legitimate part of the wedding service, "because such as marry are to marry in the Lord, and . . . have special need of instruction, direction, and exhortation, from the word of God, at their entering into such a new condition, . . . we judge it expedient that marriage be solemnized by a lawful minister of the word." This sermon is clearly addressed to the whole congregation. The unmarried are instructed on how they are to seek a husband or wife. The married are admonished to acknowledge God's providence that they might recognize God's blessing. The sermon even has words of comfort for those who have lost a husband or wife. Manton has clearly recognized the pastoral opportunity provided by preaching at a wedding.

In much the same way, funerals were considered appropriate times to witness to the Christian belief in the resurrection of the body and the life everlasting. At the funeral of Mistress Jane Blackwell, the wife of a fellow minister, Dr. Manton selected the text, "Blessed are the dead who die in the Lord" (Rev. 14:13), and developed from it a three-point sermon. First, he tells us what it is to die in the Lord; second, he tells us what the blessedness is of those who die in the Lord; and third, he tells us how the Christian comes to be blessed with dying in the Lord. This sermon like all of Manton's sermons is marked by a straightforward analysis of the text of Scripture. Here we have a perfect example of what the Puritans meant by a "plain style of preaching." The beauty of the sermon is the clarity with which it draws from the Bible the Christian teaching on the hope of eternal life. There is in the whole sermon a remarkable pastoral tone of a minister who recognizes what the Christian needs to know when faced by death.

As a preacher Thomas Manton is distinguished by his profound insight into the meaning of the text of Scripture. Simply in his mastery of the Scriptures Manton surpasses other preachers. One is amazed at his resourcefulness in bringing parallel passages to the illumination of his text. His sermons are great because he was a most able interpreter of Scripture. The greatest example of his ability as an expositor is his commentary on the epistle of James. This commentary is an adaptation of a series of sermons he delivered on weekday mornings at Stoke Newington. We find in it a perfect balance between a clear analysis of the text and practical application to the Christian life. Today, almost 350 years later, this commentary can be bought in two or three different editions. It remains unsurpassed, the great classic commentary on the epistle of James. Surely the preaching ministry of Thomas Manton proves to us once again that the greatest preaching is that which most clearly sets forth Scripture.

PIETISM AND THE GREAT AWAKENING

With the coming of eighteenth-century Pietism, the preaching of a considerable number of Protestant pastors took a very different direction. The Pietists continued to develop the Puritan concern for inward piety, but they developed it to the point where they began to lose interest in the text of Scripture in itself. One sometimes gets the impression that they were interested in Scripture primarily because it produced religious experience. This was particularly the case with German Pietism. At the beginning of the Pietist movement Philipp Spener (1635–1705) had advised the preacher not to waste too much time talking about the text of his sermon, but to move as quickly as possible to the discussion of religious experience. Reformed pastors who had been heavily influenced by Pietism began to lose interest in expository preaching. This was true to some extent of Jonathan Edwards in New England; and at times we get the same impression it was true of American Presbyterians such as Gilbert Tennent and Samuel Davies. One certainly gets this impression from the Wesleys and Whitefield in England. For the Pietists of the eighteenth century, the chief concern of preaching was conversion. Among some of the Pietists the teaching of moral principles or the teaching of doctrine might have a significant place, but none of the major Pietist preachers could really be called an expository preacher.

If the Pietists were not great expositors, they were great evangelists. John Wesley (1703–91) particularly seemed to have a feel for the fact that whether one was a Cottsfield coal miner or the Countess of Huntington, we all hunger and thirst for the bounty of the Spirit. Wesley developed a very different approach to preaching. Unlike John Chrysostom and John Calvin, who spent a lifetime preaching through the whole of Scripture to a single congregation, Wesley developed a barrel of sermons on certain central themes that he preached again and again to many different congregations. Like Francis of Assisi before him or, for that matter, the apostle Paul, John Wesley developed an itinerant preaching ministry. Truly the world was his pulpit. He preached in hundreds of towns, cities, villages, and even in the open countryside in fields, cemeteries, and public parks. During the week he always preached at least once, maybe twice, a day. On the Lord's Day he might preach four or five times. Since Wesley lived to a great age, Wesley probably preached as many sermons as any preacher who has ever lived. Yet, even at that, he had a barrel of around fifty sermons that he preached again and again. These sermons typically treated such subjects as the new birth, justification, repentance unto life, sanctification, and the way to eternal life. Sometimes he departed from his standard sermons, but those fifty standard sermons were the heart of his preaching, and they were repeated again and again. These basic sermons produced a revival that changed the whole character of England.

George Whitefield (1714–70) brought the Methodist Revival to America. Whitefield had been part of the original Methodist cell group at Oxford. Coming to America in 1739, he toured the English colonies on the eastern seaboard with his evangelistic preaching. His preaching united a group of religious revivals that had been developing in the Connecticut River valley of New England and in the Raritan River valley of New Jersey. Under Whitefield's leadership these rivers of renewal converged into the Great Awakening. Whitefield, much more flamboyant than the very careful and meticulous Wesley, relied on extemporaneous preaching. He was probably the greatest orator of his century, but the chief strength of his preaching was a sort of spontaneous fire that fell from heaven as unplanned as lightning. Whitefield's approach to preaching was to have a great influence on the American church. His freewheeling, dramatic oratory would be cultivated for the next two hundred years. It somehow seemed particularly appropriate to the robust spirit of young America. Even Benjamin Franklin, who was far from being a believer, was an enthusiastic admirer of Whitefield's oratory. Ever since Whitefield a host of American Protestants has been convinced that a preacher who has to depend on a manuscript is not a real preacher at all.

The Great Awakening brought thousands of new members into the churches of colonial America, and yet it raised a great number of questions as to the true nature of the Christian faith. In New England such men as Jonathan Edwards (1703–58) of Northampton and Benjamin Colman (1673–1747) of the Brattle Street Church in Boston recognized this enthusiastic outburst of evangelical faith as a divine work, even if there had been excesses. They set to work guiding this new enthusiasm into a deeper moral integrity and a greater concern for the reform of the institutions of society. Pietistic preaching may have begun with concentrating on conversion, but it quickly moved to preaching on moral and social issues. Jonathan Edwards, for example, may have provoked the complacent village of Enfield to repent with his famous sermon "Sinners in the Hands of an Angry God," but before long he was preaching through 1 Corinthians 13 with a series of sermons entitled *Charity and Its Fruits*.

Much the same thing was happening in New Jersey and Pennsylvania. Gilbert Tennent (1703–64), pastor of the Presbyterian church in New Brunswick, had come to admire the ministry of his Dutch Reformed colleague Theodorus Jacobus Frelinghuysen (1692–1747), who had been deeply influenced by Continental Pietism before being sent out to America to organize churches in rural New Jersey. Frelinghuysen had drunk deeply from the Pietism that was springing up with such vitality in Germany and the Netherlands at the very beginning of the eighteenth century. Gilbert Tennent, the son of Scotch-Irish Presbyterianism, cultivated the type of evangelistic preaching he had learned from Frelinghuysen, and when Whitefield arrived from England, Tennent soon became Whitefield's most trusted lieutenant and the leader of the Great Awakening in the middle colonies. The Great Awakening split the Presbyterian church. The Old Lights could not abide the enthusiasm of the New Lights, and so they simply threw them out of the church. This had a sobering effect on Gilbert Tennent and the other New Light preachers. Called to Second Presbyterian Church in Philadelphia, Tennent began to reemphasize the importance of solid doctrine and to preach through the Westminster Shorter Catechism as a means of bringing to maturity the religious enthusiasm of the Great Awakening.

Colonial America was producing more and more capable young preachers. The Great Awakening produced several important educational institutions for the training of ministers, such as the Log College on the banks of Neshaminy Creek in Bucks County, north of Philadelphia. The Academy at Faggs Manor was another such institution, as were the College of New Jersey at Princeton and Dartmouth College in New Hampshire. One of the most distinguished young preachers to be produced in America was Samuel Davies (1723–61), who prepared for the ministry at Faggs Manor. Finishing his work at Faggs Manor, he was called to Hanover County in Virginia. Davies had been endowed with all the enthusiasm of the Great Awakening, but just as importantly he had been blessed with an amazing amount of tact. Using great diplomacy, he was able to organize the Presbyterian church in Virginia without antagonizing the Episcopalians who were officially established in Virginia in the same way as they were in old England. The Virginia authorities felt much happier about ministers who were the settled pastors of particular congregations. Itinerant preaching in the style of Wesley and Whitefield the Virginia authorities regarded with considerable suspicion. Davies was glad to give the impression of being a settled preacher, but in fact he did a great deal of itinerating. He planted churches for several counties around. Davies's sermons were typical of eighteenth-century Pietism. His itineration influenced his sermons, just as it had Wesley's. Davies's sermons did not follow the *lectio continua* or any other lectionary. They treated the principal Pietist themes of repentance, justification by faith, sanctification of life, and the hope of glory. There were plenty of sermons on practical piety and sound doctrine, but the systematic exposition of Scripture seems to have escaped Davies's homiletical concerns. With Davies the dramatic oratory of the Great Awakening flowered. His sermons are well thought out and well organized. They have all the spiritual vitality of Whitefield and all the intellectual discipline of Edwards. William Sprague, who wrote a monumental history of American preaching something over a century ago, considered Samuel Davies the greatest American preacher up to that time.

MORE RECENT TIMES

The nineteenth and twentieth centuries with their rapidly expanding world began to take the preaching of Reformed churches in yet another direction. The frontier began to produce its own ministers, who had not really been spawned by the sacred traditions of classical Protestantism and its usual schools and universities. On the American frontier Methodist circuit riders proved once again the utility of itinerant preaching. Preachers like Peter Cartwright (1785–1872) could match the devices of any brawler or heckler who might challenge his right to preach. Once again God had obviously raised up persons fit for the challenges they would have to meet. Typical of the new type of preacher who was beginning to appear was Charles Finney (1792–1875). He was brought up on the frontier of western New York in the first decade of the nineteenth century when the forests

were being cleared and the first corn fields were being planted. He grew up knowing how to fell trees, split rails, and hunt deer, but without the least notion of
what might have been between the covers of a Bible. Then he got converted and
began to study for the ministry. A Presbyterian minister tried to guide him
through the paces of a classical theological education, but to Finney all that
seemed to impede the gospel rather than promote it. Calvinism seemed inconsistent with the wide-open possibilities of the frontier, where anyone with a
strong back and a stout heart could build a future for himself. Finney had great
success at bringing people to conversion, and once he converted them, he turned
them to converting society. The slave trade and the liquor traffic were regarded
as the chief obstacles to bringing in the kingdom of God.

Assured that their vigorous preaching would bring the millennium, Henry
Ward Beecher (1813–87), Philips Brooks (1835–93), Matthew Simpson
(1811–84), and a host of evangelistic social reformers like them began to make
the pulpit a powerful force for social change. Evangelism and social reform went
hand in hand. That was the nature of evangelical American Protestantism in the
early nineteenth century. More and more the pulpit was devoted to the support
of causes that the optimism of the age was sure were destined for success. Preachers searched the Bible for every conceivable text to support these causes, but the
causes soon exhausted even the Scriptures, and all too often the relation between
Scripture and sermon became hardly more than a formality.

In Scotland the social concerns of an increasingly evangelical Presbyterianism
were advanced by such capable men as Thomas Chalmers (1780–1847) in Glasgow and Thomas Guthrie (1803–75) in Edinburgh. Advancing against the problems of city slums, these preachers stayed much closer to the Reformed tradition
of expository preaching than their American cousins. The Scottish evangelicals
often preached a *lectio continua* of major books of Scripture. At the same time
that Thomas Chalmers was organizing his model parish in one of Glasgow's most
blighted areas, he preached through the Gospel of John Sunday by Sunday.
Thomas Guthrie's series of sermons *The City, Its Sins and Its Sorrows* is a conscientious exposition of Colossians 2:14–17. All the scenes of Charles Dickens
come to life in the pulpit of Guthrie—the disgrace of poverty, the shame of igno-
rance, the ravages of alcohol, the tyranny of child labor—yet it is always the Word
of God that speaks to the problem. When Alexander Whyte (1836–1921), the
son of an unmarried teenage mother, mounted the pulpit of St. George's West in
Edinburgh, the power of the gospel to transform human life was manifested as
clearly as it ever has been in the whole history of Christian preaching.

In England men like Joseph Parker (1830–1902), Alexander Maclaren (1826–
1910), and above all, Charles Haddon Spurgeon (1834–92) began to draw enormous crowds. These preachers had never spent their time in Oxford or Cambridge, and when they preached it was not the Queen's English that came out. In
an era that was rapidly becoming the age of the common man, preachers like
Spurgeon and Whyte became folk heroes. They did not belong to the British
establishment. They were Dissenters. Chalmers, Guthrie, and Whyte were Free

Presbyterians, Parker was a Congregationalist, and Maclaren and Spurgeon were Baptists. These Evangelicals, as they were increasingly called, represented a sort of resurrection of seventeenth-century Puritanism. They were Calvinists through and through. Probably no one has ever soaked up Puritan preaching quite like Spurgeon. It was from William Perkins, Richard Sibbes, and Thomas Manton that Spurgeon learned to preach. Although he was a child prodigy as an orator, he deepened his natural ability to speak in public with a profound study of Scripture. No one was ever able to crack open the inner meaning of a text of Scripture quite like Spurgeon. While he did not have the advantages of a formal theological education, he studied the Scriptures and the biblical expositors like John Calvin and Matthew Henry. Even as a boy he had loved to read in his grandfather's library. A Congregational minister, his grandfather had an extensive collection of the Puritan classics. Young Spurgeon probably got a better theological education from his grandfather's library than he could have gotten from any theological seminary of the time. As he grew older, he continued to collect the writings of the Puritans, building up a vast private library and becoming the chief authority of his age on the preaching of Puritanism.

The nineteenth-century Evangelicals of England and Scotland brought back the Reformed tradition of expository preaching. Spurgeon, probably the most brilliant preacher of modern times, was a poet in his ability to make clear the significance of the biblical imagery. His ability with the language, even more remarkable because it was self-taught, flowed with a masterful simplicity from his understanding of the Word to his proclamation of the Word. Spurgeon never followed any kind of preaching plan. Each sermon was complete in itself. He preached on a great variety of texts. In fact, he was rather remarkable in that he remained an expository preacher although he moved from one text to another without any apparent connection from one sermon to the next. For Spurgeon it was important for the Holy Spirit to give him the right text every time he went into the pulpit. Most of the other great expositors of that age were considerably more systematic in their exposition. Alexander Whyte was remembered for preaching his way through the Psalms for three years. It was a brilliant series of sermons that opened up the Psalms as Christian prayer and pointed the way to a life of devotion. Joseph Parker one time preached his way from Genesis to Revelation, taking seven years to do it. Alexander Maclaren in his older years managed to produce a series of sermons that went through the whole Bible in something like thirty volumes.

The British expositors were bound to have their effect on the American preachers of the period. Dwight L. Moody (1837–99) was an avowed disciple of Spurgeon. Moody, like Spurgeon, had never studied in a university. He had been brought up in a small country town in New England by his widowed mother and as a teenager went off to the big city to be a shoe salesman. In Boston he joined the Congregational church and set himself to being a faithful Christian. Just before the outbreak of the Civil War he came to Chicago, and before long the shoe salesman was gathering a Sunday school class of street boys.

Moody was made of the same stuff Chicago was made of. What could have been more natural? The market town of the West produced the consummate salesman of the gospel. If God had called Charles Finney (1792–1875), a man of the sprawling frontier, to take the gospel to frontiersman, God had now called a man of the boom town to preach to the masses that were now pouring into America's cities.

Unfortunately some of America's evangelists, as much as they professed devotion to the Bible, never dug very deeply into Scripture. They never learned the biblical languages or the cultural context that produced the Bible. They may have constantly read their Bibles, but they were ignorant of the history of its interpretation. Yet they became folk heroes and magnificently demonstrated the possibility of a Christian way of life in a very distinctive culture. Their approach to preaching was unique. It centered on evangelism and social reform. These evangelists approached the unchurched masses with a simple message: Repent of your sin, believe in Christ, and clean up your life. With incredible vigor they preached abolition of slavery, the missionary endeavor, prohibition of strong drink, and women's rights.

In order to reach the unchurched, some evangelists—like Moody, Sam Jones (1847–1906), George Truett (1867–1944), and Billy Graham (b. 1918)—preferred to preach in tents, theaters, and arenas rather than in churches. Consequently their preaching was perceived to be something other than worship. Any hymnody or sacred music that might have been part of the program was understood as a sort of sacred entertainment. In order to win the interest of the masses, the typical American sermon made an excessive use of human interest stories. The tear-jerking tale, the homiletical joke, and the sentimental reminiscence became standard sermon material. But whatever shortcomings these evangelists may have had, they did get the simple basic gospel over to millions of Americans at a very important time in our national history.

America produced a great school of preaching in the century and a half between the rise of the circuit riders and the fall of the television evangelists. There was a wide variety in this school. The revivalists were not the only ones who influenced the Reformed pulpit. Walter Rauschenbusch (1861–1918) and Washington Gladden (1836–1918) were leading contenders for the social gospel. They picked up on the populism of the frontier preachers and took it in the direction of the new political and economic theories of the day. Then there were the apostles of American optimism like Harry Emerson Fosdick (1878–1969), Norman Vincent Peale (1898–1993), and Robert Schuller (b. 1926). Fosdick was a Baptist, the voice of liberal Protestantism during the '20s and '30s. His most famous sermon, "Shall the Fundamentalists Win?" stirred up theological controversies for a whole generation. He was sure the ideologies of the future would bring a better world, and he hastened to call into question any traditional Christian doctrine that stood in the way of progress. "Fearless" Fosdick was the very model of modernism. His liberal gospel shocked the churchgoing public of America, yet he drew large crowds because of his revolutionary pulpit rhetoric.

It was a commonsense, self-evident sort of rhetoric. It was a rationalistic, no-nonsense, business executive's sort of rhetoric. Fosdick, bankrolled by John D. Rockefeller, was, above all, successful. Incongruously he built a Gothic skyscraper for a church, and there he preached a modern, up-to-date morality that many found helpful. Regardless of denomination Fosdick's approach to preaching, as well as his liberal gospel, became the standard of American mainline Protestantism.

At the same time, Donald Grey Barnhouse (1895–1960), Robert Munger (1910–2001), and Louis H. Evans (1897–1981) preached significant expository sermons, but they were something of an exception. Two very exceptional preachers of the mid-twentieth century were Henry Sloane Coffin (1877–1954), pastor of New York's Madison Avenue Presbyterian Church, and his successor, George Buttrick (1892–1980). In later years Buttrick served as preacher to Harvard University. Here was a preacher who could make a biblical text shimmer with transcendent light even to a congregation of the most sophisticated and worldly Christians of the day. Still, toward the end of the twentieth century expository preaching in the Reformed tradition had virtually disappeared from the mainline American pulpit.

Seventeen years ago I finished the first edition of this book. At the time preaching seemed to have fallen on hard times. Yet with the beginning of the third millennium there seems to be a stirring. The dry bones seem to be moving. It may just be that once more the Spirit is being poured forth. It is too early to tell which of these stirrings will be finally recognized as Reformed tradition.

Chapter 6

The Ministry of Prayer

One of the most informative passages of Scripture on the subject of corporate prayer is Solomon's prayer for the dedication of the Temple (1 Kings 8:23–53). In the course of this long prayer he outlines the uses for which the Temple had been set apart. It is clear that Solomon dedicates the Temple as a house of prayer. This primary purpose of the Temple is affirmed again and again. Jesus himself understood the Temple as "a house of prayer for all the nations" (Mark 11:17). Let us look at this prayer for a picture of the ministry of prayer as it was carried out in the Temple.

Solomon begins the prayer by remembering at length the covenant promises of God. God is, above all, one who keeps covenant and shows steadfast love, or, to use the Hebrew word, *hesed,* which means God's covenant faithfulness with his people. Solomon remembers God's covenant with the house of David and the promises that were given him concerning a Temple where God would make his name to dwell. That is, the Temple was built in obedience to the Word of God and with the expectation that when the Temple was so built, God would honor the prayer that was offered in the Temple. What is abundantly clear at this point is that the theological foundation of prayer is the doctrine of the covenant.

Having remembered before God the covenant promises, Solomon mentions seven instances for prayer in the Temple. Particularly important among these are prayers in time of drought, pestilence, or military defeat. It is assumed that such things come about because the people have sinned; so Solomon prays, if the people "turn again to thee, and acknowledge thy name, and pray and make supplication to thee in this house; then hear thou in heaven, and forgive the sin of thy people Israel" (1 Kings 8:33–34). What is in question here is public sin, public confession, and the forgiveness of the whole people. What Solomon seems to envision is holding fast days, days of public repentance.

Several other places in Scripture enliven our picture of this public penitential prayer that took place in the Temple. The lamentations in the book of Joel exemplify the sort of prayers offered in the Temple when some national catastrophe occurred. The calamity that fell upon Israel on that occasion was the destruction of the land by a plague of locusts. Trumpets were blown, the priests cried and wailed before God, wearing sackcloth and besmearing themselves with ashes. Jeremiah 14 records for us the prayers that were offered in the Temple on the occasion of a drought. A certain order is to be noted in these prayers. First there is the song of lamentation:

> "Judah mourns
>   and her gates languish;
> her people lament on the ground,
>   and the cry of Jerusalem goes up.
> Her nobles send their servants for water;
>   they come to the cisterns,
> they find no water,
>   they return with their vessels empty;
> they are ashamed and confounded
>   and cover their heads.
> Because of the ground which is dismayed,
>   since there is no rain on the land,
> the farmers are ashamed,
>   they cover their heads.
> Even the hind in the field forsakes her newborn calf
>   because there is no grass.
> The wild asses stand on the bare heights,
>   they pant for air like jackals;
> their eyes fail
>   because there is no herbage."
>
> (Jer. 14:2–6)

This is followed by a penitential prayer that acknowledges the sin of the people and asks God's mercy. The prayer pleads the covenant relation Israel has with God, who is addressed as the "hope of Israel."

> "Though our iniquities testify against us,
>   act, O LORD, for thy name's sake;
> for our backslidings are many,
>   we have sinned against thee.

> O thou hope of Israel,
>   its savior in time of trouble . . ."
>   (Jer. 14:7–8)

After this prayer of confession and supplication, the people awaited an oracle from one of the Temple prophets. Doubtless in many cases there was an oracle that was an assurance of pardon and forgiveness, but in this case (Jer. 14:10), the prophet was bound to announce there was no forgiveness.

A less vivid although happier example of this liturgy of penitential prayer we find in Psalm 12. In the first two verses we hear the lamentation, in verses three and four the supplication for mercy, and in the fifth verse the prophetic oracle in which God promises justice to the afflicted, "'Because the poor are despoiled, because the needy groan, I will now arise,' says the LORD; 'I will place him in the safety for which he longs.'" The liturgy achieves completion then in a hymn of thanksgiving, "The promises of the LORD are promises that are pure." The liturgy has these four parts: (1) song of lamentation in which the people cry to the Lord, (2) prayer of confession and supplication for mercy, (3) the divine oracle of forgiveness and assurance of redemption, and (4) the hymn of thanksgiving. This four-part prayer liturgy, as well as individual parts of it, we discover in a good number of the prayers of the book of Psalms.

As we have seen, Solomon's prayer of dedication has particularly in mind the prayer of the whole nation in time of national emergencies but Solomon also has in mind the prayer of "any man . . . each knowing the affliction of his own heart" (1 Kings 8:38). Every day many Israelites must have come to the Temple as private individuals with a great variety of very personal troubles about which they wanted to pray. The priests stood in attendance to assist such people in their prayers; they led them in prayer, offered sacrifices in their name, and surely on occasion delivered to them a word of promise from God. The prayer of the Temple served not only public concerns but the personal and private needs of anyone who sought the Lord.

A particularly moving example of this is the story of Hannah's prayer for the gift of a son (1 Sam. 1:1–2:11). To be sure, the story unfolds in the sanctuary of Shiloh rather than in the Temple of Jerusalem, but we can be well assured that much the same thing would have happened in Jerusalem. First we hear of how Hannah wept bitterly before the Lord. This lamentation is a natural part of prayer, and we find prayers of lamentation throughout Scripture. Then she made a vow that if God would give her a son she would dedicate him to God's service. She mentioned her lamentation deep in her heart. All this was done before Eli the priest, who, finally, in a conversation with her discovered the deep tribulation of her heart. Eli gave her a benediction or prophetic oracle, "Go in peace, and the God of Israel grant your petition" (1 Sam. 1:17). Hannah returned home, and in due time the child for whom she had prayed was born. Then, when the child grew old enough to be taken to the Temple, Hannah led her son, whom she had named Samuel, up to the sanctuary at Shiloh. With her she brought a bull to be presented for sacrifice. Then in fulfillment of her vow she delivered the child to Eli the priest and gave her witness that God had answered her prayer. She sang the votive thanksgiving psalm that is recorded at the beginning of chapter 2. (*Votive* means "in regard to a vow." A votive sacrifice was a sacrifice made in fulfillment of a vow. The votive thanksgiving psalm was sung when the votive sacrifice was presented.)

In reading this votive thanksgiving psalm, one is somewhat surprised to find that it is not particularly appropriate to the occasion. It is a stereotyped prayer that would be appropriate to many different kinds of people who came to the Temple to make a votive sacrifice. Doubtless this prayer was a standard votive thanksgiving prayer, rather than a prayer composed for Hannah. The Temple must have had a collection of prayers of lamentation and a collection of votive thanksgiving psalms that were used on ordinary occasions. Surely special occasions would from time to time demand a new composition, but in most cases the standard prayers must have been used. In this way, the private prayers of individuals were inserted into the prayer of Israel. Private prayer became public prayer.

This sort of thing must have happened frequently in the Temple. Relatives must have come to the Temple to pray for the members of their family who were ill. Farmers surely came to pray for good crops, as well as any number of others in a multitude of different needs. The vows did not have to be made in the Temple, as the story of Jonah makes clear. The vows could be made anywhere, and then when the suppliant was delivered from danger, he or she would make a pilgrimage to Jerusalem and there pay the vows. In Psalm 107 we have a sort of corporate votive thanksgiving psalm. This psalm must have been used at one of the great annual festivals when there were many people who all wanted to pay their vows at the same time. They wanted to witness to how God had heard their prayers when they were lost in the desert, in trouble at sea, suffering in prison, or facing some other calamity. All these individual prayers and private concerns mingle together in a single hymn of thanksgiving to God, who is the savior of his people and "whose mercy endureth forever." All the personal concerns like little streams finally join into a great river of corporate prayer.

We need to look carefully at the relation between private prayer and corporate prayer in the worship of the Temple. In the book of Psalms it is not always clear whether the prayer is intended for individual use or for corporate use. There is good reason for this. The fact that one came to the Temple to pray meant that one was appealing to the whole community for support in one's prayer. It is a most natural thing for people facing very individual and personal problems to ask the support of others in their prayers. When as Christians today we assemble together for prayer, we appeal to the whole Christian community to support us in our prayer.

Personal prayer relates to corporate prayer in still another way. In the book of Psalms some prayers are centered around the person of the king. Some of these are coronation prayers or prayers for military success. There is even a royal wedding psalm. Although scholars speculate much about these royal psalms, it is quite clear that prayers for the king and his well-being were in fact intercessions for the whole nation. It has often been suggested that many of the prayers that appear in personal and individual terms are really intended for the king. David was among other things a champion of prayer. Those who want to learn to pray have only to follow his example. The prayers of David are the "type" of the prayers of the people. The life of prayer becomes an imitation of the life of David. David prayed for Israel and Israel prayed for David; even more Israel prayed in David. That is why so many of the psalms have superscriptions telling us about the situation in the life of David that gave rise to the prayer. In the book of Acts we see how the primitive Christian church developed this idea. Since David was understood as the type of Christ, the prayers of David, the prayers for David, and the prayers for David's kingdom were adopted as the prayers of Christ and his church (Acts 4:23–31). The Christian prays in the name of Jesus, Christ prays for the church, and the church prays in Christ. One thing this means is that the Christian inserts his or her own prayers into the prayer of Christ. Another thing it means is that the Christian appropriates the prayer of Christ. The ascended Christ at the right hand of the Father intercedes for the church and presents our individual prayers at the throne of grace, as part of his own prayers. Our prayer mingles with the sweet incense of his prayer.

The prayer of the synagogue developed in a very different way from the prayer of the Temple. The central prayer of the synagogue was the *Amida* or, as it is sometimes called, the Prayer of the Eighteen Benedictions. The prayer was fairly well formulated by the first Christian century, and we can be fairly certain that Jesus and the apostles followed this form of prayer. At that time, the *Amida* was a form of prayer rather than a formula. The exact text was not set; however, the arrangement and themes of each of the eighteen parts of the prayer were clearly established. When a well-known rabbi or a particularly venerated holy man led the prayer, it was expected, however, that he would extemporize on the various themes. The prayer began with three benedictions of praise and thanksgiving. In the center of the prayer were six supplications or petitions of a more personal nature, followed by six intercessions for the well-being of the nation of Israel. The final three benedictions concluded the prayer with praise and thanksgiving and introduced the giving of the Aaronic benediction.

Characteristic of this prayer is the way its supplications and intercessions are couched in praise and thanksgiving and each supplication or intercession is concluded with a benediction or thanksgiving. For example, the sixth benediction is a supplication for mercy:

> Forgive us, our Father, for we have sinned; pardon us, our King, for we have transgressed, for thou art good and forgiving. Blessed be thou, O Lord, who art gracious and dost abundantly forgive.[1]

The eleventh benediction is an intercession for the Jewish civil authority:

> Restore our judges as at first, and our councillors as at the beginning and
> reign thou over us, O Lord, alone, in grace and mercy and righteousness
> and judgment. Blessed be thou, O Lord, the King who lovest righteousness
> and judgment. [2]

The concluding sentence is, properly speaking, the benediction, "Blessed be thou, O Lord, the King who lovest righteousness and judgment." The subject of the benediction matches the subject of intercession. The prayer asks for the establishment of a just civil authority and at the same time blesses God for his love of justice. When the apostle Paul told the Philippians to make their prayers and supplications to God with thanksgiving (Phil. 4:6), he must have had in mind something quite similar to this prayer.

Now let us turn to the prayer of the New Testament church. When one has a clear picture of how this Prayer of the Eighteen Benedictions was prayed, one begins to see many indications or hints in the New Testament of how the infant church exercised the ministry of prayer. The prayer of the primitive Christian church bears the marks of the liturgical mold of the synagogue. First, let us look at the teaching of Jesus regarding prayer in light of what we have learned about the *Amida.* The Sermon on the Mount preserves for us a number of Jesus' teachings about prayer. Jesus, in criticizing the Jewish practice of prayer, very specifically has in mind the way some of his fellow Jews prayed the *Amida,* for we read, "for they love to stand and pray in the synagogues and at the street corners" (Matt. 6:5). *Amida* means "standing," that is, it is the prayer that is said standing. The point of Jesus' criticism is that the truly devout should not make a show of their praying; aside from that, Jesus probably had in mind that the prayers which were said would not differ so very much from the traditional *Amida.* For the *Amida* itself, as a form of prayer, there is no criticism. Jesus will add to the content, as we shall see, but the basic form will pass into the prayer of the church. The practice of standing for prayer would be maintained in the church for many centuries.

Jesus goes on to teach a specific form of prayer. This form we call the Lord's Prayer. The Lord's Prayer has many similarities to the *Amida* in both form and content. Like the *Amida,* it begins with praise, "Our Father who art in heaven, hallowed be thy name." If the traditional doxology, "For thine is the kingdom and the power and the glory, for ever," is indeed original, then the Lord's Prayer, like the *Amida,* ends with praise and thanksgiving. The central portion is made up of two intercessions and three supplications. From the standpoint of form, the Lord's Prayer might be called a very short Christian version of the *Amida.*

With the basic form of the *Amida* in mind, some of the teachings of Jesus on prayer become much more striking. Jesus particularly taught his disciples to pray for their enemies and for those who persecuted them. He exemplified this when he prayed on the cross, "Father, forgive them." In the Sermon on the Mount he taught, "For if you forgive men their trespasses, your heavenly Father also will forgive you" (Matt. 6:14). The Prayer of the Eighteen Benedictions had no prayer for the Gentiles or for the persecutors of Israel; it prayed for the salvation of Israel alone. Jesus very specifically taught his disciples otherwise.

The intercessory prayer of Jesus in John 17 is very interesting in this respect. This prayer is also a list of intercessions. Jesus prays for the church that his disciples are to gather out of the world. He prays for the unity of the church, the continuity of the church, and the holiness of the church. Jesus teaches us here that the prayers of his disciples should embrace a much broader concern than the traditional nationalistic concerns of the *Amida*. Jesus wanted his disciples to pray for the coming of his kingdom among all nations and the doing of his Father's will over all the earth as it is in heaven.

Now let us look at several passages in the letters of the apostle Paul. Of first importance is the passage in 1 Timothy in which the apostle instructs his young assistant.

> First of all, then, I urge that supplications, prayers, intercessions, and thanksgivings be made for all men, for kings and all who are in high positions, that we may lead a quiet and peaceable life, godly and respectful in every way. This is good, and it is acceptable in the sight of God our Savior, who desires all men to be saved and to come to the knowledge of the truth. (1 Tim. 2:1–4)

In light of the concern of Jesus that the ministry of intercession reach out beyond the confines of Israel, the instructions of Paul to Timothy take on much greater clarity. Paul instructs Timothy to see that the prayers of the church include prayers for all peoples, for kings, even for the Gentile rulers of the world. Paul underlines this by stressing that God's will is for the salvation of all peoples and that therefore we should pray to this end. The *Amida* never included prayers of this scope, and so Paul instructs Timothy in this way, lest the prayers of the church follow too closely the prayers of the synagogue.

Paul frequently requests his churches to include particular intercessions in their common prayer. He asks the church at Ephesus to pray for all the saints and also to pray for him as a minister of the gospel (Eph. 6:18–19). He asks the Colossians to support him and his fellow workers in their ministry, "that God may open to us a door for the word, to declare the mystery of Christ" (Col. 4:2–3).

A number of passages in the epistles of Paul indicate how the apostle was accustomed to pray. Frequently he begins his letters by telling the church to which he is writing that he regularly makes mention of them in his prayers. Paul writes to the Philippians, "I thank my God in all my remembrance of you, always in every prayer of mine for you all making my prayer with joy, thankful for your partnership in the gospel" (Phil. 1:3–5). To the Thessalonians we find very similar words, "We give thanks to God always for you all, constantly mentioning you in our prayers, remembering before our God and Father your work of faith and labor of love and steadfastness of hope" (1 Thess. 1:2–3). In both examples we find that Paul's regular intercessions for his churches were combined with thanksgiving. We gather that when Paul and those who were with him offered their prayers, the specific churches were remembered particularly. The passage in 1 Thessalonians indicates that the prayers in question were common prayers, not just personal, private devotions. For Paul, these intercessions were a duty, a ministry of prayer that he felt he and his colleagues were "bound" to perform (2 Thess. 1:3).

The introductory prayer of the letter to the Ephesians is particularly festive.

> Blessed be the God and Father of our Lord Jesus Christ, who has blessed us in Christ with every spiritual blessing in the heavenly places, even as he chose us in him before the foundation of the world. . . . I do not cease to give thanks for you, remembering you in my prayers, that the God of our Lord Jesus Christ, the Father of glory, may give you a spirit of wisdom and of revelation in the knowledge of him. (Eph. 1:3–4, 16–17)

Here we undoubtedly have the wording of the apostle's customary prayer. It is clearly in the tradition of the Prayer of the Eighteen Benedictions. It is a benediction worthy of the school of Gamaliel.

Having given a picture of the ministry of prayer in the earliest Christian church, the church of the New Testament period, let us turn now to finding how this ministry developed in the centuries that followed.

All things considered, we have good documentation for the second and third Christian centuries, at least for this aspect of the history of Christian worship. The First Epistle of Clement, written in Rome about the year 90, concludes with a prayer that undoubtedly reflects the liturgical prayer of that church. It is, like the *Amida*, a prayer of supplication and intercession beginning and ending with praise and thanksgiving. It may well be that what we have in this letter has been abbreviated to some extent and perhaps somewhat adapted to the more specific concerns of the letter, but the general liturgical form is nevertheless clear. The opening words of the prayer seem to be missing, but the first paragraph of what has been preserved for us is a solemn prayer of praise to the source of all creation, "who in wisdom and justice governs the affairs of all men and nations," and who has chosen from out of all the peoples of the earth a people to serve him. Then follows a list of intercessions for the afflicted, the fallen, the needy, the sick, the wandering, prisoners, and the salvation of all nations. Again meditating on God's mercy and faithfulness to his people, the prayer asks for mercy to those who have sinned and peace "for us and to all that dwell on the earth." The next paragraph blesses God as sovereign ruler of the world and then intercedes for those "to whom God has entrusted the government of this world." It is an intercession for the civil authority as well as the leaders of the church. The prayer ends with a doxology praising God through Jesus Christ, the high priest and guardian of our souls. After a few other matters are mentioned regarding the delivery of the letter, there is an elaborate benediction, which, like the ascriptions of praise and benedictions at the end of the New Testament Epistles, may well reflect the benediction that concluded the prayer of the synagogue as well as the prayer of the church.

In the writings of the church fathers of the second and third centuries we find a number of remarks about the church prayers. From Justin Martyr (ca. 100–ca. 165) we learn that one of the cardinal components of the worship of the church on the Lord's Day was a Prayer of Intercession, not only for the spiritual growth of Christians but for all people everywhere. Justin clearly indicates that this general prayer comes after the sermon and before the Communion service. This prayer, like the *Amida* of the synagogue, is given with the congregation standing. It is clearly a different prayer from the Prayer of Thanksgiving said at the Communion service. Then we notice with particular interest that having finished his description of the Sunday worship, Justin speaks of the ministry of the deacons, the giving of alms, and the care of the poor. This too obviously belongs to the worship of the Lord's Day.

By the middle of the fourth century we begin to get a much clearer picture of Christian worship. We even get the complete text of some of the prayers. The Prayer of the Faithful or the Great Prayer of Intercession is a regular feature of the liturgy. The *Apostolic Constitutions,* dating from the end of the fourth century, provides us with a complete text of the liturgy of the church of Antioch. In this liturgy we find a fully developed intercessory prayer for the whole church throughout the world, the local church of Antioch, the ministry, the local bishop, presbyters, deacons, and other church leaders. There are prayers for married people, the celibate, women expecting children, the sick, the exiled, and those in prison. There are prayers for enemies, those who persecute the church, and those who are outside the church. Finally there are prayers for those who are present and for the preservation in grace of every Christian soul. One finds in this prayer the influence of both the old Jewish Prayer of the Eighteen Benedictions and the specific concerns of Jesus and the apostles flowing together in such a way that the prayer is a comprehensive prayer for the salvation of all peoples.

Having flowered into a very full and comprehensive prayer of intercession, the Prayer of the Faithful began to fade as the Middle Ages progressed, in the West at least. By the end of the Middle Ages the Prayer of the Faithful had all but disappeared from the Roman Mass. Certain of the intercessions were to be found in the canon of the Mass, but the Latin Mass of the Middle Ages had lost a separate general prayer of intercession. In a vestigial form it was still found in the prayers of Good Friday, to be sure, but during the rest of the year these intercessions were missing.

With the strong ascetic tendency that so influenced Christian spirituality in late antiquity, prayer more and more turned away from the practical concerns of life and concentrated on achieving union with God, influenced by various forms of Platonism and Neoplatonism. Instead of the concerns of the community, the family, and everyday life, prayer began to focus on a mystical ascension to spiritual reality. Mental prayer was cultivated, especially in monastic communities, as a means of escaping the material world. Anselm of Canterbury (1033–1109) in his work *Proslogion* gives us a particularly clear outline of this approach to prayer. Another famous advocate of meditative prayer was Meister Eckhart (ca. 1260–1327). His disciple, Johann Tauler (ca. 1300–1361), did much to develop the understanding of mystical union with God and the sort of prayer that led to it. Catherine of Siena (ca. 1340–80) was well known for her concept of mystical marriage. The concept of mental prayer was further developed by the Brethren of the Common Life. Thomas à Kempis (ca. 1380–1471) is the best known of the Brethren, yet it was another disciple of this group, Wessel Gansfort (ca. 1420–89) who did most to work out the techniques of mental prayer. It has to be said, however, that prayer of this sort was largely limited to the cloister. It was for spiritual athletes and had little connection with the public worship of those who remained active in the world.

With the coming of the Reformation there was a radical reform of public prayer. The disciplines of prayer that had developed during the Middle Ages had broken down. This often happens with methods of prayer. They are developed with a great deal of fervor by one generation, but after a few generations the old prayer forms grow moribund and calcified and break down. The Reformers gave themselves to an intensive study of the prayers of Holy Scripture to discover what the prayer that is according to Scripture should be. It took some time for the new evangelical forms of prayer to evolve. At first many of the old Latin prayers from the Mass and the daily office were simply translated. In Strasbourg, for instance, when it was decided to reform the daily prayer services, the old daily collects were gone over, and those that were found suitable were translated into German. Some of the collects were not found suitable, so new prayers were written to take their place. At first these new collects were in form quite similar to the old collects, but within a few years the Reformers' approach to prayer had so completely changed that even the collect form was largely bypassed.

Over the course of a dozen years or so, the Reformed church of Strasbourg developed two basic prayers for common worship, the Prayer of Confession and Supplication and the Prayer of Intercession. The Prayer of Confession and Supplication started out as a sort of Protestant Confiteor. The Confiteor of the Roman Mass, so heavy with the intercession of the saints, was rewritten so that it was a rather simple and straightforward confession of sin. In time the prayer began to be influenced by the psalms of lamentation, particularly Psalms 25 and 26. When we meet the Prayer of Confession and Supplication in the *Strasbourg Psalter* of 1537, it has become a comprehensive prayer of confession of our sin and supplication for God's mercy. It has followed very closely the pattern we found in the Temple. First is the lamentation and confession of sin, then a supplication for forgiveness and an assurance of pardon spoken by the minister, and finally a psalm of thanksgiving sung by the congregation.

The recovery of a comprehensive Prayer of Intercession became an important feature of the regular worship of the church of Strasbourg. Here, above all, Martin Bucer (1491–1551) was responsible for the writing of the liturgical texts. In Bucer's final form of the liturgy of the Reformed church of Strasbourg we find a long Prayer of Intercession that resembles the intercessory prayers of the patristic age. First there is a prayer for the civil authority, then a prayer for the ministry of the gospel, a prayer for the conversion of all peoples, a prayer for the perfection of the saints, and finally a prayer for the afflicted. Bucer phrases the text of his prayers in such a way that we recognize quite clearly he has built the prayer on those admonitions of Jesus and the apostles directing Christians to include specific concerns in their prayer. The influence of Paul's instructions to Timothy (1 Tim. 2:1–8) shines through unmistakably. Likewise, Ephesians 6:18–19, James 5:13–18, and Philippians 1:9–11 have all clearly influenced Bucer in the construction of his prayer. Bucer, who had a good knowledge of patristic literature, knew well that the Christians of an earlier age had included such concerns in their prayers. Bucer's reform was based on Scripture, to be sure, but it was also informed by his knowledge of the practice of the early church.

These two core prayers, the Prayer of Confession and Supplication and the Prayer of Intercession, were translated into French and through Calvin's (1509–64) influence were made part of the liturgy of the church of Geneva, as we discover in the *Genevan Psalter* of 1542. From that point on, these two core prayers became a regular feature of Reformed worship. John Knox (1513–72) used these two prayers as patterns, and so we find an elaboration of these same two prayers in the *Book of Common Order* of the Church of Scotland.

From the earliest *Strasbourg Psalters* there is evidence that the evangelical pastors wanted to allow for the developing of the gift of some sort of free or extemporaneous prayer. At the same time they recognized that prayer forms were needed as well. What developed was that the two core prayers were used pretty much as they appeared in the printed text of the Psalter, but then there were other prayers in the service that were supposed to be formulated by the minister. In a way quite similar to their other liturgical activities the Reformers were trying to get away from a mere *opus operandi* saying of prayers. It was not a matter of wanting to be original or creative in their prayer. To them it was important to pray as Christ had taught them to pray. From Romans 8 they learned that prayer was a sanctifying work of the Holy Spirit in their hearts. Learning to pray and growing in holiness went together.

Calvin was quite clear that not every minister could be expected to have the gift of leading in public prayer. Evidently Calvin normally led the Prayer of Confession and Supplication and the Prayer of Intercession pretty much out of the book. It was the same thing with the accustomed prayers at matins and vespers on weekdays. On the other hand, after preaching, the reformer was accustomed to extemporize. Hundreds of the extemporized prayers of Calvin have come down to us. These prayers were offered at some length after the sermon at morning or evening prayer and were carefully taken down by the stenographer who was responsible for recording the sermon. For Calvin, hearing the Word of God naturally leads to prayer. When we search the Scriptures, it becomes clear there are things in our lives that need to be set in order and things in the church or in the community that need to be corrected. For example, when Calvin was preaching through the book of Amos, he dealt in one sermon on the stubbornness of Israel in refusing to follow God's commandments. In the prayer that followed the sermon Calvin prayed "that we might turn our hearts to thy service and submit ourselves to the yoke of thy word." As one studies these extemporaneous prayers of Calvin, one sees that through prayer one moves from the Word to the world.

That was why the major prayer of the service followed the sermon, so that the preaching of the Word called forth and shaped the prayer.

There is a certain symmetry in the discipline of public prayer as it is found in the worship of the *Genevan Psalter.* Not only do we find a balance between prayer forms and free prayer, we also find a balance between the Prayer of Confession and Supplication and the Prayer of Intercession. Each represents a distinct aspect of Christian prayer. The Prayer of Confession and Supplication is by nature more subjective and introspective. It is turned inward while the intercessions are turned outward, directed toward the building up of the church and the redemption of the world. The Prayer of Confession and Supplication is baptismal prayer while the intercessions are Communion prayers. In baptisms we are baptized unto the forgiveness of sins. Baptism is the sign under which we pray that we may die unto sin and live unto righteousness. Baptism calls us to prayers of repentance and supplications for growth in grace. On the other hand, the intercessions are more closely related to Communion. The intercessions look forward to and pray for the consummation of the kingdom, to the wedding feast of the Lamb. The intercessions pray for the building up of the church, the conversion of the nations, and the perseverance of the saints.

There is yet another dimension to this symmetry. Balancing these liturgical prayers of the church are the metrical psalms, particularly the psalms of praise and thanksgiving. The *Genevan Psalter* shows an awareness of the great variety of Christian prayer.

With the seventeenth-century Puritans the order of prayers at the ordinary Sunday service was changed considerably. The Westminster Directory for Worship outlines the content of the prayers for the Sunday morning service. It provided for a short Invocation at the beginning of the service and a short prayer after the sermon. The main prayer of the ordinary Sunday service, however, was to be a full, comprehensive prayer including the elements of praise, confession, petition, intercession, and thanksgiving. The prayer in many ways reminds one of the *Amida*, the Prayer of Eighteen Benedictions so popular in the synagogue. There is no question that this prayer had strong biblical roots. The desire of the Puritans for this kind of prayer arose from the Congregational wing of the Puritan movement rather than the Presbyterian wing. In fact the position found in the Westminster Directory for Worship represents a compromise made by the Westminster Assembly, which decided in favor of the Congregationalists and compensated the Presbyterians by conceding that there might be an Invocation at the beginning of the service and a prayer after the sermon. The Congregationalists would have been happy to have had quite simply one long comprehensive prayer. Nevertheless, the full, comprehensive prayer became the regular prayer of churches that followed the Westminster Directory for Worship from that point on. Even in Presbyterian Scotland the new Westminster arrangement of prayers supplanted the old Genevan arrangement. This comprehensive prayer, or pastoral prayer as it was called, was to be said between the Scripture reading and the sermon. It came before the sermon rather than after it.

There were some real weaknesses to the arrangement of prayers provided by the Westminster Directory for Worship. In the first place, it made for an unbearably long prayer that only the most mature Christians could follow with profit. In the second place, it disturbed the very ancient order of the dominical service by putting the prayer between the Scripture lesson and the sermon rather than in its more accustomed place between the sermon and the Communion service. It tended to have the effect of diminishing the intercessory character of the prayer. It was no longer so much a prayer for the peace of the world, the progress of the gospel, and the salvation of all people, but rather a general all-purpose prayer. Finally, because the prayer was supposed to be "framed" by the minister in his own words, it was very much dependent upon the gifts of the minister leading the prayer. Unfortunately too many ministers neglected developing this gift, and in the popular imagination the minister's long prayer was apt to be a rather tedious part of the service.

There were masters of the pastoral prayer; when it was done well, it was done very well! Developing the gift of leading in public prayer needed preparation, just as developing the gift of preaching needed long study and practice. The Puritans gave special attention to what they called "conceived" prayer. While the Puritan pastor did not read his prayers from a prayer book or even write out his prayers beforehand and then read them at worship, he prepared them meditating on the subjects that needed to be treated for several days beforehand. This, as William Perkins had taught, was part of the prophetic ministry. Just as the pastor was to proclaim the Word of God to the people, so he was to offer the prayers of the people to God. Moses and Jeremiah were both examples of this dimension of the prophetic ministry.

There were a number of manuals for this purpose. Isaac Watts (1674–1748) and John Wilkins (1614–72), the Anglican bishop of Chester, produced such works, but by far the most influential was Matthew Henry's *A Method for Prayer*. More than thirty editions of this work appeared between 1712 and 1865. The work takes up in turn the different aspects of prayer: praise and adoration, confession, thanksgiving, petition and supplication, and finally intercession. Henry (1662–1714) had gone through the whole of Scripture studying all the prayers, teachings about prayer, and examples of prayer in order to make clear the nature of each of the various prayer genres. Henry's knowledge of Scripture was prodigious. Today, almost three hundred years later, his commentary on the complete Bible is as popular as ever. What Henry attempted to do was to learn the biblical language of prayer. He well understood that one learns a language by imitation, and so he gathered together the biblical language of praise, the biblical language of supplication, and the biblical language of intercession. In Henry's seminal work he suggests how we can deepen our experience of prayer by turning to the Scriptures and saturating ourselves with the biblical language of prayer. Still today such an approach will help us to develop disciplines of prayer that are Reformed according to Scripture.

By the beginning of the eighteenth century Pietism began to shape the worship of Protestantism. Pietism had begun to appear in French Catholicism during the previous century as a reaction against the domination of religious life by the court of Louis XIV. Such figures as Blaise Pascal (1623–62) and Madame Guyon (1648–1717) emphasized the private dimensions of religious experience over against a secularized state religion. By the end of the century the movement began to appear in Germany under the leadership of Philipp Spener (1635–1705) and August Hermann Francke (1663–1727). Here Pietism took on a much more Protestant flavor. Characteristic of German Pietism was the development of small prayer groups. Not wanting to break with the official state church, the German Pietists developed little fellowships within each local church that met at people's homes on Sunday afternoons or in the evening. These people shared their personal religious experiences, held informal Bible studies, sang hymns, and prayed about each other's needs. This *ecclesiola in ecclesia*, or church within the church, was not supposed to conflict with the official church, but in fact it tended to become the center of religious life in such a way that the official Sunday morning celebration of worship in the established church was apt to be regarded as a dry formality. At the small-group prayer meetings the warmth of Christian fellowship was found, and the prayers of formal, public worship were looked upon as perfunctory.

The prayers of the Pietist fellowship meetings were popular, intense, and spontaneous. Emphasizing Luther's doctrine of the priesthood of all believers, every member of the fellowship was encouraged to voice his or her own prayer concerns. The Puritan idea of conceived prayer was replaced by an emphasis on spontaneous prayer. It was the spontaneous prayer of the heart that was clearly sincere. Those who were really filled with the Holy Spirit did not have to prepare prayers. Unlike the Puritans, the Pietists saw no need for studying the Scriptures to learn what they were to pray about or to seek guidance in developing prayer disciplines. A formal ministry of intercession drawn from the teachings of Scripture interested them no more than reading the set prayers of the official liturgy. The Puritan insight that prayer was part of the prophetic dimension of the gospel ministry faded before the concern that every member of the fellowship should have a chance to participate. Psalm prayer tended to lose its place in Protestant worship, and with it the sense of awe and majesty of the experience. But if Pietism lost some of these important aspects of prayer, it did bring an intimacy and a fervor that democratized the prayer life of Protestantism.

Emblematic of Protestant Pietism was the religious community of Herrnhut. Fleeing the religious persecutions of the Austrians, a group of Czech Protestants had settled on the estate of Count Nicholas von Zinzendorf (1700–1760). These Moravians, as they were called, claimed the heritage of the Bohemian reformer Jan Hus (ca. 1369–1415). Zinzendorf, a member of the high German aristocracy, had been educated in Halle, by that time the center of the Pietist movement. Devout by nature, the young count dedicated himself to the shepherding of these Moravians. On his lands and under his guidance the Moravians built a utopian community they called Herrnhut. There the life of prayer, as it was understood by Pietism, prospered. Prayer and work went hand in hand. The farming, the handcrafts, the care of children, and the marketing were organized around the devotional life of the community. Each member of the community belonged to a small-group fellowship organized according to age, sex, and marital status. These fellowships fostered intense personal prayer. Hymnody kept the whole community in joyful harmony. All day long Moravians sang and prayed, all to the accompaniment of lively brass choirs. The Moravians were among the first Protestants to take seriously the work of foreign missions, and the community set aside regular days of intercession for these missionaries. Groups of missionaries were sent to India, Greenland, the Caribbean islands, North Carolina, and Pennsylvania, constantly supported by an intense ministry of intercession.

The story is often told of how John Wesley (1703–91) on his voyage to America in 1737 was inspired by the deep faith, fervent prayer, and joyful singing of a group of Moravians. At the time Wesley was bent on maintaining the formal religious practices of Anglicanism, but the devotional life of the Moravians began to melt his heart. He began to realize there was more to prayer than the *Book of Common Prayer* had taught him. Wesley's mission in Georgia was a disaster as he tried to impose his High Church Anglicanism on the American colonists. Returning to England, he once more came in contact with the Moravians and with their help finally experienced conversion. Once converted, Wesley found himself shut out of the typical Church of England pulpit, and so he began to preach in the fields and, particularly interesting to us at this point, began to organize the small-group prayer fellowships so characteristic of German Pietism. These "class meetings," as Wesley and his followers called them, were the cell groups from which the Methodist church finally developed. The Methodist Revival popularized the Pietist approach to prayer wherever its influence was felt, and of course its influence was strongly felt in America.

Pietist prayer now began to shape the prayer life of American Protestantism. Even in the Congregational, Presbyterian, and Dutch Reformed churches Pietist prayer gained headway, but by the middle of the nineteenth century other influences began to appear. Samuel Miller (1769–1850), professor of theology at Princeton Theological Seminary, wrote a book on the ministry of prayer that assumed much of the Pietist approach to prayer but nevertheless maintained an appreciation for more formal corporate prayer. Miller follows very closely the concerns of Matthew Henry for developing a biblical language of prayer. Like the Westminster Directory for Worship he gives careful attention to the different genres of prayer. Obviously for Miller conceived prayer, rather than either extemporaneous prayer or reading prayers from a liturgical book, is the preferred method. But most interesting for the history of Reformed worship are his remarks about the masters of public prayer in his own day. For special approval he singles out Timothy Dwight (1752–1817), the grandson of Jonathan Edwards and president of Yale University. He also recounts the teaching of John Witherspoon (1723–94) on the subject of devotional composition. For Witherspoon the preparation of prayer was a devotional act.

Charles W. Baird (1828–88), born in Princeton, New Jersey, the son of a Scotch-Irish Presbyterian father from western Pennsylvania and a French

Huguenot mother from Philadelphia, was brought up in France, where his father served as a fraternal worker among the Protestant minorities of Catholic Europe. The young Baird discovered the liturgical heritage of Continental Protestantism. He found a strength and a depth in the more formal prayers of classical Protestantism. After returning to America to study at the University of the City of New York and Union Theological Seminary, he became pastor of a Dutch Reformed church in Brooklyn. In 1855 he published a book containing the prayers of various Reformed liturgies of the past. He gave particular attention to the prayers of the *Genevan Psalter*, John Knox's *Book of Common Order*, Richard Baxter's *Reformed Liturgy* and the prayers used by the Dutch Reformed church in America before the Great Awakening. There was nothing dry about this book. It painted fascinating pictures of the liturgical life of the Huguenots of France, the Puritans of England, and the Covenanters of Scotland. It envisioned the legitimate liturgical heritage of Reformed Protestantism. Although the book was at first published anonymously under the title *Eutaxia*, it made quite a sensation and was republished in Great Britain the following year by the Congregational minister Thomas Binney. Not long after, Baird was called to be pastor of the Presbyterian church in Rye, New York. Sad to say, his pastoral responsibilities prevented him from pursuing further his liturgical studies, but the work he had done was destined to have a profound effect on American Protestant worship.

Benjamin Morgan Palmer (1818–1902), the distinguished pastor of First Presbyterian Church in New Orleans during the Civil War, wrote one of the classics of American liturgical literature, *Theology of Prayer*. A remarkable feature of this book is its strong covenantal understanding. Typical of the whole Reformed approach to worship, Palmer's work sees prayer as both a covenant responsibility and a covenant privilege. Again, solidly in the Reformed tradition, he gives attention to the various genres of prayer—adoration, praise, petition, thanksgiving, confession, supplication, and intercession.

Most remarkable of all, however, is the way Palmer understands prayer in terms of the inner Trinitarian conversation. Prayer is based on the communion of the persons of the Trinity. As Palmer presents it, prayer has to do with the providential care of the Father for his children, the intercessory ministry of the risen and ascended Son at the right hand of the Father, and the illuminating ministry of the Spirit as well as with the Holy Spirit as our Comforter and Advocate. Palmer's rich theology of prayer confirms the historic Reformed teaching that prayer, as worship in general, is the work of the Holy Spirit, in the body of Christ, to the glory of the Father.

For Palmer, prayer as it was taught and exemplified by Jesus and the earliest Christians is part of the eternal economy. Because prayer is shaped by the relationships between the persons of the Trinity, it is something that endures for eternity. The life of prayer is part of our eternal existence. In fact, to pray is to join with the worship of the angels as they worship before the heavenly throne of God.

Henry van Dyke (1852–1933) built on the work done by Charles W. Baird. Van Dyke, of both Dutch Reformed and Old School Presbyterian heritage, was minister of New York's Brick Presbyterian Church. Later a professor of English literature at Princeton University, he was a distinguished American author in his own right and had an appreciation for the value of using the language well. His superb language not only in his books, but also in his sermons, his hymns, and his prayers, set a high standard for literary excellence in worship. Henry van Dyke became the leader of a significant group of Presbyterians who wanted to produce a service book for the Presbyterian Church similar to the liturgical books that Baird had spoken of in his pioneering book. The first edition of the *Book of Common Worship* appeared in 1905, and successive revisions appeared for several years. Strangely, the book turned out to resemble the Episcopalian *Book of Common Prayer* more than it did the *Genevan Psalter*. Whatever faults it may have had, the actual prayers were beautifully written, particularly those composed by van Dyke himself. They gave a new seriousness and dignity to public prayer wherever the *Book of Common Worship* guided the prayer life of the congregation. Henry van Dyke was honored by being elected a moderator of the Presbyterian General Assembly. He was even appointed American ambassador to the Netherlands by his old Princeton colleague President Woodrow Wilson. Above all, van Dyke was known as a writer of such tales as *The Other Wise Man*. He enjoyed the respect of being at the top of the American literary establishment. Living in his beautiful home, Avalon, not far from the campus of Princeton University, he finished his years with a sense that the *Book of Common Worship* was his most important contribution to the cultural life of America. It must be admitted that the *Book of Common Worship* did not do much in the way of encouraging the prayer life of individual Presbyterians. It remained largely a service book for ministers. During the middle of the twentieth century among Presbyterians, as generally among mainline American Protestants, the life of prayer languished. There are, however, a number of hopeful signs that things are beginning to improve. American Protestants have been fascinated by the liturgical renewal among Roman Catholics. Charismatics, on the other hand, have put a great emphasis on prayer, and, then again, among certain Protestant groups there have been attempts to restudy the prayer disciplines of classical Protestantism. It remains to be seen which of these movements will bear fruit.

Chapter 7

The Lord's Supper

The roots of the sacrament of the Lord's Supper go back to the very dawn of the biblical tradition, as far back as the covenant meals of the patriarchs. One thinks of the story of Melchizedek bringing out bread and wine to share a meal with Abraham after his victory in the battle of the kings. Then there were Abraham's meal with the three heavenly visitors and the meal Jacob prepared for his father Isaac when he sought from him the covenant blessing. These meals were covenant meals that established a profound relationship among those who shared them.

THE PASSOVER

Even more significant, however, is the Passover meal that the children of Israel ate before leaving Egypt. In Exodus 12 and 13 we have a detailed description of how the Passover feast was to be celebrated. The narrative makes clear that it was not a feast eaten once at a time way back in history, but rather was to be a perpetual memorial.

"This day shall be for you a memorial day, and you shall keep it as a feast to the LORD; throughout your generations you shall observe it as an ordinance for ever." (Exod. 12:14)

The eating of the feast itself was the service of worship. Each of the foods eaten had its particular meaning, and much of the meaning of the feast had to do with understanding the meaning of the foods that were eaten.

The two most important foods in the Passover service were the roasted lamb and the unleavened bread. As we shall see, other foods will appear in the paschal rite as time goes on: the wine, bitter herbs, the fruit purée, and so forth. Each of these foods was invested with a particular meaning, much as an American Thanksgiving feast is made up of foods that have particular significance. The turkey is a bird unique to North America; the pumpkins used for pumpkin pie were unknown in Europe; the same was true of the corn for the corn bread. When we Americans eat the turkey, we can think of the Pilgrims going out into the woods with a blunderbuss in hand to hunt that extraordinary bird. When we eat the corn bread and the pumpkin pie, we remember how the Indians taught the settlers to plant that strange new cereal and how in the same field at the same time one could grow both corn and pumpkins, foods that could be stored all winter long. Without that essential instruction in the local agriculture, the Puritans would never have survived. Each food we eat at Thanksgiving reminds us of the Pilgrims and the hardships they went through to found our land. It was the same way with the lamb and the unleavened bread for the Passover.

Scholars will tell us that behind the celebration of Passover there must have originally been two separate feasts and that what we find in Exodus 12 and 13 is the splicing together of a primitive nomadic lambing feast and an agricultural firstfruits feast. The joining together of these feasts must have happened a long time ago, and it is almost impossible from the texts that have come down to us to reconstruct the two separate feasts. Let us look at the meaning given to these two central foods.

In Exodus 13:1–2 and 11–16 we read of the consecration of the firstborn. Presumably behind this is the idea of the sacrifice of the firstfruits or the firstborn of the flocks. A lamb that had been born that same season the year before was to be prepared for the feast. Whatever undertones of sacrifice there may have been in this story, the eating, not the sacrificing, of the lamb was central. The blood of the lamb was to be put on the lintels of the house in which the lamb was eaten. When this was done as God had directed, the angel of the Lord would spare all those in the house. The angel seeing the blood would pass over the homes of the Hebrews while going through the land of Egypt executing judgment on the Egyptians. The blood on the doorposts was a sign of the covenant that those who were within had with God. They were to be spared because God had graciously put a covenantal mark upon them. In later generations, however, the lamb was to remind those who ate of the whole story of the Passover and exodus. It was to remind generations of Jews how God strengthened his people for their journey and protected them from his judgment on Egypt and led them out of the land of bondage. Whatever traces there may be of a primitive nomadic lambing festival, the text in Exodus makes the memorial of the history of God's saving acts central.

The unleavened bread likewise had both memorial and covenant significance. It was to be eaten "because on this day I brought you out of the land of Egypt." It was to remind Israel of the haste with which the Jews had left Egypt. Somewhere in the background there must have been the thought of offering the firstfruits of the year, but in our text the nature rites have been succeeded completely by the memorial of God's act of redemption from Egypt. Furthermore, we find very clear evidence that the eating of the unleavened bread had covenant significance, "for if any one eats what is leavened, that person shall be cut off from the congregation of Israel" (Exod. 12:19).

In Exodus 12:43 we read that no foreigner is to eat of the Passover meal. Slaves or sojourners or hired servants may eat of the Passover only if they have first been circumcised. Having gone through these rites, they are members of the community and therefore they may participate in the Passover. All this makes very clear that the Passover is a covenant meal and that to participate in the meal is constitutive of the community.

An important part of the rite of Passover was recounting the saving acts of God that the meal celebrated.

> "And you shall tell your son on that day, 'It is because of what the LORD did for me when I came out of Egypt.' "(Exod. 13:8)

The account in Exodus carefully provides the retelling of the story of God's redemption of Israel from servitude in Egypt. Three times the account directs that the father on the day of the feast is to tell his children the story of the deliverance from Egypt (Exod. 12:26; 13:8; 13:14). It should be carefully noted, however, that the father is to *tell* his son. Nothing is said about dramatizing the event. Nothing is said about redoing the exodus in our day. There is nothing here resembling the Mesopotamian creation myth that was reenacted each year to make the power of creation relevant to a new year. There is no cyclical interpretation of history! The events of the exodus remain firmly attached to the past. What God did then was done once for all. The exodus did not need to be repeated. Quite to the contrary, each generation needed to be made a part of that unique saving event. "It is because of what the LORD did for me when I came out of Egypt." By participating in the meal, each new generation was added to that people who had been saved from the armies of Pharaoh and the slave masters of Egypt.

To understand what the Passover was really about, it is essential to see its relation to time. The rites of Passover did not involve any magic tampering with time, as though the rites of Passover were some sort of time machine that made an event in the past leap the intervening centuries. Nor was it a retrogressive time machine that magically took us back to the days of old. It was, rather, the forming of a covenant with an eternal God who revealed himself in the past as the Savior of his people and seeks with us that same redemptive relationship in our own time and our own age.

THE LORD'S SUPPER

The Synoptic Gospels tell us of how Jesus celebrated the Passover with his disciples at Jerusalem just before his passion. The Jewish Passover as it was celebrated at the time, while it retained much that was prescribed in the account of Exodus, had been modified in certain respects. From rabbinical sources we are able to reconstruct much of the Passover liturgy of the time with fair probability, and the account we find in the Synoptic Gospels becomes increasingly clear when set beside a reconstruction of the Passover Seder.

Let us look at the account in the Gospel of Mark. While Jesus customarily stayed in the suburban village of Bethany when visiting Jerusalem, he moved into the city itself for the celebration of the Passover (Mark 14:3, 12–16). The Passover meal needed to be eaten in the precincts of the holy city. The Synoptic Gospels make a great point of the providential nature of the choice of the room in which the meal was to be eaten. The room, the text tells us, would be "furnished and ready." In this sacred hour, there is nothing casual or happenstance. It has all been arranged by the plan and foreknowledge of God.

Mark recounts that in the course of the meal Jesus took the bread, blessed it and broke it, and gave it to the disciples. It is the unleavened bread that is taken. The short benediction over the bread that Jesus, following the Passover Seder, must surely have said was:

> Blessed art thou, O Lord God, King of the Universe, who hast brought bread from the earth.

It is a prayer of thanksgiving for creation. To this was added a blessing of the feast day, that is, a blessing of the feast of Passover. Whether the blessing of the feast day is really that old is not altogether clear, but if both were in use at that time, then we have a short prayer of thanksgiving for the works of both creation and redemption.

Jesus then takes the bread and says, "This is my body broken for you" (Mark 14:22; Matt. 26:16; Luke 22:19). At this point the Passover haggadah explained that the bread was unleavened because of the haste with which they had left Egypt. Jesus, however, gave yet a new meaning to the bread. He broke the bread as a prophetic sign of the giving of his life for his disciples on the day that was to follow, much as Jeremiah had broken the potter's vessel as a prophetic sign of the fall of Jerusalem. Jesus, by means of the covenant meal, joined his disciples to himself before he offered himself up as a sacrifice for their sin and the sin of the world. He joined them to himself because what he was about to do he was doing for them. He shared that meal with them that they might be joined to him in his death.

Nothing is said here about the eating of the Passover lamb. It is mentioned a few verses earlier that it was "the first day of Unleavened Bread, when they sacrificed the passover lamb" (Mark 14:12), but nothing is said of the Passover lamb in the actual meal. The Passover liturgy did not have a special blessing for the lamb. Undoubtedly roast lamb was part of the meal. It should be carefully noticed that the sacrifice of the lamb had taken place well before the meal began.

The account of the Passover in Exodus had said nothing about wine, but the Passover Seder in the first Christian century gave great attention to the drinking of the wine. There were four different cups in the course of the meal. The major blessing was said over the third cup, the cup of blessing. The prayer started out:

> Blessed art thou, O Lord God, King of the Universe, who bringeth forth
> fruit from the vine.

The blessing goes on to mention the covenant with Abraham and the gift of the promised land. It gives thanks for the kingdom of David and God's covenant with David to preserve his son upon the throne and to establish his holy city Jerusalem.

This prayer of thanksgiving, first for creation and then for these major acts of the history of redemption, has profound significance. By giving thanks for God's gifts, one appropriated them to one's own use (see 1 Tim. 4:3–4). This is an old principle of biblical prayer. Giving thanks blesses or consecrates the gifts one has received so that one may use those gifts for one's own enjoyment and profit. In the Passover benedictions the devout Jews gave thanks for the history of salvation and thereby made it the history of their salvation. By giving thanks for the release from bondage in Egypt, they claimed their own freedom; by giving thanks for the gift of the land, they made it their land; by giving thanks for the kingdom of David, they were assured of their place in it.

Here again Jesus invests the sacramental food with a new meaning. "This is my blood of the covenant, which is poured out for many" (Matt. 26:28). The covenant aspect of the meal is here underlined by Jesus just as clearly as it had been indicated by the account in Exodus. Just as each Israelite family had been sealed in a covenant relationship by the blood on the doorposts of their homes in Egypt before the night of judgment, now Jesus bound his disciples to himself in this covenant meal before he went to the cross and passed from death to life.

"And when they had sung a hymn, they went out to the Mount of Olives" (Mark 14:26). This undoubtedly refers to the singing of the Hallel, Psalms 113–18, which was already, in the days of Jesus, part of the Jewish Passover Seder. This series of psalms is a remarkable prayer starting out with an invocation of the name of the Lord (Ps. 113). It moves to a hymnic recounting of the Exodus (Pss. 114–15). Then in a full votive thanksgiving psalm the prayer recognizes the obligation that receiving God's mighty acts of salvation had put upon Israel. "What shall I render to the LORD for all his bounty to me?" (Ps. 116:12). In Psalm

117, all nations are called to worship the Lord, and then in Psalm 118 is unfolded the messianic hope. The stone rejected by humanity has been chosen by God and has become the foundation stone of a new kingdom. With confidence in the covenant faithfulness of God, Israel cries out "Hosanna! Save now we beseech thee, O Lord. Blessed is he who comes in the name of the Lord" (cf. Ps. 118:25–26). This is how Jesus and his disciples prayed, as Joachim Jeremias so aptly puts it, when Jesus went to the cross.

In the Gospel of Luke we find among the stories of the appearances of the risen Jesus the story of two disciples who met Jesus on the road to Emmaus (Luke 24:13–35). The story takes place on the afternoon of the first Easter Day. It is in many ways a story about the Lord's Supper and what it meant to the first Christians. As they go along, Jesus joins them and opens to them the Scriptures. And beginning with Moses, the Psalms, and all the Prophets he explains to them how it was necessary for the Messiah to suffer and to rise again. So, having studied the Scriptures, they finish the day by sharing a meal together. They did not yet know that it was Jesus who was explaining the Scriptures to them, but when they sat at the table together and Jesus blessed the bread, then their eyes were opened and they recognized that it was Jesus with whom they were eating. One wonders if there was something unique in the way Jesus broke the bread or in the prayer of thanksgiving that he used to bless the bread. Perhaps already Jesus had transformed the prayers said over the bread and wine so that they were not only prayers of thanksgiving for creation, but also prayers of thanksgiving for God's acts of redemption in his own death and resurrection. There is something even more significant about the story of this supper with the Lord: the time when it took place. It took place on the first day of the week, on the first Lord's Day. Just before Jesus went to the cross, he joined himself to his disciples by means of the Supper that they might participate in his suffering and its redemptive power. Now the risen Jesus once more shares a meal with his disciples that they might participate in his victory over death and his resurrection unto eternal life (cf. John 21:9–14).

Now let us turn to the apostle Paul. That the Communion is a covenantal meal is particularly evident in 1 Corinthians 10. In an argument to show the Corinthians that they should not participate in pagan cultic meals, he gives the following reason: "The cup of blessing which we bless, is it not a participation in the blood of Christ? The bread which we break, is it not a participation in the body of Christ? Because there is one bread, we who are many are one body, for we all partake of the one bread." Paul goes on to say, "You cannot drink the cup of the Lord and the cup of demons" (1 Cor. 10:16–17, 21). The reason is simple; partaking of the meal was the act of entering into a covenant with the Lord. If the Christian had entered into a covenant with Christ, how could he or she enter into a covenant with the pagan gods?

In the following chapter, Paul again returns to the subject of the celebration of the Lord's Supper. He introduces his remarks by saying, "[W]hen you assemble as a church, I hear that there are divisions among you" (1 Cor. 11:18). The Greek here is very interesting. It might be translated, "when you come together to be the church." The text seems to imply that it is in the meeting together for the purpose of sharing the meal that these individuals become the church, the body of Christ. This Supper constitutes the church. Once again it is clear that the Lord's Supper is a covenant meal. Those who participate in it become members of the covenant community.

Here let us think for a moment about the fact that the service is called "the Lord's supper" (1 Cor. 11:20). Very few things in the New Testament are called the Lord's. We hear of the Lord's Supper, the Lord's Table, the Lord's Cup, and the Lord's Day. That is about it. These things all belong together. The Lord's Day is distinguished by the fact that it is the day for the celebration of the Lord's Supper at the Lord's Table, sharing all together the Lord's Cup. Why are all these things called the Lord's? It is because here, above all, we celebrate the memorial of our Lord, the memorial he instructed his disciples to observe. It was the Lord's Table, the Lord's Cup, and the Lord's Supper because he was the host. By means of these through his Holy Spirit he was present among them. It was the Lord's Day because this was the day on which he chose to meet them again and again.

Going on, Paul recites the oral tradition he had received, using the formula a rabbi normally used when reciting oral tradition. "For I received from the Lord what I also delivered to you" (1 Cor. 11:23). Was this oral tradition always recited at the Lord's Supper as the Passover haggadah was recited in the Jewish Seder? It would seem to have been, yet, it is not completely clear that it was. "The Lord Jesus on the night when he was betrayed took bread, and when he had given thanks, he broke it, and said, 'This is my body which is for you. Do this in remembrance of me'" (1 Cor. 11:23–24). The Jewish Passover haggadah had explained the meaning of the meal by recounting the story of the exodus from Egypt. The Passover had been a memorial of the redemption of God in freeing the children of Israel from Egypt, but now the eating of the sacred meal is to celebrate not only that act of redemption but, even more, God's act of redemption in Christ.

"Do this in remembrance of me" (1 Cor. 11:24). Quite important to a true understanding of the sacrament of Communion is an understanding of what is meant by celebrating "in remembrance of me." "Do this in remembrance of me" is in effect Jesus' interpretation of the fourth commandment, "Remember the sabbath day, to keep it holy" (Exod. 20:8). We have already spoken about this at some length. Something else needs to be said here. Neither Jesus nor Paul had in mind a simple mental recollection. They had in mind far more. The text says *"Do this* in remembrance of me." They had in mind holding a religious service. In a true celebration of a covenant meal the remembering of God's saving acts had an essential function. Through these gracious acts of redemption, God laid claim to his people; by remembering those saving acts, one confessed and acknowledged that claim. In holding the memorial, one acknowledges God's lordship and the service that one therefore owes to God. In the hymnic remembering of the history of redemption, one pledges allegiance to God and claims the benefits of those redemptive acts. In so doing, one lays hold of the covenant and assumes both the obligations and the prerogatives of the covenant people.

Paul goes on to explain, "For as often as you eat this bread and drink the cup, you proclaim the Lord's death until he comes" (1 Cor. 11:26). How was it precisely that this proclamation was made? Was the proclamation done in the context of the elaborate prayer over the cup in which the main events of salvation history were recounted? That might have been in Paul's mind. We have already spoken of how the thanksgiving prayer by which Jesus blessed the bread and wine mentioned the cardinal events in the history of salvation. Certainly the first Christian eucharistic prayers contained a hymnic recounting of the acts of creation and redemption. There was undoubtedly more than this, however. Surely Paul had in mind as well the preaching that normally preceded the celebration of the Lord's Supper. We remember how Jesus met the two disciples on the road to Emmaus and explained the Scriptures at length before coming to the inn and sitting down to supper with them. It would seem more than likely that the central proclamation of the Lord's Day worship was in preaching!

Finally, for Paul the dimension of the fellowship of the Christian community was extremely important. This is, after all, the main point of this passage in chapter 11. The celebration should express the mutual concern of the members of the church one for another. It was important to discern the Lord's body and to wait for one another. It was not like eating in a cafeteria, where each one eats the food one has chosen or where each one has as much as one can pay for. Those who had plenty were to share with those who did not have enough. It was a covenant meal wherein the individual entered into a covenant not only with God but with the total Christian community. Paul's concern for the poor of the community was completely in keeping with the nature of the covenant meal.

Having very briefly gone over these passages of the apostle Paul, let us take a look at the Gospel of John to see what it tells us about the Lord's Supper. In the Gospel of John we do not have an account of the celebration of the Last Supper, but a number of passages show us how John understood the celebration of the sacrament.

The story of the wedding feast of Cana has important sacramental implications. Jesus uses the simple village wedding as a sign of the coming of the kingdom, showing himself to be the true bridegroom by providing the wine, a wine delicious beyond the expectations of the guests. In that feast, the new Solomon played on the themes of the Song of Solomon. The messianic son of David provided a foretaste of the wine of heaven and the wedding feast of the Lamb (2 Sam. 7:1–17; Prov. 9:1–6; Matt. 22:1–14; Rev. 19:9). Here the Fourth Gospel emphasizes the eschatological dimensions of the Eucharist. From the story of the wedding at Cana we understand that the sacrament is a celebration of the joyful life of the coming kingdom.

The Gospel of John specifically calls the changing of the water into wine at Cana a sign. As C. H. Dodd has so beautifully shown, John's use of the word *sign* draws on the rich meaning of the word that we find all the way through Scripture. Again and again God reveals his will through signs. The rainbow that God set in the heavens after the flood, the burning bush from which he spoke to

Moses, the opening up of the sea, the pillar of cloud and fire that led Israel through the wilderness, the manna that nourished the children of Israel, the sweetening of the waters of Marah, and the water from the rock were all signs of God's redemptive presence among his people. It is clear that for John the sign at Cana, as well as the feeding of the multitude, are signs of a very similar sort. When we speak of the sacraments being signs, we should have in mind the profound force of the word *sign* found in the Gospel of John.

In Johannine eucharistic teaching the story of the feeding of the multitude (John 6:1–14) with the five loaves and two fish and the bread of life discourse (John 6:35–65) that follows it are of central importance. Here we must pay careful attention to two elements of Old Testament tradition. The first of these is the wisdom tradition. Sapiental themes abound in the Gospel of John. The Prologue to the Gospel presents Jesus as the Word of God, that is, the divine wisdom from on high. We have already suggested that the first sign of Jesus recounted by John, the turning water into wine, is to be understood from the standpoint of the wisdom tradition. When we get to the story of the multiplication of the loaves and the feeding of the multitude, we find the wisdom theme recurring. The scene John recounts evokes the memory of Moses delivering the law to Israel. Then, in the bread of life discourse, Jesus interprets the text from Exodus 16:4–15, "He gave them bread from heaven to eat." The text comes from the story of God feeding the children of Israel with manna in the wilderness. Following the Alexandrian exegesis, the manna is presented as a sign or sacrament of the divine wisdom revealed in the law of Moses. Jesus tells his listeners that in his feeding of the multitude there was a sign to be seen, just as there was in the manna. The sign Jesus gave, however, points to a teaching that leads to eternal life (John 6:26–27). The prophets had spoken of the day when God himself would teach his people (Isa. 54:13), and that day has now come. The Word of God, who was God from the beginning, is now revealed as the bread of life. This teaching of the Word of God is of far greater value than the teaching of Moses. "Your fathers ate the manna in the wilderness, and they died." The teaching of the gospel of Christ, unlike the teaching of the law of Moses, gives eternal life. Jesus tells them, "I am the bread of life" (John 6:47–49). By this he means that those who receive his teaching will receive eternal life. Repeatedly Jesus urges his hearers to believe. Justification by faith is one of John's recurring themes. Just as they ate the loaves that were a sign of the divine wisdom or a sacrament of the Word, so now they should believe the gospel. Eating and believing go together. In fact, eating the bread and drinking the wine of the Eucharist is an act of believing.

The bread of life discourse has far more in mind than telling us that the teachings of Jesus on the good moral life will nourish us unto eternal life. "I am the living bread which came down from heaven; if any one eats of this bread, he will live for ever; and the bread which I shall give for the life of the world is my flesh" (John 6:51). It is to be sure the gospel of his saving death and resurrection that is meant. When Jesus tells us that his flesh is the bread which he gives for the life of the world, he refers to his sacrificial death. He gives himself up for the life of

the world (John 3:16). At the very beginning of the Gospel of John, Jesus is identified as the sacrificial Lamb of God who takes away the sin of the world. To those
who first read the Gospel of John, there was nothing obscure or novel about the
idea that the eating of a sacrificial meal was a sign of receiving the divine wisdom. It was along this line that the Alexandrian exegesis had interpreted the sacrifices of the law long before the Gospel of John appeared on the scene. Even
before that, as Raymond Brown has pointed out, we find in the book of Proverbs
that wisdom invites her children to the sacrificial feast, "Wisdom has built her
house, she has set up her seven pillars. She has slaughtered her beasts, she has
mixed her wine. . . . 'Come, eat of my bread and drink of the wine I have mixed.
Leave simpleness, and live, and walk in the way of insight' " (Prov. 9:1–6). Essential for understanding the bread of life discourse is the recognition that it is the
Lamb of God who is the Word of God. It is the crucified and risen Christ who
is the divine wisdom. We are not to be offended by the death of Christ. We are
to accept his death as God's act for our salvation. In it the wisdom of God is
revealed. When this wisdom is received, it nourishes us to eternal life. For John,
to eat the bread and drink the wine, the signs of Christ's sacrifice, is to receive
the wisdom that nourishes unto eternal life.

The second thing we need to consider in our attempt to understand John 6
is Passover. Allusions to the Passover and the events that Passover celebrated recur
constantly in the chapter. We are specifically told that the feeding of the multitude took place at the Passover season. Then Jesus in the bread of life discourse
interprets the feeding of the multitude in terms of Israel receiving manna in the
wilderness. The theme of Passover involves of course the Passover meal itself
(Exod. 12–13). It also involves quite naturally the meal of manna (Exod.
16:1–36). There is a third meal involved in the Passover traditions, the covenant
meal on the top of Mount Sinai (Exod. 24:3–11). That this third meal is alluded
to is very clear from the fact that the Gospel tells us that Jesus "went up on the
mountain" and there fed the multitude (John 6:3). Let us look at this story. After
the law had been given, Moses proclaimed the law to Israel, and the people
vowed, "All the words which the LORD has spoken we will do" (Exod. 24:3). Sacrifices were made, half the blood was sprinkled on the altar, and half the blood
was sprinkled on the people, and Moses said, "Behold the blood of the covenant
which the LORD has made with you in accordance with all these words" (Exod.
24:8). Then Moses and the seventy elders of Israel went up on the mountain and
there "they beheld God, and ate and drank" (Exod. 24:11). In that meal with
God on the top of Mount Sinai the covenant was sealed. God became their God,
and they became his people. John 6:52–59 plays on these themes.

Here then is John's understanding of the Lord's Supper. Through the Lord's
Supper, the covenant meal of the New Covenant, the Christian is joined to the
crucified and risen Christ and therefore has eternal life. What John says here is
very similar to what the apostle Paul said in 1 Corinthians 10 and 11. When we
ask how Jesus can give us his flesh to eat, the answer is that he gives us his flesh
by becoming our Passover lamb, the Lamb of God, and offering himself up for

us. His death and his resurrection are for us because we have been joined to him in a covenant relationship; what is his is ours, and what is ours is his. Through eating the bread we share in his broken body, through drinking the cup we become partners in the New Covenant. We have been consecrated for the new life of the kingdom of God.

This whole discourse underlines the importance of understanding that Christ is present at the eucharistic meal. With a covenant meal everything turns on with whom the meal is shared. When Jesus fed the multitude "on the mountain," they ate with Jesus. At the heart of the sign was the belief that the meal they shared, they shared with God himself. The discourse on the bread of life puts in high relief the close relation of word and sacrament. It makes clear that when we participate in the covenant meal, we engage ourselves to live by the Word of God.

Before leaving our consideration of the celebration of Communion in the New Testament, we must ask one very important question. Did the church of New Testament times understand the celebration of Communion to be a sacrifice?

Undoubtedly the earliest Christians understood that participation in the Communion united them to Christ in his sacrificial death. Paul put it this way: "The cup of blessing which we bless, is it not a participation in the blood of Christ?" (1 Cor. 10:16). This does not mean that the bread and wine that have been blessed are then offered to God as a sacrifice. It means that the covenant meal of bread and wine unites us to the one who gave himself as a sacrifice. At the Passover in the time of Jesus the lambs were sacrificed at the Temple but eaten in the home. The Passover meal itself was not a sacrifice. To be sure, without a sacrifice there could have been no covenant meal, but the sacrifice took place before the Passover Seder began. "Christ, our paschal lamb, has been sacrificed. Let us, therefore, celebrate the festival" (1 Cor. 5:7–8). Christ was sacrificed at one particular time and place in history, yet the feast is celebrated in many times and places.

Undoubtedly the earliest Christians understood that praise and thanksgiving had taken the place of the Temple sacrifices (Rom. 12:1–2). Their prayers were the spiritual sacrifices of the royal priesthood they offered daily (1 Pet. 2:1–10). One could therefore logically move from this general understanding of prayer and thanksgiving as a spiritual sacrifice to understanding the prayer of thanksgiving over the bread and wine as a sacrifice, although the New Testament does not specifically indicate that the earliest Christians had come to such conclusions. Nowhere does the New Testament speak of the Supper as a sacrifice of praise and thanksgiving.

The Scriptures provide us with a very full theology of thanksgiving, particularly in the thanksgiving psalms that accompanied the thank offerings of the Temple. A thank offering was not propitiatory. Such a sacrifice did not atone for sins; it was far more an appropriation of God's grace and favor that one had already received. Having received the blessing of God, one was obligated to witness to God's blessing in a public act of thanksgiving. This was done by presenting at the Temple a thanksgiving sacrifice, an important part of which was the recitation of a psalm of thanksgiving. For the Jews of the first century it was the "spiritual sacrifice," that is, the psalm or prayer of thanksgiving, and the public witness of recounting God's favor was regarded as more important than the actual animal sacrifice. The thanksgiving consecrated the gracious acts of God to one's own use (1 Tim. 4:4–5). The earliest Christians, however, seem to have understood the thanksgiving over the bread and wine not so much in terms of the thanksgiving sacrifices of the Temple as in terms of the thanksgiving prayers of the Passover Seder (1 Cor. 10:16). There is quite a difference between regarding the prayer of thanksgiving at Communion as an appropriation of Christ's atoning sacrifice on the cross for our salvation and regarding that thanksgiving as a sacrifice for the forgiveness of sin. There is no evidence that the early church confounded the two in such a way that they regarded the Communion as a repetition of Christ's sacrifice. Rather, the New Testament, in the clearest possible terms, speaks of Christ's death on the cross as the unique sacrifice, which never needed to be repeated and which once and for all put away sin (Heb. 10:12–14).

We summarize this cursory investigation of the celebration of the Lord's Supper in the New Testament with the following observations. The celebration by the earliest Christians was in liturgical form very much like the Passover Seder. It was, like the Passover meal, a covenant meal, but it was shared with the risen Christ as a celebration of his passage from death to life and as a prophetic sign of the heavenly banquet in the last day. By the end of the New Testament period the Christian celebration of this meal had undergone a number of modifications. First, it had become a weekly celebration held every Lord's Day morning in celebration of Christ's resurrection. Second, it was no longer a rite observed by a small group of ten people, but a celebration of the whole Christian community in a given area. By means of this service Christians came together as the church. Third, the celebration was closely connected with the proclamation of the gospel. It is not clear whether the service of the Word and the service of the Supper had been joined into a single liturgy in New Testament times, but surely this was beginning to happen. Fourth, the sacrament already had diaconal significance. The meal was to be shared with the poor, the widowed, and the hungry. It was a sign of concern for those who were in need. Fifth, the content of the prayers had been changed so that they were a thanksgiving for God's mighty acts of redemption in Christ. Finally, the whole service was a memorial of God's mighty acts that the church proclaimed to the world "until he comes."

THE EARLY CHURCH

One hesitates to embark on a brief and simple account of the historical development of the eucharistic liturgy. To do this requires going over much detailed work in a most summary way. Every author whom we must treat is capable of a wide variety of very subtle interpretations. The subject of sacramental theology has been treated by some of the greatest minds of Christendom, and as yet there is far from being any unanimity. We must approach the subject with a sense of humility. It is with only the greatest apologies that one ventures to write on the subject in such a summary fashion.

The most important document we have concerning the celebration of Communion in the earliest days of church history is a small collection of directions for ordering the affairs of the church called the *Didache*. From this document we discover that the Christians of the late first century or the early second century celebrated a Communion service that liturgically was very close to the Passover Seder. The form of the service seems to have remained the same, with separate prayers over the bread and the wine at the beginning of the meal and a longer prayer over the cup of blessing at the end of the meal. The theological content of the prayers is different. The prayers of the *Didache* are a thanksgiving for creation and for our redemption in Christ as well as the celebration of the Christian hope for the consummation of the kingdom. Although the full text of the prayers is given, there is no mention of the words of Jesus being repeated as part of the prayers. For this reason many scholars insist that what the *Didache* reports is not a celebration of the sacrament. Surely this opinion is in error, even if it means we are faced with the fact that in the oldest eucharistic liturgy we have no words of consecration. The dominical words may have been repeated elsewhere in the liturgy, but they were obviously not part of any of the three eucharistic prayers.

Here in the *Didache*, rather than in the New Testament, we find the first hint of the doctrine of the eucharistic sacrifice that begins to develop in the following centuries. We read toward the end of the document that before partaking of the Communion, Christians were to confess their sins in order that "their offering be pure." What seems to have been meant, however, is simply the idea, already mentioned, that prayer is the Christian sacrifice of praise and thanksgiving. The passage goes on to allude to the prophecy of Malachi 1:11, "in every place and time offer me a pure sacrifice"[1] Christians often understand this as a prophecy of the worship of the church, the spiritual sacrifice of the royal priesthood (1 Pet. 2:1–10). In other words, what is being said is not that the Communion is a sacrifice but that it is analogous to the Jewish sacrifices. The sacrifices of the law were the types or foreshadowing of the Christian forms of worship. The Christian Eucharist may have succeeded the Jewish offerings but that did not mean it really was a sacrifice.

Shortly after the middle of the second century Justin Martyr (ca. 100–ca. 165) gives us a picture of the way the Communion was celebrated. The several blessings of the Passover Seder have been consolidated into a single prayer of praise to the Father and thanksgiving for his works of creation, providence, and redemption. This prayer has not yet been codified into a formulated canon. The one presiding followed certain customs as to what was to be included in the prayer, but he prayed in an extemporary fashion and at length. When he was finished, the whole congregation said the Amen. This prayer of thanksgiving forms the heart of the liturgy Justin describes. When the prayer has been said over the bread and wine, this food has thereby been blessed or in some sense consecrated. It is the "eucharist," that is, "thanked-over" bread and wine.

One would like to say more about how Justin understood this consecration, but he seems to be purposely vague and ambiguous. Justin seems to indicate that the words of institution were recited as part of the liturgy, but it is not clear at what point in the service. For Justin they are words of institution in that they communicate that what is done is at the bidding of the Savior and thereby receives his promised blessing. They are not a formula of consecration. Justin does not suggest that he considers the sacrament a sacrifice, although he does understand it to fulfill the prophecy of Malachi that the Gentiles will offer up pure sacrifices to God's name (Mal. 1:11). The covenant aspect of the celebration is evident. Those who participate are baptized and keep or intend to keep God's commandments. Special significance is given to the fact that the whole Christian community gathers together in one place for the celebration and that the Eucharist is celebrated on the Lord's Day.

By the beginning of the third century we notice further developments. Hippolytus (ca. 170–ca. 236) in his *Apostolic Constitutions* gives us considerably more detail as he writes down what he understands to be the apostolic tradition for the celebration of Communion. First, we notice that the bread and wine that are brought to the bishop are called an offering or oblation. The presenting of the bread and wine at the table has come to have special significance; it is an offertory. The prayer over the bread and wine gives thanks for the sending of a Savior who was "born of Holy Spirit and a Virgin," a Savior who suffered that he might abolish death and demonstrate the resurrection. Here we recognize the Logos theology of Hippolytus. This portion of the prayer was no doubt marked by the author's particular understanding of the person and work of Christ. Yet the text of the prayer was supposed to be flexible enough to allow for such individual expressions. There was as yet no formulated canon. Notice that the words of Jesus concerning the bread and cup are recited in the midst of the prayer. This is done in such a way that they function as words of consecration. Then the bread and wine are offered to God, "because thou hast bidden us to stand before thee and minister as priests to thee." The Communion has clearly become a sacrifice. It is not completely clear in what sense it was considered a sacrifice. Much has been written on the subject, but exactly how Hippolytus understood the sacrament remains uncertain. Furthermore Hippolytus seems to have some idea that the saying of the eucharistic prayer did something to the bread and wine, but again it is not too clear whether it was through the recitation of the words of Jesus, "This is my body . . . this is my blood," or because of the invocation of the Holy Spirit. From this point on, the Communion service begins to become more and more an act of consecration and sacrifice. The eucharistic prayer begins to occupy greater and greater importance as the act of consecrating or transforming the bread and wine and presenting them as an oblation or sacrifice to God.

At the end of the fourth century, sometime between 380 and 390, we have a series of sermons on the sacraments preached at Milan by its great bishop Ambrose (ca. 339–97). This series, entitled *De sacramentis,* was an explanation of the rites of baptism that the new converts had received at the paschal vigil, followed by their entry into the church and first Communion on Easter morning. From this document we learn much about how Communion was celebrated at the time and how it was understood. One of the most beautiful things about the sermons of Ambrose is the poetic use they make of the Old Testament types of the sacraments. Explaining the sacraments by means of the Old Testament types goes back to the New Testament itself and ever since has been one of the most important means of trying to perceive the meaning of the signs. In the *De sacramentis* we find for the first time a number of the prayers that eventually found their way into the canon of the Roman Mass. Ambrose makes the point that before the words of Jesus, "This is my body . . . this is my blood," what we have is bread and wine; but after those words of Jesus, we have the body and blood of Christ. Very clearly, then, Ambrose understands that when the words of Jesus are quoted in the eucharistic prayer, they are words of consecration by which bread and wine are transformed into the body and blood of Christ. The eucharistic prayer goes on, "Therefore remembering his most glorious Passion and his Resurrection from Hell, and his Ascension into Heaven, we offer to thee this immaculate host, reasonable host, unbloody host, this holy bread and cup of eternal life, and we desire to pray that this oblation be accepted at thy sublime altar."[2] It is equally clear that for Ambrose the consecrated bread and wine are offered as a sacrifice to God in the course of the eucharistic prayer. One notices, however, that with his increased emphasis on consecration and oblation, the aspects of thanksgiving and covenant have receded into the background.

Toward the end of the fourth century, another important series of developments begins. Christians come to church to see the Communion service performed but do not participate in it by receiving the bread and wine. Both John Chrysostom in the East and a bit later Augustine in the West began to admonish their congregations against the growing practice of watching the liturgy but not taking part in the holy meal. In vain they exhorted. Their preaching inhibited the growing practice in no way. This reticence to participate was partly due to the fact that Christian preachers and teachers were putting such a strong emphasis on worthy participation that weaker Christians were discouraged from receiving Communion for fear that it would be to their judgment. In addition, the liturgy was beginning to take on elements of the drama. This is particularly noticed in the explanations of the liturgy given by Cyril of Jerusalem (ca. 315–386) in the second half of the fourth century. One also finds this tendency in the pilgrimage journal of a Spanish nun, Etheria (fl. 410), who told of the services of worship in the city of Jerusalem toward the end of the same century. It was natural perhaps that the worship of the city of Jerusalem should begin to develop in this direction. Pilgrims from all over the Christian world flocked to the Holy Land and made up a large portion of the worshiping congregation in the Church of the Holy Sepulchre. Particularly during the Easter season the pilgrims came to see the room where Jesus had eaten the Last Supper, the garden where he had prayed before his passion, the place where he had been crucified, and the sepulchre from which he rose again. It was only natural that on Good Friday the pilgrims would retrace the footsteps of Jesus, stand beneath the cross, and wait before the tomb. The idea of reenacting the passion of Christ came easily, particularly to a Greek-speaking culture that had so much love for the theater.

In Cyril of Jerusalem's *Mystagogical Catechism* we begin to get a clear picture of an increasingly important conception of the liturgy. The very title of the work makes clear what is beginning to happen. A mystagogical catechism was the explanation of the sacred rites of one or another of the Greek mystery religions. The Hellenistic world was filled with these mystery religions. The Mithras cult, the Eleusinian mysteries, the Orphic rites, and the mysteries of Isis were among the most popular. One obtained salvation in these mystery religions by going through a sacred initiation in which one was illuminated in the teachings of the cult by experiencing them in a sacred drama or ceremony. These initiation services still survive in a rather pale form in the initiations of college fraternities and sororities or various lodges. A mystagogical catechism was an explanation of the sacred mystical rites. The Greeks loved these dramatic rites, and it could have been expected that Christians would begin to understand their sacraments as though they were Greek mysteries. The idea behind these mysteries was that the dramatic representation of the redemptive event made that past event contemporary so that its redemptive power was available to those who were being initiated. The great paschal baptisms of the fourth century were indeed dramatic with their preparatory rites during the weeks leading up to Easter, their dramatic immersions in the dark of night, their anointing with perfumed oil, their robing in pure white gowns, and their solemn procession into the church to receive first Communion at dawn. One can see real similarities to the cult mysteries of the day. It was an easy way for a Christian preacher to explain things to a popular audience. The question is whether Cyril (ca. 315–86) was leading the church into a profoundly Christian understanding of sacraments or whether he was confusing the Christian sacraments with the pagan mysteries.

About the same time another attitude toward the liturgy began to develop that also had great consequences for the development of worship. It was the introduction of a devotional attitude of sacred fear. One of the first places we see this is in the works of Theodore of Mopsuestia (ca. 350–428). This attitude became very popular with the Christians of Syria and the churches of the East. The celebration of the Eucharist was an awe-filled mystery. "Let All Mortal Flesh Keep Silence and with Fear and Trembling Stand," a hymn we sing today, was translated from one of the Oriental liturgies from this period, the *Liturgy of St. James*. It expressed this devotional posture quite well. In the course of time the most sacred part of the service tended to be hidden from human eyes and spoken in a reverent hush. In the East the most holy moment of the consecration of the host was moved behind the iconostasis, a screen constructed of sacred pictures or icons. In the West the prayer of consecration came to be spoken with such profound reverence that it was inaudible to the congregation. The moment when the consecration had been performed was marked by the ringing of bells and the prostration of the celebrants. When the host was offered up, the people could not hear the prayer in which the offering was made; they could only see the elevation of the host from afar as they bowed deeply to the ground.

Augustine (354–430), one of the most fertile thinkers of Christian antiquity, had a tremendous effect on the sacramental theology of the Western church. His thought developed in a very different direction from Cyril's. He reemphasized the fundamental biblical teachings regarding the Lord's Supper, including the covenantal aspects. The Latin word *sacramentum,* which originally signified a sacred oath of allegiance, naturally lent itself to the reemphasizing of the covenantal aspects of the Supper. Augustine also highlighted the initiative of God in the sacrament. The sacrament was a God-given sign. Against the Donatists he stressed that it was the work of God in the sacrament that made it effective, not the worthiness of the minister. Against the Pelagians he stressed that the sacrament was a sign of God's grace. Augustine gave the classic definition of a sacrament as an outward and physical sign of an inward and spiritual grace. The most interesting aspect of Augustine' s sacramental teaching is the way he returned to the themes of the Gospel of John and explained the sacrament as the Word of God made visible. As we shall see, the Reformers found Augustine's insights at this point very helpful. Unfortunately these insights of Augustine were to fall on hard days. Even as Augustine was preaching his last sermon, the Vandals were destroying classical civilization in North Africa. Learning was in retreat before the barbarians. In the centuries that followed, much that was said by Augustine and other church fathers would be either misunderstood or understood in a magical and superstitious way.

THE MIDDLE AGES

By the time of Charlemagne (742–814), the power of Christendom had moved north across the Alps. Islam had begun to eclipse the influence of the Christian East, but the barbarian tribes of France and Germany were infusing fresh vigor into the Christian faith. Although for these northerners Latin was a foreign language, they wanted their religion to be Roman, just as they wanted to make their barbarian empire Roman. So they maintained Latin, the Roman language, giving to their worship a mystique of learning and culture. Because many Christians did not understand the liturgical language, ceremonies, symbols, vestments, pictures, and images began to be more and more important. About the year 800, Amalar of Metz (ca. 780–850/51), one of Charlemagne's bishops, wrote a commentary on the liturgy that gave an allegorical meaning to every gesture, every movement, every act. More and more the faithful understood the liturgy as a sacred drama to be watched with awe. The allegorical explanations, which began to multiply from this time on, had the effect of inspiring even more ceremonials that could be interpreted and read by the spectators. Even though the worshipers might not understand the liturgical language, they could understand the visual ceremonies.

By the end of the Middle Ages, the Lord's Supper had already a long time before become the sacrifice of the Mass. It was a sacred drama that reenacted the sacrifice of Christ on the cross, a most solemn mystery celebrated in a language unknown by the common people. It was, in the eyes of many, a magical ceremony that transformed bread and wine into the body and blood of Christ and made God present on the altar, there to be worshiped and adored in sumptuous religious rites. The awesome idea of eating Christ's flesh and drinking his blood led to the practice of receiving Communion but once a year; even then, only the bread was eaten, and the cup was withheld from the people. Many churches were filled with dozens of altars, and every day flocks of priests would offer the sacrifice of the mass for the salvation of the living and the dead. The private mass had become an institution. The whole concept of covenant fellowship among the faithful was lost. The splendid celebration of the Roman Mass in a Rhineland cathedral in the year 1500 had developed into something quite different from the celebration of the Passover Seder that Jesus observed with his disciples in the upper room.

THE REFORMATION

Toward the end of the Middle Ages, the need to reform the worship of the church was generally felt and widely expressed, but with the beginning of the Protestant Reformation the cry for specific liturgical reforms became increasingly urgent. For the Reformers of classical Protestantism—Martin Luther (1483–1546), Philipp Melanchthon (1497–1560), Ulrich Zwingli (1484–1531), Martin Bucer (1491–1551), and John Calvin (1509–64)—there was agreement about the most pressing liturgical reforms needed in the celebration of the Communion service. The first thing was to translate the Communion prayers into the language of the people and for the celebrant to speak them in a loud and distinct voice. The second was to remove from the liturgy the sacrificial elements both in regard to the offertory prayers that were said when the bread and the wine were brought to the table and those prayers in the canon of the Mass in which the consecrated bread and wine were offered to God as a sacrifice. Third, the Reformers were agreed that when Communion was celebrated, all the faithful had to both eat the bread and drink the cup. It was not sufficient for the priest alone to commune, nor was it enough for the congregation to receive only the bread. No more was the Communion to be a show for worshipers who simply watched but did not participate. The first stage of the liturgical reform, then, was to translate the text, remove the prayers of sacrifice, and to emphasize the actual communing of the faithful.

Late in 1523 Luther published his *Formula missae,* a proposal for the reform of the celebration of the Communion service. In some ways it was a rather moderate proposal. It advocated a gradual introduction of German into the liturgy and provided that there would always be occasions for the use of Latin in worship. The first part of the service, up to the offertory, was to remain unchanged, but from that point on, as Luther put it, the whole thing "reeked with sacrifice." For the Reformers generally, the removal of the elements of sacrifice from the Mass was one of the most pressing of reforms. The offertory, that is, the ceremony by which the bread and wine were brought to the altar and offered to God, Luther felt should be completely discontinued. The canon of the Mass, that is, the prayer of consecration said over the bread and wine, Luther wanted to rearrange completely so that any prayers implying the presenting of the consecrated bread and wine as a sacrifice to God should be omitted. For Luther the sacrament of Communion was not to be understood as a sacrifice to God but as a gracious gift from God.

What did Luther and the other classical Protestant Reformers object to so much in the doctrine of the eucharistic sacrifice? At the very core of Protestant theology is the affirmation that the sacrifice of Christ on the cross was full, sufficient, and perfect. Christ offered himself up once for all. His sacrifice never has to be repeated. His sacrifice is more than sufficient to redeem the whole of the human race from all its sin. Once a doctrine of a eucharistic sacrifice has developed, then the doctrine of the sufficiency of Christ's sacrifice has been compromised. Equally important to classical Protestantism is the doctrine of the substitutionary atonement. Christ died for us and in our place. He made the sacrifice that we could not make. Christ's sacrifice was unique because he was the lamb without blemish. Once the Mass is regarded as a sacrifice, the uniqueness of Christ's sacrifice disappears. In this question, what is really at issue is the Reformers' Augustinian theology of grace.

In Wittenberg there seemed to be no hurry to implement the suggestions made in Luther's *Formula missae,* but in Strasbourg it was another matter. A few months later, in February 1524, Diebold Schwarz, Matthew Zell's assistant at the Cathedral of St. Lawrence, celebrated a German Mass much like the service Luther proposed. The entire service was conducted in German, the offertory was removed, all prayers from the canon implying any doctrine of eucharistic sacrifice were struck out, and Communion in both kinds was offered to the congregation. Although the *Strasbourg German Mass* of Diebold Schwarz was not a Reformed Communion liturgy but an expurgated Mass, it was an important step toward a truly Reformed celebration of the sacrament.

The first important attempt to celebrate a Reformed Communion service took place almost a year later. At the end of 1524 Bucer published a work, *Grund und Ursach,* in which he explained the liturgical reforms that he and his colleagues were trying to achieve. In the succeeding months several editions of the *Strasbourg Psalter* appeared. These writings witness to the liturgical changes that were gradually taking place.

First, the Communion itself is emphasized. The sharing of the bread and the cup by the whole people of God becomes the heart of the service. The Reformers place the emphasis here rather than in the consecrating, the sacrificing, or the adoring of the bread and wine. The altar is replaced by a table. Here we see the Reformers' concern for the recovery of a basic biblical sign. The Communion is to look like a meal.

Second, the Strasbourg Reformers strove to restore the basic unity between word and sacrament. The words of Jesus are to be proclaimed as the promises of the gospel rather than recited as a formula of consecration. When the sacrament is celebrated, it is essential to preach the gospel. Sermon and Supper go together.

Already we notice that the Reformers are beginning to turn to the Old Testament concept of covenant to understand the Lord's Supper. The covenantal nature of the holy meal is underlined by an attempt to get the whole church to participate in one celebration of Communion each Lord's Day. The Communion Invocation that follows the Prayer of Intercession draws on and develops the themes of the covenant. In the earliest Strasbourg psalters the Communion Invocation asks the Holy Spirit to write the law upon our hearts, that Christ live in us and we in him, that we be members of Christ's body and serve him in the building up of his church. In later editions of the Psalter it is put even more expressly. In Communion we are to become partakers of the eternal testament, the covenant of grace.

If the Word of God is to be visible, as Augustine had taught, then it is to be visible in terms of the bread and wine of Communion, not in terms of liturgical art. All statues of the saints, pictures of Christ, and liturgical images or icons have been removed from the churches of Strasbourg. We see from this document that from the very beginning the use of images in worship is completely antithetical to a Reformed concept of worship. It is clearly forbidden by Scripture. Reformed theology, like both the Old Testament and the New Testament, understands that we are to serve God not by our creating images of God but by our being the image of God. The glory of God is not reflected in our works of sacred art but in holiness of life, sharing with those in need and in the witness to a life of peace and justice. Clearing the churches of those images and icons that God had forbidden put the emphasis on the visible signs which God had commanded.

Finally, the connection between Eucharist and Lord's Day is underlined. The celebrations of the sacrament are reserved to the Lord's Day. Here again we find the same concern at work—the concern to recover the basic biblical signs of the liturgy. The Lord's Supper is to be celebrated on the day of resurrection so that both Christ's death and resurrection are observed and so that the sacrament is received as a sign of the last day, the day of consummation. The reform that these documents of the church of Strasbourg envision has much that is truly consequential.

Ulrich Zwingli (1484–1531) drew up another attempt at a Reformed eucharistic liturgy. It was celebrated in the church of Zurich at Easter in 1525. The service is very short. We note the following things. The "dominical action," that is, the sharing of the bread and the cup, occupies the central position in the service. The doxological and eucharistic aspects of the service are likewise put in high relief through the reciting of the Gloria, the Apostles' Creed, and Psalm 113. Zwingli is quite aware that this is the first of the Hallel psalms traditionally used in the Passover Seder. Finally, the ecclesial or covenantal aspect of the service is emphasized in the Communion Invocation. The Communion is seen as a sign of the uniting of the whole church in the body of Christ. Zwingli's Communion rite has often been misunderstood by an attempt to understand it from his "sacramentarian" theology. Theologians have often tried to show that this service demonstrates Zwingli's teaching that the sacrament is "only a subjective memorial." A more helpful key to understanding Zwingli's liturgical reform is the title he gave to the service, *The Act or Way of Observing the Memorial or Thanksgiving of Christ*. Obviously even for Zwingli the celebration of Communion was not just a subjective remembering. It was a quite objective act of thanksgiving. It was the observing of the memorial Christ had appointed.

In the city of Basel, a bit later that same year, John Oecolampadius (1482–1531) attempted to develop a celebration of Communion following much the same principles adhered to by his colleagues in Strasbourg and Zurich. Oecolampadius, as we have already had several occasions to remark, was not only an outstanding biblical scholar but an outstanding patristic scholar as well. Oecolampadius realized that one of the great problems in the history of the liturgy was the concept of mystery. The reformer of Basel realized that the word *mystery* (Greek, *mysterion*) was the word the Greek church used for sacrament. He knew well what pagan Greeks meant by the word. He studied the usage of the word in the New Testament and showed that what Scripture meant by mystery was very different from what the mystery religions meant. As Oecolampadius understood it, the Christian mysteries are God's sending of his Son to establish a kingdom in which all things will be united under his sovereign will. The Christian mysteries are the mysteries of Christ—the gospel, our faith and God's faithfulness, the church, and the coming of the kingdom. Oecolampadius realized well that Cyril of Jerusalem and the apostle Paul had quite different understandings of the word *mystery*. It is not surprising, therefore, that the Communion service developed by the church of Basel is marked by great simplicity.

COMMUNION IN CALVIN'S GENEVA

For almost twenty years the reformers of the Upper Rhineland had been working on the reform of the Communion liturgy. When John Calvin published the *Genevan Psalter* of 1542, he drew on the experience of his predecessors. Let us look briefly at this service. Psalms are sung as the congregation gathers. The minister begins the service with the Invocation. Then, he leads the congregation in a general prayer of confession and supplication. This is followed by the singing of a metrical psalm. The reading of the Scriptures is prefaced by the Prayer for Illumination, asking God for "the grace of His Holy Spirit to the end that His Word be faithfully preached to the honor of His name and the building up of the Church." A sermon is then preached on the lesson. After the sermon and the usual prayers of intercession, the actual celebration of Communion begins with the singing of the Creed. The Creed is a hymnic recital of God's mighty acts of creation and redemption as well as a celebration of the Christian hope of the resurrection of the body and the life everlasting. The Creed is said to testify that the people "wish to live and die in the Christian faith."

Calvin's Communion Invocation appears at different points in the various editions of the liturgy. He seems to have preferred it after the Creed. The prayer consists of three elements: first, a prayer of invocation, or an epiclesis, asking that we might receive the grace promised in the sacrament; second, a prayer of thanksgiving rendering praise and thanks to God and celebrating his redemptive work in Christ; third, a prayer in which the covenant vows are renewed. The prayer is concluded by the Lord's Prayer.

After this the Words of Institution are recited from 1 Corinthians. The Exhortation follows from the Words of Institution. In it the unrepentant are warned not to participate, and the faithful are encouraged and invited to receive the Communion. This "fencing of the table" was an attempt to take seriously the warning of the apostle Paul (1 Cor. 11:27–32). It was largely shaped by the dismissals of the catechumens and penitents, as the Reformers learned about this practice from the works of John Chrysostom. This Exhortation is in effect a short sermon setting forth the benefits of the sacrament and an invitation to come to the Table to renew the covenant vows. It ends with these words: "Lift up your hearts and minds on high where Christ is seated in the glory of his Father, whence we expect his coming at our redemption." The whole service is thereby given an eschatological dimension. It is an invitation to enter into an invisible and heavenly reality. This done, the bread and wine are distributed to the people, the ministers serving the bread and the deacons the cup.

During the distribution, a psalm of thanksgiving, Psalm 138, is sung by the congregation. The psalmody is central to the liturgical structure of the celebration. In the psalmody, sung by the whole congregation, the central act of praise and thanksgiving is to be found. When all have received, there is a prayer of thanksgiving for the sacrament, in which the people dedicate themselves to live out the rest of their lives to the glory of God and the well-being of their neighbors. Then the congregation sings a final hymn of praise and thanksgiving such as Psalm 103 or 113. The use of Psalm 113 is obviously appropriate because it was one of the Hallel psalms that even in the time of Jesus belonged to the Passover Seder. For the same reason Psalms 116, 117, and 118 were considered equally appropriate. The Reformers were well aware that the Gospels referred to the Hallel psalms when they tell us that Jesus and the disciples sang a hymn before leaving the upper room. The Communion liturgy of the *Genevan Psalter* concluded when the minister lifted up his hands and dismissed the congregation with the Aaronic benediction (Num. 6:23–26).

Let us look for a moment at the theology behind this service. While a covenantal understanding of the sacrament was clearly to be seen in the earlier Communion liturgies of Strasbourg and Zurich, it comes to full bloom in the Genevan order. Earlier, in our chapter on baptism, we spoke of the reasons for the development of Covenant theology among the High Rhenish Reformers of the early sixteenth century. It was among these theologians that biblical Hebrew was recovered by the Western church. It was quite natural that the full Semitic color of Scripture should become evident to them in a way it had not been evident to Christian theologians for over a thousand years. Moreover the Hebrew concept of covenant gave the early Reformed theologians an alternative to scholastic theology and its attempt to explain the sacraments in terms of Aristotelian philosophy. Just as the recovery of the Hebrew concept of covenant had opened up to the Reformers a more profound understanding of baptism, so it opened up a much deeper understanding of Communion as well.

One of the first places one notices this is in the relationship between word and sacrament. Calvin's writings on eucharistic theology always gave ample attention to this subject. He understood quite well how often in the Scriptures the sharing of a meal was the way an agreement was sealed. As Calvin understood it, the proclamation of the covenant promises at the celebration of Communion was an essential element of the service. Calvin reminds us of the teaching of Augustine that the sacraments are the visible words of God. The celebration should always include teaching, so that what is seen might be understood. It was important that the covenant promises be understood, because in the sharing of the bread and the cup the covenant promises were sealed. Calvin tells us that our Lord clearly had this in mind when he said, "This cup is the new covenant in my blood" (1 Cor. 11:25). It is clear from this, Calvin tells us, that the signs of bread and wine are the signs of the covenant he has made with us.[3] For Calvin, sharing in the Communion seals to us the promises proclaimed in the preaching of the Word.

If Calvin wanted to follow Augustine's maxim that the sacraments are the visible words of God, he also wanted to guard against dissolving the sacraments into words. God gave us the sacraments because our minds are not able to grasp the fullness of God's redemptive work. Again and again Calvin speaks of the mystery of the Lord's Supper being far greater than any of our attempts to explain it. The Communion itself—that is, partaking of the bread and wine—should be the heart of the service. As Calvin sees it, it is important during the celebration of the Lord's Supper to meditate on the sacramental signs of bread and wine and contemplate the deeper meaning. "As bread nourishes, sustains, and keeps the life of the body, so Christ's body is the only food to invigorate and enliven our soul. When we see wine set forth . . . we must reflect on the benefits which wine imparts to the body and so realize that the same are spiritually imparted to us by Christ's blood."[4] For Calvin the sacrament is, above all, a sign of our being fed by the body of Christ, and therefore the liturgical celebration preserves the outward sign of the meal. The celebration of the sacrament at Geneva did precisely that. The service was celebrated around a table rather than before an altar, and the receiving of the bread and wine itself was the high point of the service.

For Calvin the discourse on the bread of life in John 6 is of the greatest possible importance in understanding the sacrament. Putting the discourse in the context of the whole of the Johannine literature, Calvin reminds us that the Gospel of John begins by telling us that in Christ is life: "In him was life, and the life was the light of men" (John 1:4). Then, calling on 1 John, the reformer tells us that this life "was manifested only when, having taken our flesh, the Son of God gave himself for our eyes to see and our hands to touch."[5] Having set this context, he returns to the words of the bread of life discourse: "I am the bread of life . . . which came down from heaven . . . the bread which I shall give for the life of the world is my flesh" (John 6:48–51). Calvin tells us that Christ is life, life in itself, the life God intended. Being then that life God intended, he entered into this world so that we might be alive as he is alive. The inward grace of Communion is then the gift of life, the life of the Son of God.

Calvin is not talking about divinization or *theosis* in the sense of Neoplatonic philosophy. Reformed theology has never been much attracted by Neoplatonism and has never shown much interest in those church fathers such as Origen (ca. 185–ca. 254), Gregory of Nyssa (ca. 330–ca. 395), Dionysius the Areopagite (ca. 500), and John of Damascus (675–749) who were so obviously influenced by it. Calvin is concerned about the restoration of true human life, not the divinization of humanity.

One more thing needs to be said about the relation between word and sacrament. If for Calvin the sacraments are the visible word of God, they are effectual. The sacraments are not only signs of the Word but seals of the Word as well. The outward sign of the meal speaks of nourishment for eternal life. The worshiper taking part in the service can be sure that what the outward and visible sign promises will indeed take place inwardly and invisibly. This inward and invisible fulfillment of the signs of promise is the work of the Holy Spirit.

It is likewise from the standpoint of covenant that we can best understand Calvin's doctrine of Christ's presence at the Supper. In a covenant meal it is of the greatest significance with whom one eats. Many of the stories of covenant meals make the point in one way or another that the meal is shared with God. The fact that the Lord's Supper is a meal shared with the Lord escaped in no way Calvin's notice. Calvin, indeed, understood Christ to be present at the Supper. We need to understand the nature of that presence. According to Calvin, our Lord, ever since the ascension, has been at the right hand of the Father. Nevertheless, through his Spirit he is still present with us. We read, for example, in the Gospel of John, "I go to prepare a place for you" (John 14:2). As we read further in the Gospel of John we discover that Jesus promised the disciples the Holy Spirit, which the disciples could not receive unless Jesus left them. Nevertheless, leaving the disciples, Jesus sent his Holy Spirit that he might dwell within them. As Calvin understood it, although Christ is clearly in heaven, at the right hand of the Father, he is nevertheless present among us through the Holy Spirit. As Calvin understood it, Christ's presence at the Lord's Table is not so much a local presence as it is a personal presence. Again, it is not so much that Christ is present on the table as that he is present at the table. By our sharing a meal with him the covenant is sealed.

Here Calvin's doctrine of the Holy Spirit once more comes into play. Obviously for Calvin our union with Christ, brought about by the Holy Spirit, is of the greatest possible significance. Through the inner working of the Holy Spirit

Christ abides in our hearts. However, for Christ to abide in our hearts implies that he rules in our hearts. Calvin makes a point of our being nourished by our union with Christ, who is both crucified and risen. The Holy Spirit does not pour into our hearts some sort of spiritual fluid but, rather, makes Christ present by sanctifying us. The Holy Spirit nourishes us by uniting us to the death of Christ so that we too die to sin. The Holy Spirit nourishes us by the resurrection of Christ so that we too live in newness of life.

Another important element of Calvin's eucharistic theology is his working out of the Pauline concept of the body of Christ. Here again the biblical concept of covenant is in evidence. Calvin begins with Ephesians 1, where we read that the mystery of God's will is to unite all things in Christ (Eph. 1:9–10). Our participation, our communion, our sharing in Christ's body is indeed a great mystery. Paul is talking about the kingdom of God and the reign of Christ that God in his sovereign will ordained before creation. The creation of Adam and Eve, the giving of the covenant to Abraham, the revealing of the law to Moses, the establishment of the throne of David all built toward this plan, that in the fullness of time all things will be united in Christ. How is this unity of the body of Christ to be understood? Is it to be understood in terms of the mystery religions or in terms of the Old Testament concept of the covenant? Admittedly Paul is using a Greek vocabulary, which can very easily be understood in terms of the Hellenistic mystery religions. He even uses the word *mystery*! But Calvin understands Paul quite correctly. He sees Paul against the background of the Old Testament rather than of Greek philosophy. Calvin's commentary on Ephesians 1 makes it clear that what makes for the unity of the body of Christ is Christ's reign over that body. Of the very essence of our union with Christ is covenant faithfulness. It is "to do justice, and to love kindness, and to walk humbly with your God" (Mic. 6:8). Ever since the days of Amos, the Hebrew prophets had insistedon the integrity of worship and conduct. If true humanity is to be restored, then the human community must be healed. Human life as God intended it is life in community.

For Calvin the Lord's Supper had profound ethical and moral implications. The communion is not only with God in heaven; it is participation in the Christian community as well. The Lord's Supper was both an invitation to the rich banquet of the grace of God and a call to the righteousness and justice of Christ's kingdom. Just as the sharing of the Passover meal in Egypt was to strengthen the children of Israel for their passage to the promised land, so, for Calvin, the Supper nourishes us in our pilgrimage to the heavenly Jerusalem. Hungering and thirsting after righteousness, we have cried out for the grace of God, and we have been granted that grace. We have been granted, through the death and resurrection of Christ, new and eternal life. We have been joined to Christ in his death to the old life and in his resurrection to new life. Now, using covenant terms once again, we are obligated to give thanks to our Savior and to confess the obligation this lays upon us. This confession is a witness, recounting the story of God's mighty acts of redemption and, at the same time, a vow dedicating one's life to the service of the ever-faithful God who has heard our cry. This is how the prayer of dedication at the end of the service is to be understood.

> Now grant us this other benefit: that thou wilt never allow us to forget these things; but having them imprinted on our hearts, we may grow and increase daily in the faith which is at work in every good deed. Thus may we order and pursue all our life to the exaltation of thy glory and the edification of our neighbor.[6]

Having received Communion, we are obligated to live in holiness, justice, and peace.

It would be a mistake to regard the service used by Calvin in Geneva as the ideal Reformed Communion liturgy. The *Genevan Psalter* offered many significant liturgical reforms, but still others needed to be made.

VERMIGLI'S EUCHARISTIC THEOLOGY

The Italian Reformed theologian Peter Martyr Vermigli (1500–1562), had a profound effect on the Reformed doctrine of the Lord's Supper and on the way the sacrament has ever since been celebrated in Reformed churches. His writings are perhaps the most thorough treatment of eucharistic theology by any Reformed theologian. Vermigli was born in Florence to a family that had been greatly influenced by the famous reformer of that city, Savonarola (1452–98). Joining the Augustinian order, Vermigli became prior of an Augustinian community at Naples in the early 1530s. While in Naples he came to know Juan de Valdes (1500–1541), who was already recognized as the most eminent of the Spanish reformers. De Valdes introduced Vermigli to a circle of prominent Spaniards and Italians who hoped for the reform of the church. This group included Princess Vittoria Colonna, Cardinal Gonzaga, Benedetto Ochino, and even the great painter and sculptor Michelangelo. After some time Vermigli became prior of the important Augustinian community at Lucca and while there tried to institute reforms. Official opposition to these reforms made it necessary for Vermigli to leave Italy. In 1547 Archbishop Thomas Cranmer (1489–1556) invited him to England and had him appointed as Regius Professor of Divinity at Oxford. In 1549 he took part in the great eucharistic disputation held at Oxford and from that time on had a tremendous influence on Anglo-Saxon eucharistic theology.

Vermigli gave a lot of study to the biblical concept of sign. As Vermigli saw it, the giving of signs is part of the divine condescension involved in God's self-revelation. God graciously accommodates himself to human weakness. Humans cannot understand divine things as they are; therefore God reveals himself in signs, shadows, and types in order that by analogy we may rise to some intimation of divine truth. Following the line of thought made so popular by the fourth-century church father Hilary of Poitiers, Vermigli gave much attention to the Old Testament types as sacraments of Christ. Joseph McLelland even goes so far as to say that Vermigli's typology is his real sacramental theology.[7] In this appreciation for typology, Vermigli is typical of sixteenth- and seventeenth-century Reformed theologians. Contemporary theologians are only beginning to fathom the great depth of thought involved here.

Vermigli's doctrine of the Lord's Supper is particularly significant for his profound sense of the analogy between the Lord's Supper and the doctrine of the incarnation. For Vermigli Christ himself is the ultimate sacrament, the sign and promise of our redemption. As the Italian reformer so often put it, it is important that in our doctrine of the Supper we respect both the divinity and the humanity of Christ. Appealing to Chalcedonian Christology, Vermigli reminds us that we should not confuse, mix, or separate the true humanity and the true divinity of Christ. Christ's humanity remains even after the resurrection and ascension. His humanity is not turned into divinity. His divinity does not destroy or efface his humanity. Rather, it redeems it, sanctifies it, and glorifies it. In the same way, at the Lord's Supper bread is not changed into God. Bread remains bread, but it becomes a sign of the body of Christ. At the Lord's Table, by means of the signs of bread and wine, we encounter the body of Christ. In the incarnation, the humanity of Christ is not turned into divinity but rather sanctified. Likewise, we come to Communion not for divinization, but rather that through this communion with Christ we may become holy as he is holy. Our human flesh and blood remain human flesh and blood, but being sanctified, we become the humanity God always intended us to be. We become true children of God, heirs and joint heirs with Christ, "the first-born among many brethren" (Rom. 8:29). As true children of God we inherit eternal life.

Another feature of Vermigli's sacramental theology is his profound appreciation of the biblical theology of thanksgiving. Vermigli liked to use the word *eucharist* in referring to the sacrament, because that word emphasized that the Lord's Supper is a feast of praise and thanksgiving. As Vermigli understood it, one of the cardinal actions of the liturgy is the eucharistic prayer, in which the church gives thanks in joyful profusion for God's mighty acts of creation and redemption. Vermigli, like the other Reformers, very much opposed making the sacrament into a sacrifice. To be sure, the sacrament is a memorial and a thanksgiving for Christ's sacrifice. To be sure, Christians, having received the benefits of Christ's sacrifice, owe to God the sacrifice of thanksgiving and the offering of their lives to his service, but it is by Christ's sacrifice alone that our salvation has been won. Vermigli distinguished carefully between a propitiatory sacrifice that saves us from our sins and a eucharistic sacrifice that gives thanks to God for the salvation God has already granted us. Our giving of ourselves to his service, our giving of alms, our self-dedication are entailed by Christ's obedient sacrifice of himself, but these responses must not be confused with his sacrifice.

This concern to respect the uniqueness of Christ's sacrifice explains a number of the features of the Reformed Communion service. It explains the absence of what in the Mass is called the offertory. The early Reformed liturgies studiously avoided anything that looked like or even sounded like the offering of bread and wine to God. If bread and wine were brought to the table during the service, it was done in a manner that could not possibly be considered an offering. In order to avoid confusion, alms were collected at the end of the service. The same concern explains the fact that during the Eucharistic Prayer itself there is no kind of oblation nor any offering of "ourselves, our souls and our bodies." We do find quite typically a post-Communion prayer of thanksgiving and dedication in which the worshipers give themselves to God's service. This comes quite intentionally after the congregation has received the bread and wine. Thus it is made clear that we give ourselves to God because he first gave himself to us. "We love, because he first loved us" (1 John 4:19).

Where Vermigli's influence was especially strong, one normally finds, particularly in the early Anglo-Saxon Reformed liturgies, two distinct prayers. The Eucharistic Prayer is a hymnic setting forth of God's mighty acts of creation and redemption. With this central prayer of the liturgy devoted to extolling Christ's death and resurrection, his humiliation and exaltation for our salvation, there is no question as to the eucharistic and doxological emphasis of the service. These early Reformed liturgies do indeed "proclaim the Lord's death until he comes" (1 Cor. 11:26). After all have participated in the meal, there is a prayer that thanks God for the benefits received from the sacraments and dedicates the congregation to a faithful confession before the world, the doing of good works, and the advancement of God's glory.

JOHN KNOX AND THE SCOTTISH REFORMATION

With the Reformation of the Church of Scotland in 1560 John Knox was given the responsibility of drawing up a Reformed liturgy. While the intention of John Knox was to follow the Genevan liturgy, he improved it considerably, particularly in regard to the Eucharistic Prayer. The prayer is a thanksgiving for the works of creation and redemption and a celebration of both the grace and mercies we have received in life and those to which we look forward in the kingdom of heaven.

> O Father of Mercy, and God of all consolation! Seeing all creatures do acknowledge and confess thee as Governor and Lord: It becometh us, the workmanship of thine own hands, at all times to reverence and magnify thy godly Majesty. First, for that thou hast created us in thine own image and similitude: But chiefly in that thou hast delivered us from that everlasting death and damnation, into the which Satan drew mankind by the means of sin, from the bondage whereof neither man nor angel was able to make us free.
>
> We praise thee, O Lord! that thou, rich in mercy, and infinite in goodness, hast provided our redemption to stand in thine only and well-beloved Son, whom of very love thou didst give to be made man like unto us in all things, sin excepted, in his body to receive the punishment of our transgression, by his death to make satisfaction to thy justice, and through his resurrection to destroy

him that was the author of death; and so to bring again life to the world, from which the whole offspring of Adam most justly was exiled.

O Lord! we acknowledge that no creature is able to comprehend the length and breadth, the depth and height of that thy most excellent love, which moved thee to show mercy where none was deserved, to promise and give life where death had gotten the victory, to receive us in thy grace when we could do nothing but rebel against thy justice.

O Lord! the blind dullness of our corrupt nature will not suffer us sufficiently to weigh these thy most ample benefits; yet, nevertheless, at the commandment of Jesus Christ our Lord, we present ourselves at this his table, which he hath left to be used in remembrance of his death, until his coming again: to declare and witness before the world, that by him alone we have received liberty and life; that by him alone thou dost acknowledge us thy children and heirs; that by him alone we have entrance to the throne of thy grace; that by him alone we are possessed in our spiritual kingdom to eat and drink at his table, with whom we have our conversation presently in heaven, and by whom our bodies shall be raised up again from the dust, and shall be placed with him in that endless joy, which thou, O Father of Mercy! hast prepared for thine elect before the foundation of the world was laid.

And these most inestimable benefits we acknowledge and confess to have received of thy free mercy and grace, by thine only beloved Son Jesus Christ: for the which, therefore, we thy congregation, moved by thine Holy Spirit, render all thanks, praise, and glory, for ever and ever. Amen.[8]

This Eucharistic Prayer has been composed with a very clear understanding of the biblical theology of thanksgiving. It celebrates in hymnic terms God's mighty acts for our redemption in the incarnation, redemptive sacrifice, and life-giving resurrection of Christ. It declares and witnesses before the world what God has done of his own mercy and grace. For Knox, as for the English Puritans, an important part of the sign was the actual breaking of the bread, the pouring out of the wine, and actually sitting about the table. In fact Scottish churches were often built in such a way that the congregation sat around three sides of the table. When the congregation had received the bread and wine, there was a prayer of thanksgiving for the sacrament in which the worshipers dedicated themselves to live in praise to God and love toward their neighbors. This was followed by singing a psalm of thanksgiving. Psalm 103 is specifically indicated. In the course of Scottish liturgical history the use of this psalm became almost invariable. The great emphasis Knox put on the eucharistic aspects of the service is clear. Knox was very conscious that the Gospels tell us that when Jesus took the bread and wine, he gave thanks.

THE PURITANS

The English Puritans developed a number of the insights of the sixteenth-century Reformers in a most positive manner. During the Puritan period, not only in England but in Scotland and New England as well, a distinctive eucharistic piety began to develop. In the middle of the seventeenth century we find the following instructions in the Westminster Directory for Worship. First, either on the Sunday before the Lord's Supper or during the week immediately beforehand, there is to be a preparatory service that "all may come better prepared to that heavenly feast." Then, when the day comes for the administration, the sermon being completed, the minister is to give a brief exhortation on the proper use of the sacrament. The people are to sit about or at the table, and then the minister is to set apart the bread and wine "by the Word of Institution and Prayer." The words of institution are to be read out of the Gospels or from 1 Corinthians. Then follows the Eucharistic Prayer. The prayer is to give thanks for all God's benefits, "and especially for that great benefit of our redemption, the love of God the Father, the sufferings and merits of the Lord Jesus Christ the Son of God, by which we are delivered; and for all the means of grace." This prayer included a very clear invocation of the Holy Spirit "to sanctify these elements both of bread and wine, and to bless his own ordinance, that we may receive by faith the body and blood of Jesus Christ crucified for us, and so to feed upon him, that he may be one with us, and we one with him."[9]

What is most notable here is the elaboration of the invocation or epiclesis. Richard Baxter (1615–91), one of the most influential of the Puritans, further elaborated the epiclesis in his *Reformed Liturgy* of 1662.

> Most Holy Spirit, proceeding from the Father and the Son: by whom Christ was conceived; by whom the prophets and apostles were inspired, and the ministers of Christ are qualified and called: that dwellest and workest in all the members of Christ, whom thou sanctifiest to the image and for the service of their Head, and comfortest them that they may shew forth his praise: illuminate us, that by faith we may see him that is here represented to us. Soften our hearts, and humble us for our sins. Sanctify and quicken us, that we may relish the spiritual food, and feed on it to our nourishment and growth in grace. Shed abroad the love of God upon our hearts, and draw them out in love to him. Fill us with thankfulness and holy joy, and with love to one another. Comfort us by witnessing that we are the children of God. Confirm us for new obedience. Be the earnest of our inheritance, and seal us up to everlasting life. Amen.

The invocation of the Holy Spirit was a characteristic liturgical concern of the Puritans. Indeed, the element of invocation is to be found in the prayers of Strasbourg, Zurich, and Geneva, but in nothing like the fullness we find here.

Returning to the Westminster Directory for Worship we find that the bread and wine are distributed much as in other Reformed liturgies. The sharing of the bread and wine complete, there follows a post-Communion prayer. One assumes that the Westminster Directory for Worship has in mind the usual Communion psalmody but it is not specifically mentioned. By this time there were well-established traditions in regard to which psalms were appropriate for Communion. Among the favorites were Psalms 23, 24, 34, 103, 113, 116, 118, and 133. Something is mentioned, however, that is of great importance: the collection of alms for the poor. This had been an important aspect of the eucharistic piety of Continental Reformed churches, although it is not often specifically mentioned in the liturgical documents. It is a long-honored practice of Reformed piety that on Communion Sundays there is a special collection of alms that is turned over to the deacons for distribution to the poor.

From this presentation it should be clear that the classic Reformed Communion service should include a number of different facets: the covenantal, the eucharistic, the epicletic, the eschatological, the kerygmatic, and the diaconal. Each of these the Reformers discovered in Scripture, and each was emphasized at one point or another in the development of the tradition.

THE COVENANTERS

In Scotland toward the end of the seventeenth century the celebration of Communion began to develop a very distinctive character. When King James VI of Scotland became King James I of England, Scotland gradually came under English rule. The English government was determined to subject the Church of Scotland to the liturgical practices of the English *Book of Common Prayer*. The Scots were not about to conform to Anglicanism; to make clear to the world their intention, they signed the Solemn League and Covenant in 1638. This ushered in the age of the Covenanters, a struggle for religious independence that lasted well into the eighteenth century. This struggle was particularly sharp at the end of the seventeenth century, when the Duke of Cumberland tried to suppress the celebration of Presbyterian worship and the faithful often had to resort to holding worship in secret conventicles in the fields and woodlands of the open countryside. With what seriousness these Covenanters celebrated the sacrament, the feast of the eternal covenant! During these days the tradition of the Communion seasons developed. A week or more would be devoted to the celebration of the sacrament. For several days, usually starting with the Sunday previous, preparatory sermons would be preached. On weekdays there were several services, which included preparatory sermons, prayers of confession and supplication, and the singing of appropriate psalms. On the Lord's Day the feast was celebrated; then Sunday evening and for a day or two following, thanksgiving services were held. Neighboring ministers were invited to preach, and the faithful from miles around would gather for the special occasion. These sacramental seasons were not held frequently—in rural parishes they might be only once a year—but when they were held, they were held with the greatest solemnity.

John Willison (1680–1750), pastor of the church of Dundee, published several works on the celebration of the Lord's Supper that show us something of the spiritual intensity of the Scottish Communion season and impress us with several remarkable characteristics. First, the Scots gave considerable attention to preparing themselves for the celebration, not only in the preparatory services, but particularly in family worship and in secret prayer and meditations. Willison published a series of thirty-three *Sacramental Meditations* designed to help communicants in their preparations. He encouraged each communicant to set things right in his or her own life, to seek reconciliation with those from whom he or she was estranged, in prayer to seek forgiveness from God, to draw closer to God in prayer, and to resolve to live a more godly life. Having made such preparation, the communicant came to the Supper to be restored and renewed in the covenant relation with God.

Second, if the week before the celebration was devoted to solemn preparation, the Lord's Day on which the Supper was celebrated was a time of sacred joy. It was the wedding feast of the king's son, the marriage of the Lamb. It is remarkable how often the Communion sermons of this period were preached on a text from the Song of Solomon. Just as every Lord's Day was understood as an anticipation of the eternal rest, so the Lord's Supper was understood as a foretaste of the feast envisioned in the book of Revelation. The Scottish Communion service was celebrated with a sense of what today we would call realized eschatology. To the eyes of faith, the bridegroom was indeed present. The worshiper ate the bread of heaven and drank from the bridegroom's cup. One feasted with a present Christ.

Third, at these Communion seasons the Scottish church did its evangelism. In these courses of sacramental sermons the central themes of the gospel were presented in their greatest clarity and simplicity. Here the congregation hearing the Word with faith made the covenant vows that established them as members of the body of Christ. At this time new communicants were admitted to the Lord's Table. The Scots did not "join the church." They became communicants by being admitted to the Lord's Table and made their vows of faith by reciting the catechism. The vows and resolves they had made in private prayer were publicly professed by participation in the sacred meal. A covenantal eucharistic theology implied a close connection between evangelism and the celebration of Communion.

THE GREAT AWAKENING

It is not surprising that in America during the Great Awakening there was a strong link between evangelism and the celebration of Communion. One often hears that it was the Great Awakening that first linked the thirteen colonies in a common spiritual bond and began to give them a sense of having a single religious destiny. Certainly the great revival swept through the whole land from New Hampshire to Georgia. It brought together such diverse figures as the Congregational theologian Jonathan Edwards (1703–58), the Dutch Reformed dominie Theodorus Jacobus Frelinghuysen (1692–1747), and the Scotch-Irish preacher Gilbert Tennent (1703–64). More importantly, the Great Awakening gave to American Protestantism a fervent dedication to the task of evangelism that has been one of its chief characteristics ever since.

Gilbert Tennent's first published sermons were entitled *Several Sacramental Discourses.* The sermons were in fact his revival sermons preached in New Jersey at a typical Communion season. First printed in New York in 1737, they were soon published in Boston as evidence that the revival reported by Jonathan

Edwards was appearing in other colonies as well. Of particular interest is the sermon preached before the actual celebration of the sacrament. It is on a text that concerns the wedding feast. Once again we observe that the celebration of the Lord's Supper is understood in terms of the imagery of the Song of Solomon and the wedding feast of the Lamb. The faith inspired by revival preaching was to be formally sealed in the celebration of Communion.

Samuel Davies (1723–61) took the Great Awakening to Virginia. Trained in the Presbyterian Academy at Faggs Manor, he had been inspired by the preaching of George Whitefield (1714–70). After finishing his studies he was called to Hanover County, Virginia, where he organized the Presbyterian church. His sermons were masterpieces of pulpit oratory. While Davies left us no treatise on the doctrine of the Lord's Supper, several of his sacramental sermons give us a good insight into the sacramental piety of eighteenth-century American Presbyterians. In these sermons one notices the same themes that we found in John Willison and Gilbert Tennent. The Lord's Supper is understood basically in covenantal terms. It is at the Supper that the covenantal vows are made, renewed, and strengthened. In Virginia even as early as the 1740s and 1750s the covenantal fellowship is understood to include white and black, master and servant, rich and poor, slave and free. The invitation is open to all. The celebration of the sacrament that we find regularly among both New England Congregationalists and Scotch-Irish Presbyterians is the wedding feast of the king's son. The invitation has been sent out to all, to the highways and hedgerows, to the plantation owners, to their black slaves, to townspeople and traveling merchants alike. This is the invitation that really counts. To accept it is to start out on a life of holiness, which through the faithfulness of God and the inner working of the Holy Spirit will bring us fully clothed in the righteousness of Christ to the heavenly banquet. One must prepare oneself for this feast. It is not simply a rash decision. Samuel Davies was as effective an evangelist as any America has produced, but his evangelism had a sacramental dimension to it. He knew that the people to whom he preached had already been claimed for Christ in their baptism. Now they must take the covenant vows for themselves. To turn down the invitation is to deny the covenant into which they had been baptized, but to accept this invitation is to affirm the covenant. Evangelists in generations to follow tended to ignore the relation of evangelism to baptism and the Lord's Supper. The sacraments were all too often regarded as mere formalities with no relation to the essential concerns of salvation. With Samuel Davies this was obviously not the case. For this evangelist the evangelistic invitation was an invitation to the Lord's Supper.

Alexander Campbell (1788–1866) was something of an exception to the nonsacramental tendency of nineteenth-century American evangelism. Seen in the larger view of Reformed theology, he takes on the figure of a liturgical reformer. While it is always recognized that Campbell was born and brought up in Scotch-Irish Presbyterianism, one seems never to have recognized the implications of his being brought up a Reformed Presbyterian. Among the Reformed

Presbyterians the Covenanter tradition was maintained with singular ardor. The covenantal understanding of the Lord's Supper would obviously have been cultivated with special devotion among Reformed Presbyterians, and one would expect that a man like Alexander Campbell would be among the last to lose sight of the relation of evangelism to baptism and the Lord's Supper. As Alexander Campbell saw it, evangelism must always be followed by baptism and the Lord's Supper. In fact he actually succeeded in reestablishing the weekly celebration of Communion. To his everlasting credit, Alexander Campbell, although caught up in the passion for evangelism so characteristic of the American frontier, was able to infuse it with a respect for baptism and the regular celebration of Communion.

THE NINETEENTH CENTURY

For the most part, nineteenth- and early twentieth-century American Protestantism tended to ignore the celebration of Communion. It was all too often regarded as a denominational concern that got in the way of more nondenominational concerns for evangelism and such issues as the abolition of slavery, temperance, universal suffrage, foreign missions, and controversies over science and religion. An exception to this were the Old School Presbyterians. We have already spoken of how the stalwarts of the Old School did much to support a more profound exercise of public prayer. Such men had much the same influence on supporting a reverent celebration of the sacrament of the Lord's Supper.

John Williamson Nevin (1803–86) in particular emphasized the importance of Communion to the Christian life. Brought up in the Old School Presbyterianism of western Pennsylvania, he found great meaning in the solemn celebrations of the Lord's Supper he had experienced as a youth. He found the anxious bench of the revival preachers hard to reconcile with Reformed theology. After having studied at Princeton Theological Seminary, he completed his theological education at the University of Berlin, where he had come under the influence of Schleiermacher and the Pan-Protestantism of the German Evangelical Church. On arriving home, he accepted a call to teach theology at the German Reformed Theological Seminary, then located in Mercersburg and later in Lancaster, Pennsylvania. In 1846 he published a book, *The Mystical Presence*, that attempted to restate Calvin's eucharistic doctrine. His teaching overlooked many of the more traditional insights of Reformed sacramental theology, becoming primarily concerned with the doctrine of the real presence. Nevin was quite correct about one very important thing: Calvin gives the sacrament of Communion a high importance, a much higher importance than was customary in the American Protestantism of the day.

Even among Old School Presbyterians Nevin's doctrine of the Lord's Supper was found eccentric. Charles Hodge (1797–1878), a most prominent leader of the Old School, rejected Nevin's interpretation of Calvin firmly. Personally, I have always been proud to claim Nevin as a relative. I find myself agreeing with Howard Hageman (b. 1921), who a generation ago was the pastor of Third Reformed Church in Newark, New Jersey. As Hageman saw it, Nevin did much to encourage American Reformed churches to reclaim their liturgical heritage. Nevin was a pioneer; his basic vision was brilliant, but, as with all pioneers, his followers were left with a lot of details to work out.

Charles Washington Baird (1828–88) was one of those followers who helped work out the details. He was, however, a more accurate historian of Reformed worship than Nevin. Although born in Princeton, he was raised in France, where his father had been sent as a fraternal worker to help the Protestant minority reorganize after the devastating persecutions they had suffered since the revocation of the Edict of Nantes. Returning to America, he finished his education at Union Seminary in New York. Then in 1855 he published a collection of studies of the worship of Continental Reformed churches. To this he added studies of the worship of the Church of Scotland and the English Puritans. He gave his work the title *Eutaxia, or, the Presbyterian Liturgies*. The Greek word *eutaxia* means "good order." As he understood it, the essence of Presbyterianism was that, everything, especially public worship, should be done decently and in order (cf. 1 Corinthians 14:40). Significantly his book provided in English the Communion liturgy Calvin had used in Geneva, as well as the Communion liturgy Knox had used in Scotland. Baird's work helped American Protestants see their worship in a much broader historical context.

Old School Presbyterianism was particularly strong in the South. The Virginia valley, Union Seminary in Richmond, and Davidson College in North Carolina were centers of a more traditional Presbyterian approach to worship. Southern Presbyterians gave considerable time to public worship. They were very thoughtful in their preaching and their prayer, but, above all, in their celebration of the Lord's Supper they were very reverent. The celebration of Communion was an occasion for the greatest seriousness and most profound awe.

Henry van Dyke (1852–1933) was another Old School Presbyterian who encouraged Presbyterians to maintain a strong sacramental piety. We have already spoken of van Dyke in relation to praise and prayer. He was a crucial figure in the history of American Presbyterian worship. His life work was the publication in 1905 of the *Book of Common Worship*. This venerable volume attempted to put in prayer book form the liturgical principles of the Westminster Directory for Worship. Sad to say, the work suffered from being too strongly under the influence of the Anglican High Church movement. While it undoubtedly had attained a high degree of literary excellence, it had not been based on solid historical research into the history of Reformed worship. Particularly in regard to the Communion service, much was simply taken over from the Anglican Prayer Book. Even features of the Anglican liturgy that Presbyterians had objected to for centuries suddenly appeared in what was supposed to be a Presbyterian liturgy.

But we can say about van Dyke, as we said about Nevin, that what he started out to do is important.

Old School Presbyterians were not the only supporters of a strong sacramental dimension of Christian worship. There were members of other Reformed churches who had similar inclinations. But we also need to recognize that among the Evangelicals there were definitely those who gave great importance to the celebration of the Lord's Supper.

During the age of Evangelicalism Charles Haddon Spurgeon (1834–92), an English Baptist, was one of the most notable standard-bearers of Calvinism. While chiefly remembered as the greatest preacher of the English language, he was a strong believer in the weekly celebration of the Lord's Supper. His weekly celebrations were often limited to a small group within his congregation, but he did celebrate the Supper weekly. A selection of his Communion sermons published by Princeton's Andrew Blackwood (1822–1966) gives us a good idea of how a typical Reformed pastor during the Victorian Age would have understood the sacrament. First, for Spurgeon the celebration of the Lord's Supper has a strong eucharistic element. The Lord's Supper is to be accompanied by the singing of psalms and hymns of praise and thanksgiving. In a sermon on the text, "And when they had sung an hymn, they went out into the mount of Olives" (Matt. 26:30 KJV), he tells us of the Jewish custom of singing Psalms 113 to 118 at the celebration of Passover. It was the means of their remembering God's saving acts in bringing them out of Egypt. If the Jews could give thanks to God for that deliverance, Spurgeon tells us, how much more can Christians rejoice at the Lord's Supper in remembering a far greater deliverance from sin? Spurgeon's knowledge of the Psalter and the traditions of its interpretation was prodigious, as anyone who has studied the pages of his *Treasury of David* knows. For him the singing of the whole Psalter is fulfilled in the eucharistic hymn, the culmination of Christian praise.

Second, Spurgeon finds great significance in the Reformed tradition that the Lord's Supper is to be served from the Lord's Table rather than from an altar. In a sermon on the text, "And when the hour was come, he sat down, and the twelve apostles with him" (Luke 22:14), Spurgeon develops the significance of table fellowship in Scripture. It establishes a covenantal bond between the participants. Even today when we come to the Lord's Table, we enter into that covenantal bond with Christ. What was true for the apostles is true for us. This table fellowship establishes the same bond with all who participate. Our covenant is with Christ and with each other. Then Spurgeon goes on to emphasize that fellowship entails a mutual pledging of faithfulness. Christ promises his faithfulness to us, and we pledge our faithfulness to him and to each other. Obviously for Spurgeon, sitting at the table is an important part of the sign, just like the breaking of the bread and the sharing of the cup.

Third, for Spurgeon in the celebration we experience the presence of Christ. Preaching on the text "I will not leave you comfortless: I will come to you" (John 14:18 KJV), he points out that the text literally says that Christ will not leave us orphans. Christ's presence with believers must be very real, or else we would be left as orphans. He comes to us at the Lord's Supper in a way more real than simply through our remembering him or simply our being granted his grace. Orphans can remember their dead parents or be supported by the provisions of dead parents, but they are still orphans. Christ is indeed present to us at the Lord's Supper, but not according to the flesh. His presence is a personal presence. This is not some sort of spiritualized presence, but rather a presence through the Holy Spirit. A spiritualized presence might leave us orphans, but a presence wrought by the Holy Spirit is a different matter. It is a true personal presence, even if it is not according to the flesh. One would have to go a long way to find a simpler or more vivid exposition of Calvin's doctrine of the eucharistic presence.

The twentieth century has made its greatest contributions to the Reformed practice of the Lord's Supper in the field of biblical scholarship. Joachim Jeremias (1900–1979) in his study *The Eucharistic Words of Jesus* led us to a much deeper appreciation of the relation of the Lord's Supper to the Jewish Passover as it was celebrated in New Testament times. While some would insist that there is more to the Lord's Supper than simply a Christian celebration of Passover, Jeremias has helped us to understand much in the New Testament narrative of the Lord's Supper, particularly as it is found in the Synoptic Gospels. In the same way Oscar Cullmann (1902–99), the Alsatian New Testament scholar, has helped us to understand the eucharistic passages of the Gospel of John. There have always been some who have thought that the Gospel of John, which does not report the Last Supper, was not interested in the Eucharist, but Cullmann has shown us quite convincingly that this is not the case. John has chosen to develop his eucharistic theology in terms of other meals, such as the wedding feast at Cana and the feeding of the multitude. Likewise the English New Testament scholar C. H. Dodd (1884–1973) has helped us understand the deep meaning of the biblical concept of sign. In the same way Gerhard von Rad (1901–71) has helped us recognize the rich biblical concept of thanksgiving. Then, too, we should speak of Eduard Schweizer (b. 1913), professor of New Testament at the University of Zurich. He has provided us with a contemporary approach to a covenantal theology of the sacrament of Communion. It is strangely fitting that four centuries after Henry Bullinger, who did so much to develop Covenant theology in the very same city of Zurich, the more recent professor of New Testament would rejuvenate a covenantal understanding of the Lord's Supper. Surely in this respect we should mention Brevard Childs (b. 1923), professor of Old Testament at Yale University, who in his monograph *Memory in Israel* has helped us come to a deeper appreciation of the biblical concept of memorial.

During the twentieth century the celebration of the Lord's Supper in the Reformed churches has come under a number of divergent influences. It is too early to say which of these will finally be accepted as truly representing the Reformed tradition. As Professor Edward Dowey (b. 1918) one time put it, a historian should never try to write the history of his or her own time. In a very provisional way, however, several things might be mentioned. The biblical scholarship of the twentieth century has done much to support a Reformed understanding of the Lord's Supper. Sometimes this research has been carried out by scholars who have clear commitments to the Reformed heritage, but certainly not always. The continuing value of twentieth-century biblical studies will no doubt be debated for some time, but for a Reformed understanding of the sacrament of Communion the biblical studies will remain fundamental.

Chapter 8

Daily Prayer

The worship of the Temple was daily worship. It had been so since earliest times. To be sure, the worship of the weekly Sabbath was especially important. The annual feasts of Passover, Pentecost, and Tabernacles were great occasions at the Temple too. But the worship of the Temple was also an everyday affair. Every morning and every evening there were sacrifices at the Temple. These daily sacrifices were called the *tamid,* the continual sacrifice. They were accompanied by prayers and particularly the singing of the psalms. The Christian discipline of daily prayer is ultimately derived from these continual sacrifices of the Temple.

In the book of Daniel we read of how faithful Jews maintained the continual sacrifices of the Temple even when they were far from Jerusalem. Three times a day, at the regular hours of the Temple sacrifices, Daniel went to his room, opened his window toward Jerusalem, and said his prayers. (When the third daily sacrifice was added is not known.)

There is another very ancient root of Christian daily worship. In the book of Deuteronomy we find an old version of the Ten Commandments followed by a summary of the law that for centuries Jews have called the Shema.

"Hear, O Israel: The LORD our God is one LORD; and you shall love the LORD your God with all your heart, and with all your soul, and with all your might. And these words which I command you this day shall be upon your heart; and you shall teach them diligently to your children, and shall talk of them when you sit in your house, and when you walk by the way, and when you lie down, and when you rise." (Deut. 6:4–7)

From very early times faithful Jews took quite literally the admonition to recite the Shema "when you lie down, and when you rise." Every morning and every evening the devout Jew would repeat the summary of the law. Rabbinical scholars of our day tell us that in the days of Jesus the reciting of the Shema included the reciting of the whole of the Ten Commandments in addition to what is regarded as the Shema. In doing this Jews kept the law constantly in their hearts and minds; they meditated on the law day and night (Ps. 1:2). Perhaps, if people had had inexpensively printed Bibles as we do today, they might have read a chapter of their Bibles each morning and evening. Copies of the Torah were very expensive in the days before printing, and only very rarely would an individual have a personal copy. It was therefore important to have a summary of the law, such as the Shema, which every man, woman, and child could memorize. Each morning and evening this core of the law was recited as a religious duty or devotional practice. From earliest times daily prayer included a portion of Scripture.

By New Testament times the Jews had well-established customs for daily worship. In fact, from the time of the council of Jamnia (A.D. 110) the maintaining of the discipline of daily prayer was considered obligatory. The service of daily prayer consisted of three parts: the repetition of a number of psalms, the saying of the Shema with its introductory and concluding prayers, and the Prayer of the Eighteen Benedictions. It is quite certain that Jesus and the apostles maintained this prayer discipline and that in the earliest Christian church daily prayer was maintained much as it was in the synagogue. In fact, when the apostle Paul tells us to pray continually or to pray without ceasing, he surely has in mind that we are to maintain the daily discipline of morning and evening prayer (Rom. 12:12; 1 Thess. 5:17; 1 Tim. 5:5).

One of the places we most clearly see the first Christians maintaining the discipline of daily prayer is in the Acts of the Apostles (Acts 4:23–31). After Peter and John were released from prison, they went to find their friends, and they knew just where to find them. They were gathered together for daily prayer as they were each morning and evening. The contents of that prayer meeting follow amazingly closely the pattern of daily prayer as it was practiced by the synagogue. The congregation, we are told, lifted up their voices together in prayer. A line from Psalm 146 is quoted. We can take this to mean that the service began with the congregation chanting several psalms. The synagogue normally began morning prayer with the chanting of Psalms 145 through 150. A passage of Scripture was quoted at length and the meaning of that passage of Scripture to the situation of the church at that time was discussed. This was followed by a prayer of intercession for the needs of the church. This prayer service held by the apostles, like the prayer service of the synagogue, was made up of three elements: the chanting of psalms, a passage of Scripture, and prayers of supplication and intercession.

A good number of early Christian documents witness to the practice of holding daily prayers at the church, as well as to the fact that Christian families maintained daily prayers at home. The *Didache,* for example, tells us that Christians were expected to pray the Lord's Prayer three times a day. We learn from Hippolytus (ca. 170–ca. 236) that about the year 200 daily morning and evening prayer was regularly held at the church. From the *Apostolic Constitutions* we get a rather full report of the daily prayer services in Antioch at the end of the fourth century.

With the development of monasticism the service of daily prayer began to be cultivated with great care. Even from the very beginning the monks of the Egyptian desert gave great attention to the memorizing and praying of the Psalter. Anthony (ca. 251–356), one of the founders of Egyptian monasticism, knew the whole Psalter by heart and in this respect was typical of the desert saints. The monks often understood one of their main reasons for existence to be the service of daily prayer. They understood the saying of daily prayer to be their "office," that is, the work that God had called them to perform. Monks still refer to their services of daily prayer as the saying of the "daily office."

At the beginning of the sixth century, Benedict of Nursia (480–550) led a reform of monasticism that aimed at organizing the monks into Christian communities. Benedict had a keen perception into one of the fundamental truths of the Christian faith. Christian life is life in community, and Christian prayer is essentially common prayer. Christian prayer is more truly Christian when it is shared with others. At the heart of Benedict's monastic reform was the organization of the daily prayer services and his division of the Psalter so that in the course of time the whole Psalter would be said. The cultivation of daily prayer reached such a high point in the Middle Ages that the monks held a series of seven services of prayer each day. This "liturgy of the hours," as it was called, developed elaborate musical settings. The artistic perfection that was frequently achieved in the saying of the liturgy of the hours must have been remarkable. It was in the Eastern church, however, that the saying of daily prayer reached its most sublime form. The story goes that in the Church of Hagia Sophia in Constantinople the service of daily prayer became so rich in its musical setting that it required three choirs of monks working in relays to provide the music.

Unfortunately, with this elaborate development the saying of daily prayer became almost a monastic prerogative. Those not engaged in "religious vocations" hardly had either the training or the leisure to maintain such a complicated discipline of daily prayer.

With the Reformation it was necessary to restore the service of daily prayer to the regular members of the church. This entailed simplifying the service so that it could be maintained by those who were engaged in secular work and family responsibilities. Again Strasbourg led the way in the reorganizing of the daily prayer services. The series of seven services that began at earliest morning and ran through the whole course of the day was reduced to a very simple program of morning prayer and evening prayer. Why it was reduced to two services—rather than a single service or to three services, morning, noon, and night—is not explained. Be that as it may, the custom of holding daily prayers at morning and evening became characteristic of the Protestant reform of the daily office. Each service began with the singing of one or more psalms. Great attention was given to the production of a collection of metrical psalms and canticles that could be sung to simple tunes and in the German language. The daily prayer services in Strasbourg included a program of daily preaching. There were two main prayers. At the beginning of the service was a prayer of confession and supplication. After the sermon there was a comprehensive prayer of intercession for the needs of the church, for the Christian magistracy, for the perseverance of the saints, and for those suffering from any adversity. The service was concluded with another psalm and the giving of a benediction by the minister.

Very similar daily prayer services were held in the Reformed church of Augsburg. Augsburg developed its own Psalter, although in other ways the worship of the church of Augsburg was greatly influenced by Strasbourg. In time Geneva too developed daily morning and evening prayer services.

In the seventeenth century it became more and more the practice to emphasize the discipline of daily family prayer. Particularly in England and Scotland the maintaining of the discipline of daily prayer was understood as a family responsibility. Richard Baxter (1615–91) in his *Christian Directory* wrote at considerable length on how daily morning and evening prayer was to be conducted by the father of each family. Baxter insists that daily family prayer is one of the divinely ordained functions of the family. A family, Baxter tells us, is a little church. Family prayer should include the following things: the singing of one or more psalms, the reading of a chapter of Scripture, and a full and comprehensive prayer by the head of the house.

The General Assembly of the Church of Scotland drew up a special chapter on secret and family prayer that it added to the Westminster Directory for Worship shortly after its adoption in 1647. The fact that the Scottish General Assembly found it necessary to add such a chapter to the Westminster Directory for Worship is interesting itself. Originally the chapter was much longer than what we now have. According to the Directory, family prayer should be held morning and evening each day. It should include prayer, reading the Scriptures, and singing praises.

Matthew Henry (1662–1714), pastor of a Presbyterian church in Chester, England, had a pastoral concern for cultivating family prayer. He produced a number of aids for those who bore the responsibility of leading family prayers. First, there was his classic, *A Method for Prayer.* Then there was a collection of psalms and canticles, *Family Hymns,* an anthology of the best metrical psalms Henry was able to gather from a number of collections then available in the English language. In addition to these, Henry wrote several popular essays on the subject of daily prayers, which give us an insight into how the English Puritans understood this important devotional discipline. For Matthew Henry the discipline of daily morning and evening prayer was the fulfillment of the continual sacrifices of the Temple. These daily services were the spiritual sacrifices of praise and thanksgiving offered by the royal priesthood. He saw a very definite devotional rhythm in morning and evening prayer. In the morning we go to God in praise and adoration. We ask his guidance through the course of the day. Such an approach was natural for a Reformed theologian for whom the doctrine of providence was so important. Then, having finished the day, one comes to God again in thanksgiving for his guidance, mercies, and blessings.

Another important guide to daily family prayer in the Reformed tradition is the work of James W. Alexander (1804–59), the son of Archibald Alexander, the first professor at Princeton Theological Seminary. James was pastor in New York for many years and was one of the best preachers among the Old School Presbyterians. His book *Thoughts on Family Worship,* a tribute to the piety of his parents, makes very clear how important the discipline of family prayer was to the devotional life of that day.

For classical Reformed spirituality, morning and evening family prayer was one of the foundations of piety. It was at the heart of the day-to-day exercising of Christian faith. This made sense to those for whom Covenant theology was so formative. The unity of the family was a significant feature of Covenant theology. With the coming of Pietism, daily family prayer was unfortunately replaced with private devotions.

Pietism was very individualistic, and many of this persuasion had a hard time understanding why children should be baptized. There was no sacred unity in the family. Each single human being stood before God alone. With the demise of Pietism, private devotions began to develop atrophy. They finally became not much more than "five minutes a day." Today, as we seek to recover a Reformed spirituality, we need to reach behind Pietism and recover the older classical Protestant discipline of daily morning and evening prayer.

Chapter 9

Alms

When Martin Bucer (1491–1551) in his *Grund und Ursach* of 1524 tried to summarize what should be included in the service of worship, he appealed to the text of Acts 2:42, "And they devoted themselves to the apostles' teaching and fellowship, to the breaking of bread and the prayers." As Bucer understood this, the service of worship that aspired to follow the apostolic example should include preaching and teaching, the giving of alms, the celebration of Communion, and the service of prayer. Perhaps most of this would seem self-evident except for the second of the four parts, the giving of alms. Bucer's approach to the Greek text of the book of Acts, if a bit original, was certainly sound enough. The Greek word in question is *koinonia*, which can mean "communion" or "fellowship" or, very practically, "the sharing of material goods" with those who are in need. We can leave aside the question of whether Bucer's translation was completely appropriate. His sense of liturgical balance was impeccable. The giving of alms should always be regarded as one of the constituent elements of Christian worship.

In the days of Jesus the giving of alms to the poor was considered as one of the standard good works the faithful Jew was supposed to practice. As pious Jews understood it, the giving of alms was something quite different from the paying of tithes. Tithes were a sort of tax paid for the support of the Temple and other religious institutions. Alms were gifts to the poor. The word *alm* comes from the Greek word for "mercy." To give alms is therefore to make a gift as an act of mercy, to relieve those who are in need. Normally, when one entered or left the synagogue, there were beggars asking alms. That Peter and John should meet with a beggar on entering the gates of the Temple is not at all remarkable; there were always beggars there (Acts 3:1ff.). To be sure, this was not the only way of giving one's alms. We read in the Gospel of Mark, for example, the story of the widow's mite (Mark 12:41–44). Jesus, while teaching in the Temple, saw an obviously poor woman putting a gift into the alms chest and commended the fact that even in her poverty she gave alms. The story is witness to the fact that the Temple maintained an alms chest so that the faithful might give anonymously. No doubt similar chests were to be found in each synagogue. The giving of alms was well organized among first-century Jews. The synagogue regularly appointed some of its most respected members to be almoners. These almoners were charged with reminding people of their responsibility toward those in need, collecting alms, and distributing food and other necessities of life to the poor, the sick, the widowed, and the orphaned.

In the Sermon on the Mount Jesus turned his attention to the subject of almsgiving. He was concerned in his teaching with correcting certain abuses that accompanied the giving of alms in his day:

> "Thus, when you give alms, sound no trumpet before you, as the hypocrites do in the synagogues and in the streets, that they may be praised by men. Truly, I say to you, they have their reward. But when you give alms, do not let your left hand know what your right hand is doing, so that your alms may be in secret; and your Father who sees in secret will reward you." (Matt. 6:2–4)

What is striking, however, is that this instruction on the proper way to give alms is found in a series of teachings about prayer. Almsgiving, as Jesus evidently understood it, is an auxiliary discipline to prayer. For this reason pious Jews gave alms when they went to the synagogue or to the Temple to pray.

Very early in the life of the church it was necessary for Christians to establish something like the almoners of the synagogue. In Acts 6 we find the church doing just that. As the church had grown, the care of the poor had become an increasingly time-consuming task. The primitive church realized that the care of widows and orphans, the crippled, the blind, and the disturbed was an essential part of the ministry of Jesus, and so specific members of the church were charged with maintaining this ministry. Acts 6 makes a point of the division of labor between the apostles, who were to devote themselves to prayer and the ministry of the Word, and the deacons, who were to devote themselves to the ministry of tables. *Deacon* really means "one who serves at the table"; a deacon is a waiter. This kind of service or ministry is essential to the church. The ministry of the Christian deacon is grounded in the ministry of Jesus himself, who came "not to be served but to serve." Here Jesus was making a play on the Greek word from which the word *deacon* comes. Jesus often claimed for himself the role of the deacon, that is, the role of the servant. One place where this became particularly clear was in the upper room, where Jesus washed the disciples' feet and told them, "If I then, your Lord and Teacher, have washed your feet, you also ought to wash one another's feet" (John 13:14). So important is the diaconal ministry of the church!

Another place where we get an intimation of the place of almsgiving in the worship of the church is the apostle Paul's instructions to the Corinthians regarding the collection for Jerusalem (1 Cor. 16:1–4). The apostle directs that on the first day of the week, that is, on the Lord's Day, the day when Communion was celebrated, each one is to put aside some money for the saints of Jerusalem. One gathers that a collection was made at the worship assembly, but perhaps after the actual service of worship was over. The money was then to be kept, no doubt by the deacons, until the apostle's arrival. In this the apostle Paul was only following the teaching and example of Jesus regarding the true nature of the Sabbath. It was to be a day of release, a day of healing, and a day of charitable works. What could be more appropriate to the Lord's Day than to collect funds for the relief of the poor? How could the church more appropriately remember Jesus? In works of mercy the death and resurrection of Jesus were eloquently remembered.

During the first centuries of church history, generosity in the giving of alms was characteristic of Christians. That the church maintained funds for the care of the poor we learn from many early sources. Of particular interest is a passage in the *Apology* of Tertullian (ca. 160–ca. 225), written at the end of the second century, that makes clear the diaconal aspect of the celebration of Communion. True *koinonia* was at the same time communion with God and sharing with the poor. That marvelous Greek word meant both at the same time.

Rarely has the Christian church lost sight of the importance of almsgiving. The charitable works of the deacons of the early church often left a profound impression. Lawrence, a deacon of the city of Rome in the middle of the third century, is a particularly well-remembered example. Even the briefest remarks on the subject should mention John Chrysostom (ca. 347–407) who may be reckoned as the greatest alms preacher in the history of the church. Frequently his sermons end up with an appeal to the congregation to remember the poor as they leave the church. The monastic orders of the Middle Ages often provided Christendom with extensive diaconal services. Francis of Assisi (1181/82–1226) was perhaps the most famous of all deacons. His whole ministry emphasized the importance of the care of the poor.

The Reformation brought a radical reshaping of the church's ministry to the poor. To the Free Imperial City of Nuremberg should go the credit for taking the lead in the reform of charitable institutions during the early sixteenth century. Nuremberg, among the most cosmopolitan centers of Germany, from the very beginning of the Reformation took a strong stand for Protestantism. Hand in hand with a new baptismal rite and a translation of the liturgy into German, the city published a new order for the care of the poor. Those who were in genuine need were to be cared for at public expense. There was to be no more begging in the streets. Homes for the care of the elderly, the widowed, and the orphaned were established and maintained by the deacons with the help of the city treasury as well as the giving of alms.

Strasbourg followed the lead of Nuremberg very quickly. The eleemosynary institutions, that is, institutions supported by alms, were completely reorganized so that the city supported a comprehensive program for the care of the sick, the blind, and any others in need. The new approach to the care of the poor won widespread approval for the city of Strasbourg. Gerard Roussel, the chaplain to the queen of Navarre, reported after his visit to Strasbourg in 1526 that the care of the poor was one of the most impressive aspects of the Reformation. Much of the reorganization of the charitable institutions of Strasbourg goes far beyond the scope of this book, but a number of these reforms were clearly liturgical.

Early in the Reformation the liturgy of Strasbourg eliminated the offertory. No collection was taken in the service of worship itself. Nevertheless a chest was put in each of the churches so that on leaving the church worshipers could deposit their alms. The collection of alms as people left worship became characteristic of Reformed churches. We hear of this being the practice of the Reformed church of Augsburg. In Basel, after the minister had given the Benediction, he was to remind the congregation to contribute to the care of the poor, and as the people left the service they put their alms in one of the alms chests that stood near the door.

In Strasbourg we begin to find a reform of the ministry of the deacon. In about the fifth century, after the introduction of the hierarchical principle into the organization of the Christian ministry, the office of deacon tended to become the first rung up the hierarchical ladder. One had to become a deacon before one could become a priest. So gradually the church lost sight of the uniqueness of the diaconal ministry as a ministry of mercy to those in need. The reformers of Strasbourg did much to recover the charitable orientation of the diaconate. This was picked up by Calvin, who likewise interpreted the office of deacon in the light of Acts 6. For Calvin the deacon performed one of the distinct ministries of the church, the care of the poor. This understanding of the office of deacon soon became characteristic of the Reformed doctrine of the ministry. In England, for example, when Thomas Cartwright (1535–1603) and the Cambridge Presbyterians drew up their admonitions to Parliament, one of the specific reforms they advocated regarded the recovery of the diaconal ministry. They wanted deacons whose primary concern was the care of the poor.

Let us look very briefly at the diaconal ministry of the church of Geneva. As in most of the Protestant cities of the Rhineland, public begging, even at the doors of the churches, was discontinued soon after the city accepted the Reformation. The care of the poor was to be managed in other ways. One of the most important of these was the establishment of a hospice or hospital. Robert Kingdon (b. 1927) has given us a vivid picture of the work of this institution. In those days a hospital was a much more comprehensive institution than what we usually understand today. In Geneva it was housed in a large building in the center of the city, surrounded with stables, barns, courtyards, and gardens. Several dozen people were cared for in that building. They ranged from orphaned children to elderly widows too feeble to care for themselves. This hospital was presided over by a hospitaller and his wife. Several servants cared for the extensive gardens and the large kitchen. This was important because the garden and the kitchen provided a considerable amount of food for needy families who did not live in the hospital. There was even a resident tutor, who was usually a theology student. The tutor's job was to help care for the children in the hospital. The hospital was under the care of the deacons. It was their job to see to it that the hospital was well funded and well administered.

Another diaconal work of the Genevan church was the French Refugee Fund. This was presided over by Jean Budé (1558–1610), the son of the great Renaissance Greek scholar, Guillaume Budé (1468–1540). This fund was to care for those who had had to flee from France because of religious persecution. The fund was generously supported by a number of very wealthy French refugees living in Geneva including Jean Budé himself. Robert Estienne (1503–54), the famous printer, and Laurent de Normandie were generous supporters, and Calvin himself made regular contributions from his own salary. He too was a French refugee. According to Kingdon, the French Refugee Fund spent its money for a great variety of projects. The fund was used to help obtain housing for recently arrived refugees and to provide furniture for families and tools to help artisans set themselves up in business. It provided fees for young men who needed to enter apprenticeships and dowries for women wanting to get married. The fund supplied food and medical care for those in need and even supported the widows and orphans of Reformed pastors who had lost their lives in the service of the gospel. The fund's distributors were concerned with evangelism too. They sent missionary pastors back into France and saw to the printing and distribution of Protestant literature in the French homeland. The French Refugee Fund was precisely the sort of social service that was needed in Geneva at the time. Refugees poured into Geneva at such a rate that, while Geneva had a population of perhaps ten thousand at the beginning of the Reformation, twenty years later the population had doubled, largely because of the refugees. Geneva was kind to its refugees. More than four hundred years later Geneva is still maintaining this tradition as a haven for refugees.

Let us now turn our attention to the Directory for Worship of the Westminster Assembly. It provided for the giving of alms in three ways. First, in its chapter on the sanctification of the Lord's Day, among the duties of the day are to be reckoned the "visiting of the sick, relieving the poor, and such duties of piety, charity, and mercy." Nothing is said about a collection during the ordinary service of worship; nevertheless there might have been one. This would especially be the case when some special cause needed to be supported. Second, when Communion was celebrated, there was quite definitely to be a collection for the poor. The ancient connection between the Lord's Supper and the giving of alms is patently recognized. Third, the Westminster Directory for Worship provides for the giving of alms in the chapter on the observing of days of public thanks-giving. There we are told, "At one or both of the publick meetings that day, a col-lection is to be made for the poor, . . . that their loins may bless us, and rejoice the more with us. And the people are to be exhorted, at the end of the latter meet-ing, to spend the residue of the day in holy duties, and testifications of Christ-ian love and charity one towards another, and of rejoicing more and more in the Lord; as becometh those who make the joy of the Lord their strength." For the Puritans, almsgiving belongs to thanksgiving. It is a way of expressing holy joy. It is a way of rejoicing in all the riches of grace and all the benefits of salvation we have received from God.

The nineteenth century brought several notable developments in the diaconal ministry of the church. Thomas Chalmers (1780–1847), often called the Abra-ham Lincoln of Scotland, was one of the most remarkable preachers of the cen-tury, a man of great intellectual power and firm evangelical conviction. His writings won him not only an honorary doctorate from Oxford University but election to the Institute of France as well. He had a fervent concern for the relief of the poor in the teeming, squalid slums of Glasgow. Charged with establishing a new parish in the center of one of the city's blighted areas, he developed a var-ied ministry. The new church was named St. John's and given the care of more than ten thousand people. One of his first projects was to establish schools for the poor of the neighborhood. Concerned to provide pastoral care for each per-son in the parish, Chalmers organized it into groups of sixty to a hundred peo-ple and charged an elder and a deacon with the care of each of these groups. The deacons were particularly concerned with the material needs of the parishioners. It soon became clear that the deacons were meeting the needs of the poor with an uncommon thoroughness. The work of the deacons of St. John's Church did much to relieve the misery of one of the worst slums of Europe. In time Thomas Chalmers took a larger and larger role in the leadership of Scottish Protestantism. In 1823 he was appointed professor of moral philosophy at the University of St. Andrews and a few years later professor of theology at Edinburgh. He published a remarkable work, *Christian and Civic Economy of Large Towns,* in which he taught that religious and moral reform was the basis of social reform. His con-cern for the poor was not limited to the city. Largely through the work of Thomas Chalmers the Scottish Mission Society provided a ministry to even the most remote and isolated communities of the Highlands and Western Isles. In the min-istry of Thomas Chalmers there was an amazing balance between the liturgical, the evangelistic, the educational, and the diaconal ministries of the church.

The German pastor Theodor Fliegner (1800–1864) made a great contribu-tion to the development of the diaconal ministry by promoting the work of dea-conesses. The son of a pastor in Epstein, he studied at the University of Göttingen and then completed his theological studies at a Reformed seminary in Herborn. Called to pastor the church of Kaiserswerth in the Rhineland, he became inter-ested in prison reform in addition to his teaching and preaching. In 1836 he organized a deaconess house to serve the poor, the sick, and the young of his church at Kaiserswerth. The deaconesses maintained a hospital and lived together in an organized Christian community devoted to serving God in works of mercy. A number of related institutions were founded: a refuge for discharged female convicts, an orphanage for girls, a normal school for kindergarten teachers, and an asylum for mentally disturbed women.

The deaconesses of Kaiserswerth were an inspiration to the whole of German-speaking Protestantism, not only for their devotional intensity but for their practical Christian service. Similar groups of deaconesses sprang up throughout Germany. In Jerusalem, Constantinople, Smyrna, Cairo, and Alexandria deaconess houses were organized as well. The founder of the English nursing order, Florence Nightingale, was one of those inspired by the deaconesses of Kaiserswerth, spending several months training among them before beginning her work in London. In essence the deaconess movement was shaped by the admonition of the apostle Paul to Timothy concerning the ministry of widows (1 Tim. 5:2–16). Deaconesses were widows or unmarried women organized into religious communities but not bound by vows to remain in these communities for life. There was no stigma attached to leaving the deaconess house to marry. Deaconesses were devoted to a life of prayer and works of mercy. The deaconesses of Kaiserswerth well exemplified that basic Christian principle that the service of worship and the service of mercy belong together.

Characteristic of nineteenth- and twentieth-century Protestantism has been a strong charitable work. In fact one sometimes speaks of the benevolent empire founded and so generously supported by American church people in the last two centuries. Even the most cursory study of it could take volumes.

Chapter 10

Tradition and Practice

Having devoted all these pages to the Reformed tradition in worship, let us take a few more pages and speak of how this tradition should shape our current practice. Let us think for a few moments about what the Reformed liturgical heritage has to offer American Protestants of today.

In our considering this, we need to avoid two extremes. The first is a sort of archaeological reconstruction in the English language of the *Genevan Psalter* or a meticulous following of the Westminster Directory for Worship. Simply going back to either of these classics would not really constitute a reform of worship. One problem with doing this is that our tradition, at its most simple and at its most classical, revolves around two foci, the Continental Reformers of the sixteenth century and the English Puritans of the seventeenth century. There will always be some who tend more toward Geneva, others who tend more toward Westminster. Martin Luther (1483–1546), Ulrich Zwingli (1484–1531), Martin Bucer (1491–1551), and John Calvin (1509–64) did not always agree, nor did the Scottish Presbyterians and the English Puritans. There is quite a spread between Richard Baxter (1615–91) and Matthew Henry (1662–1714). Some are going to be more attentive to Thomas Manton (1620–77), others to Martin Bucer. The Reformed tradition has been collegial from its very beginning. This was made abundantly clear as early as the Synod of Bern in 1528. We are not the devotees of some single, star reformer. Reformed is not the same thing as Lutheran, Zwinglian, or Calvinist.

Then there is the obvious fact that there is a gap between the classical age of Reformed theology and our age. Reformed theology suffered its baroque period and its mannerist period. With the coming of Pietism and rationalism, Reformed churches began to worship in ways that were very different from those of the Reformers. That is, their worship was motivated by other considerations. Other problems arose, problems that had not confronted the Reformers. The Great Awakening and the revivals that followed it had their influence on worship. The romanticism of the High Church Movement began to have its effect about the middle of the nineteenth century. We have only spoken of these problems in summary fashion because it was our intention to be brief. Pietism, rationalism, and romanticism have all had their influence on the Reformed tradition. The Reformed tradition is richer because of it.

It would have been interesting to have spoken of Jean-Frédéric Ostervald (1663–1747) and his influence on the French Huguenot liturgy or to have become engrossed in the work of the German Reformed hymnodist Joachim Neander (1650–80) or the Czech educator Jan Komensky (1592–1670). The Dutch Reformed pastor and statesman Abraham Kuyper (1837–1920) wrote much interesting material for the liturgist. In America, Charles W. Baird (1828–88), Henry van Dyke (1852–1933), and Louis F. Benson (1855–1930) led a significant liturgical revival. John W. Nevin (1803–86), Philip Schaff (1819–93), and the Mercersberg school make a most important chapter in the history of Reformed liturgics. One should certainly mention the influence on Reformed worship of the Wesleys, Alexander Campbell (1788–1866), and the English Calvinistic Baptist Charles Haddon Spurgeon (1834–92). They often did in one respect or another a masterful job of representing the Reformed tradition.

An archaeological reconstruction rarely meets the needs of the time. Too many things have happened in the meantime. No longer can one expect a whole town or city to share a common faith, to the extent that the church can exercise any kind of discipline. Today the church cannot expect civil law to support its calendar. Today we have much more friendly feelings toward Roman Catholics, and we are not apt to avoid a religious practice simply because it appears to be Roman Catholic. We are beginning to discover much in the monastic tradition that is admirable and much in scholastic theology that we rather like. Things have indeed changed since the sixteenth and seventeenth centuries.

At one time for most people the church was the only place where one could experience music or hear an interesting speaker. Now the church is in constant competition with the entertainment industry for the attention of its members. This cannot help but affect the worship of today's church. One could go on and on in this vein, but the point has so often been made; we hardly need to repeat the obvious. Just because one seeks to recover a tradition, one is not necessarily committed to an archaeological reconstruction of the tradition.

For a Reformed theologian, any tradition, including the Reformed tradition, needs to be measured against Scripture to determine whether it is of value. It is Scripture that has authority, and the tradition has authority only when it is based on Scripture. We need to evaluate and reevaluate the tradition and then emphasize those elements in it that are most solid. In any tradition there are elements that played a significant role because of the needs of the day, but in a few generations no longer seemed meaningful. In every tradition, there are the marks of compromises with the culture. There are things the religious leaders would have liked to have done but which the state would not permit or the people would not support.

A particularly good example of this was the way the Reformers wanted to restore to the church the weekly Communion of the faithful. In Strasbourg Bucer and his colleagues tried to get the whole population of the city to come to one celebration of the Lord's Supper at the cathedral each Lord's Day. Unfortunately the Reformed pastors of Strasbourg were never able to bring about that reform. A similar thing happened in Geneva. Calvin wanted a weekly celebration of Communion in Geneva. Evidently the faithful, who had been accustomed under the old order to receive Communion but once a year, just could not make that kind of transition, and so quarterly observance became the rule. In Geneva Communion was celebrated only four times a year: Christmas, Easter, Pentecost, and the first Sunday in October. That was an advance over the medieval custom, but before too long, Reformed churches were stuck with a tradition that was not "according to Scripture." Alexander Campbell tried to set that matter in order at the beginning of the nineteenth century. We need to get back to that reform again.

Certain recurring aspects of our tradition we really do not need to continue. The Reformed liturgical tradition has usually been read as being rather ascetic in its attitude toward music. Occasionally it has gone in the direction of exclusive psalmody. This attitude still has supporters among the Reformed Presbyterians here in America and in certain Reformed churches in the Netherlands. It is a most venerable sort of hyperconservatism. It certainly has patristic support. There have been long periods when the church, or large portions of it, refused to sing anything but the psalms. On the other hand, Reformed churches of today can appeal to the example of Constance and Strasbourg to support the use of hymnody in addition to psalmody. It is much the same with the use of instrumental music. Zwingli had the organ closed up in the Zurich minster, but he never claimed scriptural support for doing so. One can only speculate what his reasons might have been. Calvin did his best to get talented musicians for the church of Geneva, but the city council constantly frustrated his desires. The city fathers were not willing to pay the salary of good musicians. What finally was taken for the tradition was a compromise with the bland musical taste of the burghers of Geneva. Luther did not have to fight that kind of opposition. Consequently German Lutherans had much better church music than the Zwinglians and the Calvinists of Switzerland.

In sixteenth-century Reformed Communion liturgies there was always a long Communion exhortation, in which unrepentant sinners were warned not to approach the Table and the faithful were encouraged to receive the sacrament. These exhortations normally went into considerable detail as to who was allowed to receive Communion and who was not. They usually elaborated the proper doctrine of the Lord's Supper at great length. Reading these exhortations must have taken ten to twenty minutes. They were quite necessary in those days, when the Reformers needed to explain again and again the reasoning behind their reforms. The Reformers strove valiantly to establish true church discipline. Besides, for the members of the congregation the exact formulation of eucharistic doctrine was of great interest. It was a matter of public discussion, and the more alert members of the congregation could be counted on to follow these exhortations with the closest attention. It would be foolish to revive these long Communion exhortations. Today most of us would find them tedious. This is not necessarily to our credit. It is much more because we have lost our church discipline and are apathetic in matters of theology. One might say that the temperature of devotion in American Protestantism is not sufficiently high to support such a conscientious approach to public worship. But we might be able to find more effective ways of fulfilling the scriptural admonition to examine ourselves before coming to the Table and being sure we discern the Lord's body. At the heart of the Reformed tradition is this witness to the moral implications of the sacrament. The Reformed tradition recognizes this to be a fundamental aspect of what Scripture teaches us about the proper celebration of the Lord's Supper. We do not have to copy everything that was done in Geneva in the mid-sixteenth century, but a celebration of Communion that ignores its moral implications has lost contact with the Reformed tradition.

The Puritans in both England and America as well as the Dutch Calvinists often developed the observance of the Lord's Day to unfortunate extremes. Surely we do not want to resuscitate all this. Nevertheless an important aspect of the Reformed liturgical heritage was the recovery of a biblical theology of the Lord's Day. The more left-wing Puritans totally rejected the liturgical year and celebrated only the Lord's Day. Reformed churches today would probably be better advised to follow the practice of the Continental Reformed churches that reemphasized the weekly celebration of the Lord's Day but also allowed for the celebration of what they called the five evangelical feast days: Christmas, Good Friday, Easter, Ascension, and Pentecost.

The recent effort to bring back the celebration of the old liturgical calendar has suspicious similarities to a revival of the nature religions, natural theology, a cyclical interpretation of life, and the resurgence of the religions of fortune and fertility. One does penance in Advent, when winter sets in, and then one rejoices at Easter, when the flowers reappear in the spring. It is all quite natural, but this fascination with liturgical seasons sometimes seems not much more than a revival of Canaanitism. The primary emphasis of any Reformed liturgical calendar should be the weekly observance of the Lord's Day. Very significantly, the seven-day cycle of the biblical week is not related to any of the nature cycles! The celebration of the resurrection is primarily the weekly celebration of the Lord's Day, not the yearly celebration, which in certain parts of the world is connected with spring. To drape the worship of any Sunday in penitential purple is contrary to the best our tradition teaches us.

There is another extreme. Archaeological reconstruction is one extreme. Liturgical romanticism is the other. On the one hand, we do not want mechanically to reproduce the tradition, but, on the other hand, we do not want to give ourselves up to perpetual liturgical revision. One often explains the name Reformed by the motto "reformed and always reforming." That motto can be understood in more than one way. It can point to the fact that "Reformed" must always mean reformed according to Scripture. At best this motto points to the fact that our obedience cannot become a static matter that was worked out in the sixteenth and seventeenth centuries and never needs to be reconsidered; it means that our church doctrine and practice must always be set against the measure of Scripture. "Reformed and always reforming" can be understood in another way, as a sort of theological Trotskyism. It can mean submitting the worship of the church to perpetual revolution. Romanticism, we remember, had a tendency to glorify revolution. To call for perpetual revolution in liturgical matters, however, is to lose sight of the value of having a liturgy.

There are good reasons for having an established liturgy, and these reasons have often been recounted. In the first place, liturgical forms are a good means of teaching the essentials of the Christian faith. When familiar liturgical forms and texts are used again and again, it gives us the opportunity to meditate on them and to penetrate their meaning more deeply. When there are well-established procedures with which everyone is familiar, it makes it easier to concentrate on the content rather than the outward form. Any athlete understands the importance of mastering form. Such simple things as breathing must be done correctly. It takes a long time to get some of these simple techniques down, but this is essential so that eventually they can be done spontaneously, without effort, without thinking about them. The concentration must be on other things. Forms are a means to an end; if they are constantly changing, they obscure the end rather than lead to it.

A tradition that gets radically changed every generation is not really a tradition. For tradition to be tradition, it must have a considerable amount of permanence and changelessness. Tradition can become tradition only when it is passed from one generation to another. That is what the Latin verb *tradere* means, "to hand over," from one hand to another, from one generation to another. Tradition cannot be invented. It can be discovered or recovered, but it must be received from someone else. A liturgical tradition cannot be concocted by a General Assembly task force. Such a task force can recognize that over the generations such and such a liturgical tradition has been passed on to us. It can evaluate traditions, asking whether they are adequate or inadequate for our day and whether they are true to Scripture. Tradition can be received or rejected, but it cannot be invented.

The story is told of a well-known Presbyterian liturgist who held a workshop in liturgy at an ecumenical study conference center. The liturgist, having all sorts of credentials in music and the arts, was instructing the workshop in the creation of liturgies. When the course drew to a close, the liturgist gave an assignment to his class. Each participant was to create his or her own liturgy. Among those in the class was a woman from the Orthodox church of Ethiopia. To her the assignment was the cause of great confusion. At last she approached the liturgist and explained her confusion. How could she write a liturgy? A liturgy was something that had developed over the centuries. How could she just sit down and make one up in the course of a few hours? The liturgist, realizing he was dealing with someone from a very primitive culture, patiently sat her down and explained that it was really all very easy. For an hour or so he worked at putting together a liturgy for matins. Since he was responsible for leading matins the next morning, he had the service mimeographed and then performed the next morning. When the performance was over, the liturgist asked the woman what she thought of it. She shook her head and said, "The liturgy can only come from many tears." She understood what liturgy really is. It is participation in a fellowship of suffering and joy that has gone on for centuries.

On the other hand, tradition must always be reinterpreted. That is the very nature of tradition. This is true for liturgical tradition just as it is for music. Today when a Mozart trio sonata is played before a modern audience, an important part of the artists' work is the interpretation of Mozart's composition. A certain amount of adaptation must be made. Today, two hundred years after Mozart, the musical instruments used will be different from those used in Mozart's day. The instruments of Mozart's day were much more delicate. Performances took place in drawing rooms or salons rather than concert halls. Then there are the matters of the phrasing and the tempo. A good interpreter recognizes subtle harmonies, contrasts, and balances. The interpreter underlines them and brings them out so that the listener hears them, too. Artists who are sensitive to the composer can make these compositions fascinating, but a poor interpretation can make them dry and boring.

There is something quite analogous to this in the celebration of the liturgy. One cannot celebrate the liturgy without interpreting it. The pastor of an American Protestant church today must evaluate the liturgical heritage of his or her church and decide what things are important to include in the time set aside for worship. The pastor must decide how to divide that time between preaching, prayer, praise, and sacraments. He or she must decide how much to be guided by the contemporary liturgical books offered by the denomination, how much by the great classics of the tradition, and how much by the capacity of the congregation. A celebration of vespers on Easter Sunday in a large city church with a well-trained choir and a professional organist will obviously be quite different from the holding of vespers on a camping trip with a group of a dozen teenagers. There is a real art to adapting the liturgical forms of vespers to such very different situations. One could of course just ignore these forms, but a far greater depth can be gained in the worship if these forms are used as a guide in the shaping of the prayers of the group.

There is great value in maintaining the tradition. More and more, this is becoming recognized today. Let us look at some reasons for maintaining the tradition.

First, we human beings feel a need to keep in contact with our roots. Often in history there has been a violent reaction against the tradition. Nevertheless one eventually gets around to going back and trying to recover the tradition. Something in us reaches out for the tradition, just as something in us pushes us to pass on the tradition. This concern for the tradition corresponds to a basic human need. For the Christian this is not at all surprising. God made us to live in community, so we find it natural that we should reach out to our neighbors. As Christians we recognize a need to maintain fellowship with Christians in other parts of the world. For the same reason we recognize a need to maintain fellowship with Christians who have gone before us. The universality of the community has dimensions in time.

The importance of having roots was illustrated by Alex Haley in his book *Roots*. As an American of African ancestry he went searching for his roots in Africa. The fact that he found them gave millions of black Americans a new appreciation for the value of their own life today. Even more, it gave millions of American whites a new appreciation for blacks.

We reach out for the tradition because we want to see who we are, where we came from, and where we are going. We want to see our own lives in a larger perspective of history. We want to know who we are as American Protestant Christians at the beginning of the third millennium.

Second, the tradition contains material of lasting value. The church has maintained great respect for the church fathers of the earliest Christian centuries, particularly those Christians of the second and third centuries, such as Irenaeus (ca. 130–ca. 200), Cyprian (d. 258), Origen (ca. 185–ca. 254), Clement of Alexandria (ca. 150–ca. 215), Lactantius (ca. 240–ca. 320), Hippolytus (ca. 170–ca. 236), and Tertullian (ca. 160–ca. 225), who did their work amidst the persecutions and harassment of a hostile civil authority. One is amazed that the church produced any literature at all during this period. Nevertheless, they preserved for us a vivid picture of the nature of the Christian life. They reveal a vitality and purity that we can only emulate. With the establishment of the church in the fourth century, the number of great Christian thinkers, preachers, and writers increased enormously. Athanasius (ca. 296–373), Hilary of Poitiers (ca. 315–367), Ambrose of Milan (ca. 339–97), John Chrysostom (ca. 347–407), Basil of Caesarea (ca. 329–79), Gregory of Nazianzus (ca. 330–ca. 389) and Gregory of Nyssa (ca. 330–ca. 395), Cyril of Jerusalem (ca. 315–386) and Cyril of Alexandria (d. 444), Augustine (354–430), and Jerome (ca. 347–419/20) were all men of intellectual prowess who provided extraordinary leadership for the church. Whenever Christians talk about tradition, the Fathers figure prominently in the discussion. The reason is not hard to discover. We respect them because of their brilliance.

It is a strange thing about the Fathers; for very few of us are they really fathers. Very few American Protestants have Italian or Greek ancestors. We have neither racial nor ethnic relation to the Fathers of the early church. Most of us can claim no saints in the branches of the family tree, not even in the most remote twigs. Some American Protestants can, after the flesh, claim Abraham and Sarah as ancestors, but most of us claim them as ancestors according to the lineage of faith. In fact, when we think about it, do we not think of Abraham and Sarah as being our ancestors far more than any proto-Germanic or Celtic tribes who might have been tramping around northern Europe in that age when Abraham was called out of Ur of Chaldees? It is an old custom to call John Chrysostom "our father among the saints." John Chrysostom, however, was a celibate. Not one of us can claim him as our ancestor. What makes him then our father? Augustine had one son, who died at the age of twelve. Besides that, Augustine was an African of racially mixed parentage. He seems to have had some Roman ancestry, but for the most part he was a descendant of Punic stock. Racially he is quite distant from most of us. How is it that we call such men Fathers?

The answer is this: Chrysostom, Augustine, and Jerome have again and again engendered spiritual children, in one generation after another, in one culture after another. The schoolmen of the high Middle Ages quoted Augustine more than anyone else. The Reformers feasted on him. In our own country the Mercersburg school paid him the highest deference. Augustine's commentaries on Scripture, his theological essays, and his introspective thoughts get great minds thinking. They have the power to inspire thought. He, like the other Fathers, was a seminal thinker. The thinking of the Fathers inspires others to think. The Fathers were the seminal thinkers of Christian theology. If it were not for this ability of theirs to speak to the most devout and fertile of minds of every age and nation, they would have been forgotten long ago.

For the American Protestant of today, the Fathers and the Reformers occupy much the same position. As Karl Barth (1886–1968) puts it, the Reformers recognized much the same sort of authority in the Fathers of the early church as the modern Protestant recognizes in the Reformers of the sixteenth century. It was inevitable that the Reformers should respect Basil of Caesarea. He was a great ethical thinker and a man of such moral integrity. He wrote about the Christian life so clearly. Ambrose of Milan could not help but capture the imagination of the Reformers. He was a man of such courage and political ability. Cyril of Alexandria's commentary on the Gospel of John is such a brilliant exposition of orthodox Christology that when the first generation of Reformers read it, they were thoroughly convinced. Cyril was a great theologian regardless of where and when he lived.

It is now approaching five hundred years since the Reformers did their work, and it is becoming very clear that they were great thinkers far beyond the accidents of time and culture that produced them. Luther is far more than a German folk hero. He is far more than a reaction against certain religious abuses of a certain age in the history of the church. Luther is not really explained or explained away by the economics and politics of his day. He gained a very fresh and clear insight into some lasting realities. He perceived the radical nature of God's grace revealed in the death and resurrection of Christ. He perceived the transcendent authority of the Word of God. He clearly perceived the priority of faith in the Christian life. Because he saw this so clearly and because he wrote about it so perceptively, we recognize his leadership in the church.

Luther was not alone. In John Oecolampadius (1482–1531) we recognize a great biblical philologist who had a profound sense of how one interprets Scripture. Oecolampadius helped bring into focus many biblical concepts that had become blurred over the centuries. An outstanding patristic scholar, he translated for the first time into a Western language a sizable portion of the treasures of Greek Christian literature. In Calvin we recognize an outstanding interpreter of Scripture. Calvin's biblical commentaries still speak to us today, even though biblical research has gone far beyond him. Thomas Manton's sermons on the epistle of James are to this day the most practical sort of instruction on the Christian life. Matthew Henry's commentaries are as popular today as they were when they were first written. In fact few people realize they are close to three hundred years old. This is the nature of the classics! They transcend the merely ethnic, the merely national, the merely cultural.

The classics, in theology or any other field, are classics because they are so good. It is a matter of quality. The tradition becomes important when we recognize that what the tradition preserves is important. The way we evaluate the tradition has certain points in common with the way we evaluate great music. Generation after generation listens to Bach simply because his music is so good. We do not listen to his music because it is German or because it is an expression of baroque culture. The more one studies music, the more the genius of Bach becomes clear. The sophisticated craftsmanship of Bach is simply unsurpassed. That Bach is among the greatest of composers is not simply a matter of subjective opinion or mystical experience. He was able to solve problems of harmony and counterpoint with a classic simplicity that amazes the musician of today. The breadth of Bach's genius is illustrated by the variety in his work. There are the choral works, the chamber music, the delicate works for harpsichord, and the mighty organ works. Another amazing thing about him is the volume of his work. This is typical of a real genius. Bach's genius was not a trickle or an occasional spurt. It was a mighty river constantly flowing in full force. The classics themselves set the standard of quality. We do not really measure the classics; they measure us. It is somewhat the same way with theology.

But to return to the Reformers. Were they really any better than the theologians of any other age? Should we really place them in some sort of golden age of theology? By what standard do we give them any more respect than theologians of any other age? These questions are often asked, but in fact it is hard not to recognize the genius of the sixteenth-century Reformers. We do not recognize them as great because they lived in a golden age and therefore have to be recognized as great. We recognize them as great because they were great! Luther, for example, sufficiently mastered both Greek and Hebrew that he was able to do an original translation of both the Old and New Testaments which has never been surpassed. That feat alone should win for Luther our abiding respect. Calvin's brilliance is recognized in the many facets of his theological endeavor. He was a most able commentator on Scripture. He was a master of the original languages and an excellent biblical philologist. He was a systematic theologian too. Few theologians have achieved distinction in both fields. In the *Institutes* he treated the whole range of Christian thought. His letters reveal him to have been an excellent pastor. He was a capable preacher as well. It is the quality of Calvin's work that has won him the respect he has enjoyed among theologians ever since the sixteenth century. Again, Luther and Calvin were not alone. Henry Bullinger (1504–75) was a man of enormous ability. Educated at the University of Cologne in pure *via antiqua* scholasticism, he knew Thomas Aquinas (1225?–74), Bonaventure (1217–74), and Duns Scotus (1266–1308) well. His knowledge of patristic, exegetical, and historical literature was encyclopedic. He had read everything in his long life. He started out as a child prodigy, succeeding Zwingli while he was only twenty-seven years old, and for more than forty years he capably directed the reformation of Zurich securing for it an international influence. It was not simply because the politics of Europe were favorable to the Reformation that it succeeded. The Reformation had very capable leadership. The Reformers were great scholars and men who exercised spiritual leadership of the highest quality. At the center of their reform was a concern for the reform of worship, and they had a profound insight into the nature of worship. That is why we are interested in what they had to say.

Third, we should maintain the tradition because it witnesses to the authority of Scripture. Above all, the leadership of both the Fathers and the Reformers is to be found in the fact that they understood Scripture so well. They were *testes veritatis,* that is, witnesses to the truth. Because the Fathers and the Reformers point us to the Scriptures so unequivocally and open up Scripture so widely, we listen to them.

Just before the beginning of the Reformation, when Erasmus (d. 1536) published his first edition of the complete works of Jerome, he was sure it was going to clear up the theological atmosphere. Jerome was the greatest biblical scholar of the ancient Latin church. He produced the standard Latin translation of the Bible. He made his translation from the Hebrew Old Testament and the Greek New Testament and devoted a lifetime to the work. The Christian humanists of the early sixteenth century who recognized Erasmus as their leader read the enormous nine-volume folio edition of the complete works of Jerome with high expectations. Here they had before them the fulfillment of the Christian humanist ideal. Erasmus in his edition of Jerome was indeed bringing his generation *ad fontes.* He was bringing them to the purest sources of the tradition. The sharpest students of Erasmus, men like Zwingli, Oecolampadius, and Bucer read Jerome, and Jerome pointed them to Scripture. They went further than Erasmus. Zwingli tells us that the ink was hardly dry before he had the first volume under his nose.

He read the whole thing with the most careful attention. Jerome opened to him the study of Scripture. When he finished Jerome, he realized it was Scripture he had to study.

Erasmus gave Oecolampadius the job of preparing the index volume for his edition of Jerome. Erasmus was a great Latinist and had also mastered Greek, but he did not know Hebrew; Oecolampadius, on the other hand, like Jerome, was a master of all three ancient languages. Erasmus set Oecolampadius at the job of preparing an index of all the Hebrew words discussed by Jerome and then an index of all the Greek words discussed by that master biblical philologist. This work of Oecolampadius opened up modern biblical philology and became a Rosetta stone for theologians. The work of Oecolampadius made it possible to see how Jerome, the master of Latin, Greek, and Hebrew, had translated the original biblical words into Latin. It made it possible to discover what those original biblical words really meant. Jerome had a passion for discovering the "Hebrew verity," and from Jerome the Reformers learned the importance of searching out the original Hebrew concepts. No wonder Oecolampadius, Zwingli, and Bullinger rediscovered the meaning of covenant! They had carefully studied Jerome, and Jerome taught them the importance of studying the Hebrew text. Jerome, like Cyril of Alexandria, like John Chrysostom, and like one father after another, pointed the Reformers to Scripture.

For us Christians of the twenty-first century the Reformers are tradition, just as the Fathers were tradition for the Reformers. To be sure, the Fathers are tradition for us, too. If we accept the Fathers and the Reformers as important constituents of our tradition, then we need to be interested in them not in themselves but interested in them because of what they point out to us about Scripture. We are interested in what they have to say about how Scripture teaches us to worship.

Reformed theology has always made a very clear distinction between Scripture and tradition. Scripture has authority, and tradition has the value of witnessing to that authority. In a chapter of his *Church Dogmatics* titled "Authority under the Word," Karl Barth shows how and in what sense tradition witnesses to Scripture. The authority of tradition is secondary, derived from and dependent upon the authority of Scripture. In the last analysis we are not as much concerned with what tradition tells us about worship as with what tradition tells us about what Scripture has to say about worship. We are concerned to hear what those great biblical scholars have had to say about worship. Few matters of concern in Reformed worship are merely matters of tradition. Most things that we do in worship we do because God has commanded us to do them. Because of this, we read the Scriptures and preach the gospel, we praise God in psalms and hymns, we serve God in prayer, we baptize and celebrate the Lord's Supper. At the same time, we do some things in worship not so much because they are specifically taught in Scripture but because they are in accordance with Scripture. What this means is that we do some of the things we do in worship because they are demanded by scriptural principles. For example, we baptize in the name of the Father, the Son, and the Holy Spirit because this is specifically directed by Scripture. It is on the basis of scriptural principles, however, that before the baptism we offer the Baptismal Invocation asking the Holy Spirit to fulfill inwardly what is promised in the outward sign. The basic acts of worship we perform because they are clearly commanded in Scripture. The ways and means of doing them we try to order according to scriptural principles. When something is not specifically commanded, prescribed, or directed, or when there is no scriptural example to guide us in how we are to perform some particular aspect of worship, we should try nevertheless to be guided by scriptural principles. As we discover in the first chapter of the Westminster Confession, such is often the case with the public ordering of worship. In fact one might say that it is the essence of the Reformed tradition that worship should be far more than merely tradition. The *adiaphora,* the indifferent things, are quite appropriately matters of merely human tradition, but the essential elements of worship are those that we do in obedience to the Word of God.

Let us look for a moment at some of the most valuable worship traditions at the heart of the heritage of Reformed Protestantism, liturgical traditions that commend themselves to us because they are, above all, according to Scripture.

1. At the head of the list should certainly be expository preaching. This has always been the glory of Protestant worship. At present it seems to have fallen on hard days, but it needs to be revived. The fifteen- and twenty-minute homilies that have become the regular practice in most American Protestant churches today amount to not much more than a surrender of the tradition. Unfortunately, far too few ministers are equipped to do expository preaching. Even worse, few congregations are willing to give their ministers the time to do expository preaching. To be sure, there should be other kinds of preaching as well. On Sunday evenings it might be well to preach a major series of catechetical sermons each year, but the preaching of the Lord's Day morning should be devoted to expository preaching. Preaching should not be neglected at weddings and funerals. Needless to say, the quality of preaching will have to be improved considerably before we can expect the faithful to support a genuine preaching ministry.

2. Very closely related to expository preaching is the use of *lectio continua.* This was one of the most significant reforms of the sixteenth century, resting solidly on the practice of both the synagogue and the early church. Nothing could have a more salutary effect on preaching than the regular, systematic preaching through one book of the Bible after another. It gives a great opportunity for both the preacher and the congregation to study the Scriptures. In time, many in the congregation will develop the habit of reading along with the preacher and will arrive for worship having studied the passage on which the sermon is to be preached. This kind of preaching needs to be done in a sensitive way, with a recognition of the capacity of the congregation. It also needs to be supported by good Bible study in Sunday school for both children and adults. After several years of using the *lectio continua,* the congregation will discover itself to have learned an amazing amount of Scripture.

3. Another Reformed liturgical tradition that needs to be cultivated is the praying of the psalms. The singing of metrical psalms and the responsive read-

ing of the psalms should both be cultivated. There are plenty of excellent versions of metrical psalms which are available. Another way of using the psalms in worship is to have a lector read the text and the congregation sing a threefold Hallelujah or some other antiphon after each stanza. Certainly we should not overlook the use of choral settings of psalms. Here we find a wealth of material. Psalm settings are available in every conceivable style of music. New arrangements of psalms should always be encouraged. So much has been learned about the Psalms in the last few decades that many of us regard psalm study as one of the most fascinating branches of biblical research. Enriched by modern psalm study, we need to approach the praying of the psalms once more. Surely this will do much to deepen the prayer life of the church today.

4. We have spoken several times of the way the Reformed tradition in worship has emphasized a full diet of prayer. This sense for the full range of prayer found implicitly in the Strasbourg and Genevan psalters is elaborated explicitly in the Westminster Directory for Worship. Here we are specifically told that prayer should include praise, confession, thanksgiving, supplication, and intercession. Today, this appreciation of the varieties of prayer has taken on new interest because of what has been learned about the various genres of the Psalms and the different theologies of prayer behind each genre. There are different prayer types in another level. We have pointed out that the *Genevan Psalter* provides for the singing of psalms as prayer, the reading of set prayers, and the use of extemporaneous prayer. Surely the ability to frame prayers appropriate to the occasion has a venerable heritage, and it is important to maintain this heritage. The Puritans learned much of value in regard to the prophetic nature of prayer and in regard to prayer being the work of the Holy Spirit. The literature on prayer, which is quite extensive, needs to be carefully restudied. Extempore prayer, as the Westminster Fathers expressly remind us, takes careful preparation.

5. The first generation of Reformers recovered a number of different aspects of the celebration of the Lord's Supper. In the first place, they rediscovered the Supper as a meal. For so long the emphasis had been on the consecrating and sacrificing of the bread and wine. The Reformers put new emphasis on the Communion itself, that is, on the sharing of the bread and wine by the whole church. They tried to make their celebration look like a real meal. They replaced altars with tables and used bread that looked like real bread. In many places they actually sat at the table. The Reformers recovered a covenantal understanding of the Lord's Supper, and here is one of their most valuable contributions. Advances in biblical theology today enormously enhance the work of the Reformers. Thanks to modern biblical research, we can appreciate the work of the Reformers in this field much more than before. The Reformers were going in the right direction when they tried to understand the Lord's Supper as a covenant meal.

6. The appreciation of the Lord's Supper as Eucharist, which we find particularly in Peter Martyr Vermigli (1500–1562) and John Knox (1513–72), also needs to be maintained. John Knox's eucharistic prayer could well serve as a model for a Reformed eucharistic prayer. It is truly a hymnic recounting of the

works of creation and redemption. So many eucharistic prayers have been obsessed with walking the tightrope of theological formulation that they have lost the doxological spirit. They have become formulas of doctrine rather than hymns of praise.

7. The epicletic nature of the Lord's Supper needs to be maintained as well. There is real genius in the tradition developed in Strasbourg and Geneva in which the Prayer of Intercession is expanded by a Communion Invocation when the sacrament is celebrated. The Prayer of Intercession gathers all Christians together about the Lord's Table in much the same way as the High Priestly Prayer of Jesus in the seventeenth chapter of the Gospel of John. In that prayer Jesus prays for the unity of the church, the sanctity of the church, and the continuity of the church. Here, in the Prayer of Intercession, is where the real epiclesis of the Reformed eucharistic liturgy is to be found. A Reformed epiclesis is a prayer for the church. It is a prayer for the consecration of the body of Christ through the work of the Holy Spirit. It is a prayer for the gathering, the uniting, the illumination, and, above all, the sanctifying of the church.

8. The diaconal aspect of the Lord's Supper is an important aspect of the tradition that needs to be clearly expressed in the contemporary Reformed liturgy. The keynote of this part of the service is the post-Communion prayer of thanksgiving and dedication. The essence of this part of the service is magnificently expressed by the hymn of Isaac Watts (1674–1748) that so often we sing after Communion:

> When I survey the wondrous cross
>   On which the Prince of glory died,
> My richest gain I count but loss
>   And pour contempt on all my pride.
> . . . .
> Were the whole realm of nature mine,
>   That were a present far too small;
> Love so amazing, so divine,
>   Demands my soul, my life, my all.

Likewise, the singing of Psalm 116 is appropriate because it makes clear that our giving is thanksgiving. Such texts remind us that our giving of tithes and alms is an act of thanksgiving for our redemption. Surely the fact that this giving of ourselves and our substance comes at the end of the service demonstrates that our charitable works are enabled and empowered by our communion with God. Collecting tithes and alms at the end of the service is a liturgical practice consistent with a theology that emphasizes grace. It is much more in accordance with Scripture than the practice of having an offertory before the Communion. This transition from the service of God to the service of the neighbor should be a clear and distinct part of every Reformed Communion service.

9. In regard to baptism, several features might be singled out. Covenant theology needs to be reemphasized. (By Covenant theology we do not of course mean any one of the very elaborate systems of theology developed by various

seventeenth-century theologians. By Covenant theology we have in mind something much more simple. We are thinking primarily of a recovery of the biblical concept of covenant and a theology of the sacraments that has this in mind.) It is important to understand baptism as a sign of the covenant. This should be the theology on which we build our baptismal practice. In fact, one can go so far as to say that Covenant theology is Reformed sacramental theology. To understand baptism in terms of the Hellenistic mystery religions may develop dramatic liturgical rites, but these rites will be neither according to Scripture nor Reformed. When baptism is understood in terms of covenant, then it is clear that the children of the covenant community should be baptized.

10. Any Reformed celebration of baptism should be very clear in maintaining the unity of the sacrament. There is one baptism for the forgiveness of sins and the gift of the Holy Spirit. No secondary rite, such as anointing, should be introduced that might suggest that those who had been merely baptized with water now needed to receive the gift of the Holy Spirit. The washing of water should be presented as an outward sign of an inward gift of the Holy Spirit.

11. Baptism should be explained as a sign given at the beginning of the Christian life of what happens to us through the whole of the Christian life. As long as we live here on earth, we are living out our baptism as we more and more die unto sin and live unto God.

12. Baptism should always entail the teaching of "all that I have commanded you" (Matt. 28:20). The Reformers were eager to revive the catechetical discipline of the early church. They had to adjust this discipline to a church that existed in a society which, in name at least, was Christian. They did this well by providing thorough catechetical instruction for children baptized in infancy, once those children had achieved sufficient age to understand basic Christian teaching. Upon completing this course of instruction, the children were admitted to the Lord's Table on the basis of a profession of faith. This historic Protestant catechetical discipline does justice to two great biblical truths. It recognizes that baptism is a sign of entrance into the covenant community and therefore should be given at the beginning of the Christian life, and it recognizes that baptism should be accompanied by teaching and a profession of faith.

13. One aspect of our tradition that particularly needs our attention is the daily service of morning and evening prayer. This needs to be cultivated both in relation to the service of daily prayer maintained by Christian families in their homes and in relation to the service of daily prayer maintained at the church. Today a revival of daily prayer at the church has become increasingly important because of the great number of Christians who live alone. Christian prayer is the prayer of the body of Christ. It is prayer in fellowship with other Christians. For many of us, single or married, if we are going to pray in the fellowship of other Christians, then the church is the place we are most likely to find that kind of prayer fellowship. Most singles need more than kaffeeklatsch fellowship. Plenty of people who live in families need stronger prayer support than they can find at home. It should be in the context of the daily prayer services that pastoral care

should take place. Let us leave counseling couches to the psychologists and make the service of daily prayer the heart of our ministry of pastoral care.

14. The Puritans developed the discipline of daily family prayer with particular insight. They understood the family to be a little church. The family is a divinely created organism, a reality established by God. As such it owes worship to God. The maintaining of family prayer demonstrates the family to have a sacred reality.

15. The greatest single contribution that the Reformed liturgical heritage can make to contemporary American Protestantism is its sense of the majesty and sovereignty of God, its sense of reverence and simple dignity, its conviction that worship must above all serve the praise of God.

This program for the renewal of worship in American Protestant churches of today may not be exactly what everyone is looking for. In our evangelistic zeal we are looking for programs that will attract people. We think we have to put honey on the lip of the bitter cup of salvation. It is the story of the wedding of Cana all over again, but with this difference. At the crucial moment when the wine failed, we took matters into our own hands and used those five stone jars to mix up a batch of Kool-Aid instead. It seemed like a good solution in terms of our American culture. Unfortunately, all too soon the guests discovered the fraud. Alas! What are we to do now? How can we possibly minister to those who thirst for the real thing? There is but one thing to do, as Mary, the mother of Jesus, understood so very well. You remember how the story goes. After presenting the problem to Jesus, Mary turned to the servants and said to them, "Do whatever he tells you" (John 2:5). The servants did just that, and the water was turned to wine, wine rich and mellow beyond anything they had ever tasted before.

Notes

Chapter 1: Some Basic Principles

1. Westminster Shorter Catechism, Q. 1.
2. Calvin, *Institutes* 2.8.16.
3. Thomas Manton, *The Complete Works of Thomas Manton, D.D.*, 22 vols. (Reprint, Worthington, Pa.: Maranatha Publications, n.d.), 1:84.
4. Westminster Shorter Catechism, Q. 88.

Chapter 2: Baptism

1. Hughes Oliphant Old, *Themes and Variations for a Christian Doxology* (Grand Rapids: Wm. B. Eerdmans Publishing Co., 1992).
2. John Calvin, *Opera Selecta*, ed. Petrus Barth and Dora Scheuner (Munich: Chr. Kaiser, 1952), 2:30–38 (author's translation).

Chapter 3: The Lord's Day

1. Calvin, *Institutes* 2.8.28.

Chapter 5: The Ministry of the Word

1. Thomas M'Crie, *The Life of John Knox* (Glasgow: Free Presbyterian Publications, 1976), 239.
2. "Of Publick Reading of the Holy Scriptures," Westminster Directory for Worship.
3. Ibid.
4. "Of the Preaching of the Word," Westminster Directory for Worship.

Chapter 6: The Ministry of Prayer

1. David Hedegård, *Seder R. Amram Gaon* (Lund: A.-B. Ph. Lindstedts Universitetsbokhandel, 1951), 88.
2. Ibid., 92.

Chapter 7: The Lord's Supper

1. *Didache* XIV, 3.
2. Ambrose, *De sacramentis* 4, 21–23 (author's translation).
3. Calvin, *Opera selecta* 2:14.
4. Calvin, *Institutes* 4.17.3.
5. Ibid., 4.17.8.
6. Bard Thompson, *Liturgies of the Western Church* (Cleveland: World Publishing Co., 1961), 208.
7. Joseph C. McLelland, *The Visible Words of God: An Exposition of the Sacramental Theology of Peter Martyr Vermigli* (Grand Rapids: Wm. B. Eerdmans Publishing Co., 1958), 94.
8. Charles W. Baird, *The Presbyterian Liturgies: Historical Sketches* (Reprint, Grand Rapids: Baker Book House, 1957), 124–26.
9. "Of the Celebration of the Communion, or Sacrament of the Lord's Supper," Westminster Directory for Worship.

Select Bibliography for the Study of Reformed Worship

Abray, Lorna Jane. *The People's Reformation: Magistrates, Clergy, and Commons in Strasbourg, 1500–1598*. Ithaca, N.Y.: Cornell University Press, 1985.

Alexander, J. Neil. "Luther's Reform of the Daily Office." *Worship* 57: 348–60.

Alexander, James W. *Thoughts on Family Worship*. Philadelphia: Presbyterian Board of Education, 1847. Reprint, Ligonier, Pa.: Soli Deo Gloria Publications, 1990.

Althaus, Paul. *The Theology of Martin Luther*. Translated by Robert C. Schultz. Philadelphia: Fortress Press, 1966.

Anderson, Marvin Walter. *Peter Martyr: A Reformer in Exile (1542–1562)*. Nieuwkoop: B. de Graaf, 1975.

Baird, Charles W. *The Presbyterian Liturgies: Historical Sketches*. 1855. Reprint, Grand Rapids: Baker Book House, 1957.

Baker, Henry. *Heinrich Bullinger and the Covenant, the Other Reformed Tradition*. Athens, Ohio: Miami University Press, 1980.

Balke, Willem. *Calvin and the Anabaptist Radicals*. Translated by William Heynen. Grand Rapids: Wm. B. Eerdmans Publishing Co., 1981.

Barth, Karl. *La prière d'après les catéchismes de la réformation*. Neuchâtel: Delachaux et Niestlé, 1953.

Battles, Ford Lewis, and Stanley Tagg. *The Piety of John Calvin*. Grand Rapids: Baker Book House, 1978.

Baxter, Richard. *A Christian Directory*. In *The Practical Works of the Rev. Richard Baxter*, vols. 3, 4, and 5. Edited by William Orme. London: James Duncan, 1830.

———. *Christian Ecclesiastics*. In *The Practical Works of the Rev. Richard Baxter*, vol. 5. Edited by William Orme. London: James Duncan, 1830.

———. *Paraphrase on the Psalms of David in Metre, with Other Hymns*. London: Printed for Richard Baldwin, 1692.

———. *The Reformed Liturgy*. In *The Practical Works of the Rev. Richard Baxter*, vol. 15. Edited by William Orme. London: James Duncan, 1830.

Beeke, Joel R. *Forerunner of the Great Awakening: Sermons by Theodorus Jacobus Frelinghuysen (1691–1747)*. Grand Rapids: Wm. B. Eerdmans Publishing Co., 2000.

Beyer, Ulrich. *Abendmahl und Messe: Sinn und Recht der 80. Frage des heidelberger Katechismus*. Neukirchen: Erziehungsverein, 1965.

Booty, John E. "The First and Second Prayer Books of King Edward VI." In *Oxford Encyclopedia of the Reformation*, 1:189–93. New York: Oxford University Press, 1996.
———. *The Godly Kingdom of Tudor England*. Wilton, Conn.: Morehouse–Barlow Co., 1981.
———, ed. *The Book of Common Prayer, 1559: The Elizabethan Prayer Book*. Charlottesville, Va.: Published for the Folger Shakespeare Library by the University Press of Virginia, 1976.
Bornert, René. *La réforme protestante du cult à Strasbourg au XVIe siècle (1523–1598)*. Leiden: E. J. Brill, 1981.
Bosshard, S. N. *Zwingli, Erasmus, Cajetan: Die Eucharistie als zeichen der Einheit*. Wiesbaden: Steiner, 1978.
Bovet, Felix. *Histoire du psautier des églises réformées*. Paris: Grossart Libraire, 1872.
Bromiley, Geoffrey W. *Thomas Cranmer, Theologian*. New York: Oxford University Press, 1956.
Bruce, Robert. *The Mystery of the Lord's Supper*. Translated and edited by Thomas F. Torrance. Richmond: John Knox Press, 1958.
Bucer, Martin. *Bericht auss der heyligen geschrift von der recht gottseligen anstellung und hausshaltung Christlicher gemeyn. . . .* Strasbourg: Matthias Apiarius, 1534. Reprint of the German text in vol. 5 of *Martin Bucers Deutsche Schriften*, Gütersloh: Gerd Mohn, 1978.
———. *Grund und Ursach auss gotlicher schrifft der neuwerungen. . . .* Strasbourg: Wolfgang Kopfel, 1524. Reprint in vol. 1 of *Martin Bucers Deutsche Schriften*, by Martin Bucer. Gütersloh: Gerd Mohn, 1960.
———. *Martin Bucers Deutsche Schriften*. Edited by Robert Stupperich. 12 vols. to date. Gütersloh: Gerd Mohn, 1960–. Of special interest are Bucer's proposals to the city council regarding liturgical reforms, 2:423–558; Bucer's treatment of liturgical subjects in the Confessio Tetrapolitana, vol. 3; Bucer's proposals for liturgical reform in the city of Ulm, vol. 4; and the Hessian church order, vol. 7.
———. *Psalmorum libri quinque ad Hebraicam veritatem traducti et summa fide. . . .* Geneva: Robertus Stephanus, 1554. This work is particularly important for understanding the Reformed theology of praise and prayer.
———. "Psalter with Complete Church Practice: Strasbourg, 1539." English translation in *Liturgies of the Western Church*, by Bard Thompson. Cleveland: World Publishing Co., 1961. For the original text of various editions of the *Strasbourg Psalter* from 1524 to 1537, see Friedrich Hubert, ed., *Die Strassburger liturgische Ordnungen*.
———. *Quid de baptismate*. Strasbourg: Matthew Apiarius, 1533.
———. *A Treatise: How Almose Ought to Be Distributed*. Reprint of 1557 edition, Norwood, N.J.: W. J. Johnson, 1976.
Bullinger, Henry. *The Decades*. 5 vols. Translated by H. I. Edited for the Parker Society by Thomas Harding. Cambridge: Cambridge University Press, 1849. Reprint, New York: Johnson Reprint Co., 1968. Of particular interest are the sermons on prayer, on the ministry of the Word, and on the sacraments.
———. *De origine erroris in negocio eucharistiae, ac missae, per Heinrychum Bullingerum*. Basel: Thomas Wolff, 1528. This work has been called the first attempt at Dogmengeschichte. It gives important insights into the earliest Reformed understanding of the Lord's Supper.
———. *Von dem vnuerschamptem fräfel. . . .* Zurich: Christoffel Froschouer, 1531. This is one of the most important documents on the Reformed understanding of baptism.
Butin, Philip. *Revelation, Redemption, and Response: Calvin's Trinitarian Understanding of the Divine Human Relationship*. New York: Oxford University Press, 1994.
Calvin, John. *Commentary on the Book of Psalms*. Translated by James Anderson. Grand Rapids: Wm. B. Eerdmans Publishing Co., 1963. For some time the preface to this

commentary has been recognized as an important statement concerning Calvin's personal life. The text of the commentary, however, gives us equally important insights into Calvin's theology of worship.

——. *Institutes of the Christian Religion.* Edited by John T. McNeill. Translated by Ford Lewis Battles. Library of Christian Classics, vols. 20 and 21. Philadelphia: Westminster Press, 1960. See particularly his explanation of the first four commandments, the chapter on prayer, and the chapters on the sacraments.

——. *Opera selecta,* vol. 2. Edited by Petrus Barth and Dora Scheuner. Munich: Chr. Kaiser, 1952.

——. *Sermons on the Ten Commandments.* Edited and translated by Benjamin W. Farley. Grand Rapids: Baker Book House, 1980. This collection of sermons is a good example of Calvin as preacher.

——. *Theological Treatises.* 3 vols. Translated by J. K. S. Reid. Philadelphia: Westminster Press, 1954. See particularly the "Form of Prayers" and the "Short Treatise on the Lord's Supper."

Capito, Wolfgang. "Brief an den Prediger . . . Leonhard von Liechtenstein. Über das Buch vom Sabbath von Oswald Glait." In *Elsass,* 1:363–93. Edited by Manfred Krebs and Hans Georg Rott. Quellen zur Geschichte der Täufer, vol. 7. Gütersloh: Gerd Mohn, 1959.

——. "De pueris instituendis ecclesiae Argentinensis." Reprinted in *Monumenta Germaniae Paedagogica,* vol., 23. Edited by Ferdinand Cohrs. Berlin: A. Hoffmann & Co., 1907.

——. *Was mann halten soll von der spaltung zwischen Martin Luther und Andreas Carolstadt.* Strasbourg: Wolff Kopphel, 1524.

Charnock, Stephen. *The Works of the Late Rev. Stephen Charnock.* 9 vols. London: Printed for Baynes, Paternoster Row, 1815.

Chester, Allan G. *Hugh Latimer, Apostle of the English.* Philadelphia: University of Pennsylvania Press, 1954.

Childs, Brevard S. *Memory and Tradition in Israel.* London: SCM Press, 1962.

Chrisman, Miriam Usher. *Lay Culture, Learned Culture: Books and Social Change in Strasbourg, 1480–1599.* New Haven, Conn.: Yale University Press, 1982.

——. *Strasbourg and the Reform.* New Haven, Conn.: Yale University Press, 1967.

Coalter, Milton, Jr. *Gilbert Tennent, Son of Thunder: A Case Study of Continental Pietism's Influence on the First Great Awakening in the Middle Colonies.* New York: Greenwood Press, 1986.

Corda, Salvatore. *Veritas Sacramenti: A Study in Vermigli's Doctrine of the Lord's Supper.* Zurich: Theologische Verlag, 1975.

Cotton, John. *Singing Psalmes a Gospel Ordinance.* London: Printed by M. S. for Hannah Allen, 1647.

——. *The True Constitution of a Particular Visible Church.* London: Printed for Samuel Satterthwaite, 1642.

——. *The Way of the Churches of Christ in New England.* London: Printed by M. Simmons, 1645.

Cullmann, Oscar. *Early Christian Worship.* Translated by A. Stewart Todd and James B. Torrance. London: SCM Press, 1953.

——. *Sabbat und Sonntag nach dem Johannesevangelium: In memoriam. Ernst Lohmeyer.* Stuttgart, 1951.

Cullmann, Oscar, and F. J. Leenhardt. *Essays on the Lord's Supper.* Richmond: John Knox Press, 1958.

Davies, Horton. *Worship and Theology in England.* 2d ed. 6 vols. bound in 3. Grand Rapids: Wm. B. Eerdmans Publishing Co., 1996.

——. *The Worship of the English Puritans.* Morgan, Pa.: Soli Deo Gloria Publications, 1998.

Davies, Samuel. *The Sermons of Samuel Davies.* 3 vols. Philadelphia: Presbyterian Board of Publications, 1854. Reprint, Pittsburgh: Soli Deo Gloria Publications, 1993 and 1997.

Davis, Thomas J. "An Intermediate Brilliance: The Words of Institution and the Gift of Knowledge in Calvin's Eucharistic Theology." In *Calvin Studies VI.* Edited by John H. Leith. Davidson, N.C.: Colloquium on Calvin Studies, 1992.

Dodd, Charles Harold. *The Apostolic Preaching and Its Developments.* London: Hodder & Stoughton, 1936.

————. *The Interpretation of the Fourth Gospel.* Cambridge: Cambridge University Press, 1958.

Dugmor, C. W. *Eucharistic Doctrine from Hooker to Waterland.* London: SPCK, 1942.

Eire, Carlos M. N. *War against the Idols: The Reformation of Worship from Erasmus to Calvin.* New York: Cambridge University Press, 1989. This is a great piece of scholarship even though the author completely misses the basic concern of the Reformers.

Farel, William. *De la sainte cene de nostre seigneur Iesus et de son Testament confirme par sa mort et passion. . . .* Geneva: Jehan Crespin, 1553.

————. *Du vray usage de la croix de Iesus Christ.* Reprint, Geneva: J. G. Pick, 1865.

————. *La Manière et Fasson.* Neuchâtel: Pierre de Vingle, 1533. Reprint, edited by Jean-Guillaume Baum, Strasbourg: Treuttel et Wurtz, 1859.

Farner, Oskar. *Huldrych Zwingli.* 4 vols. Zurich: Zwingli-Verlag, 1943–60. Of particular interest is the chapter on Zwingli's preaching.

Frelinghuysen, Theodorus Jacobus. *Forerunner of the Great Awakening: Sermons by Theodorus Jacobus Frelinghuysen (1691–1747).* Edited by Joel R. Beeke. Grand Rapids: Wm. B. Eerdmans Publishing Co., 2000.

Gagnebin, Bernard. "L' Histoire des Manuscrits des Sermons de Calvin." *Supplementa Calviniana. Sermons inédits.* 2:xiv–xxviii.

Gérold, Theodore. *Les plus anciennes melodies de l'église protestante de Strasbourg et leurs auteurs.* Paris: P. Alcan, 1928.

Gerrish, Brian. *Grace and Gratitude: The Eucharistic Theology of John Calvin.* Minneapolis: Fortress Press, 1993.

Grotzinger, Eberhard. *Luther und Zwingli: die Kritik an der mittelalterlichen Lehre von der Messe als Wurzel des Abendmahlsstreites.* Zurich, Cologne, and Gütersloh: Benzinger Verlag and Verlaghaus Gerd Mohn, 1980.

Hageman, Howard G. *Pulpit and Table.* Richmond: John Knox Press, 1962.

Hedegård, David. *Seder R. Amram Gaon.* Lund: A.-B. Ph. Lindstedts Universitetsbokhandel, 1951.

Heiler, Friedrich. *Das Gebet, eine religionsgeschichtliche und religionspsychologische Untersuchung.* 4th ed. Munich: Verlag von Ernst Reinhardt, 1921.

Henry, Matthew. *A Church in the House.* In *The Complete Works of the Rev. Matthew Henry,* 1:248–67. Edinburgh: A. Fullarton & Co., 1855. Reprint, Grand Rapids: Baker Book House, 1979.

————. *The Communicant's Companion.* In *The Complete Works of the Rev. Matthew Henry,* 1:284–412. Edinburgh: A. Fullarton & Co., 1855. Reprint, Grand Rapids: Baker Book House, 1979.

————. *The Complete Works of the Rev. Matthew Henry.* 2 vols. Edinburgh: A. Fullarton & Co., 1855. Reprint, Grand Rapids: Baker Book House, 1979.

————. *Directions for Daily Communion with God.* In *The Complete Works of the Rev. Matthew Henry,* 1:198–247. Edinburgh: A. Fullarton & Co., 1855. Reprint, Grand Rapids: Baker Book House, 1979.

————. *Family Hymns: Gathered Mostly Out of the Translations of David's Psalms.* In *The Complete Works of the Rev. Matthew Henry,* 1:413–43. Edinburgh: A. Fullarton & Co., 1855. Reprint, Grand Rapids: Baker Book House, 1979.

————. *A Method for Prayer.* In *The Complete Works of the Rev. Matthew Henry,* 2:1–95. Edinburgh: A. Fullarton & Co., 1855. Reprint, Grand Rapids: Baker Book House, 1979.

Heron, Alasdair I. C. *Table and Tradition.* Philadelphia: Westminster Press, 1984.

Hubert, Friedrich, ed. *Die Strassburger liturgischen Ordnungen im Zeitalter der Reformation.* Göttingen: Vandenhoeck & Ruprecht, 1900.

Hunt, E. W. *The Life and Times of John Hooper (c.1500–1555), Bishop of Gloucester.* Lewiston, N.Y.: Edwin Mellen Press, 1992.

Jacobs, Elfriede. *Die Sakramentslehre Wilhelm Farels.* Zurich: Theologischer Verlag, 1978.

Jenny, Markus. *Die Einheit des Abendmahlsgottesdienstes bei den elsassischen und schweizerischen Reformatoren.* Zurich: Zwingli Verlag, 1968.

————. *Geschichte des deutschschweizerischen evangelischen Gesangbuches im 16. Jahrhundert.* Basel: Bärenreiter, 1962.

Jenson, Robert W. *Visible Words: The Interpretation and Practice of Christian Sacraments.* Philadelphia: Fortress Press, 1978.

Jeremias, Joachim. "Das tägliche Gebet im Leben Jesu und in der ältesten Kirche." In *Abba: Studien zur neutestamentlichen Theologie und Zeitgeschichte.* Göttingen: Vandenhoeck & Ruprecht, 1966.

————. *The Eucharistic Words of Jesus.* Translated by Norman Perrin. Philadelphia: Fortress Press, 1977.

————. *Infant Baptism in the First Four Centuries.* Translated by David Cairns. Philadelphia: Westminster Press, 1960.

Kelly, Douglas F. *Preachers with Power: Four Stalwarts of the South.* Edinburgh: Banner of Truth Trust, 1992.

Kingdon, Robert M. "Calvinism and Social Welfare." *Calvin Theological Journal* 17(1982): 212–30.

Kittelson, James M. "Martin Bucer and the Sacramentarian Controversy: The Origins of His Policy of Concord." *Archiv für Reformationsgeschichte* 64 (1973): 166–83.

————. *Wolfgang Capito: From Humanist to Reformer.* Leiden: E. J. Brill, 1975.

Knappen, Marshall Mason. *Tudor Puritanism.* Chicago: University of Chicago Press, 1970. See particularly the discussions on the troubles at Frankfort, the doctrine of ceremonies, and the Vestiarian Controversy.

Knox, John. *The Works of John Knox.* Edited by David Laing. 6 vols. Edinburgh: James Thin, 1895. Reprint, New York: AMS Press, 1966.

————. *The Book of Common Order: Or the Form of Prayers, and Ministrations of the Sacraments, etc. Approved and Received by the Church of Scotland, 1564.* In *The Works of John Knox,* 6:275–334. New York: AMS Press, 1966.

————. *The Form of Prayers and Ministrations of the Sacraments, etc. Used in the English Congregation at Geneva, 1556.* In *The Works of John Knox,* 4:141–213. New York: AMS Press, 1966.

————. *A Narrative of the Proceedings and Troubles of the English Congregation at Frankfurt on the Main, 1554–1555.* In *The Works of John Knox,* 4:1–68. New York: AMS Press, 1966.

————. *Prayers (Edinburgh 1564).* In *The Works of John Knox,* 6:343–80. New York: AMS Press, 1966.

Kraus, Hans-Joachim. *Gottesdienst in Israel.* 2d ed. Munich: Chr. Kaiser, 1962.

————. *Psalmen.* 2d ed. 2 vols. Neukirchen: Neukirchener Verlag, 1961.

Lamb, John Alexander. *The Psalms in Christian Worship.* London: Faith Press, 1962.

Latimer, Hugh. *Selected Sermons.* Edited by Allan G. Chester. Charlottesville: University Press of Virginia, 1968.

Leith, John H. *Assembly at Westminster: Reformed Theology in the Making.* Richmond: John Knox Press, 1973.

————. "Calvin's Doctrine of the Proclamation of the Word and Its Significance for Today." In *John Calvin and the Church: A Prism of Reform.* Edited by Timothy George. Louisville, Ky.: Westminster/John Knox Press, 1990.

————. *Introduction to the Reformed Tradition: A Way of Being the Christian Community.* Rev. ed. Atlanta: John Knox Press, 1981.

Locher, Gottfried Wilhelm. *Die zwinglische Reformation im Rahmen der europäischen Kirchengeschichte.* Göttingen: Vandenhoeck & Ruprecht, 1979.

————. *Im Geist und in der Warheit: die reformatorische Wendung im Gottesdienst in Zürich.* Neukirchen: Buchhandlung der Erziehungsverein, Vandenhoeck & Ruprecht, 1957.

————. *Zwingli's Thought: New Perspectives.* Leiden: E. J. Brill, 1981.

Luther, Martin. *The Babylonian Captivity of the Church.* Translated by A. T. W. Steinhaeuser and revised by Frederick C. Ahrens and Abdel Rose Wentz. In *Luther's Works,* vol. 36. Edited by Helmut T. Lehman. Philadelphia: Fortress Press, 1959.

————. *The German Mass and Order of Service, 1526.* Translated by Augustinus Steimle. Revised by Ulrich S. Leupold. In *Luther's Works,* vol. 53. Edited by Helmut T. Lehman. Philadelphia: Fortress Press, 1965.

————. *The Order of Baptism, 1523.* Translated by Paul Z. Strodach. Revised by Ulrich S. Leupold. In *Luther's Works,* vol. 53. Edited by Helmut T. Lehman. Philadelphia: Fortress Press, 1965.

————. *The Order of Baptism Newly Revised, 1526.* Translated by Paul Z. Strodach. Revised by Ulrich S. Leupold. In *Luther's Works,* vol. 53. Edited by Helmut T. Lehman. Philadelphia: Fortress Press, 1965.

————. *An Order of Mass and Communion for the Church at Wittenberg, 1523.* Translated by Paul Z. Strodach. Revised by Ulrich S. Leupold. In *Luther's Works,* vol. 53. Edited by Helmut T. Lehman. Philadelphia: Fortress Press, 1965.

Macdonald, Alexander B. *Christian Worship in the Primitive Church.* Edinburgh: T. & T. Clark, 1934.

Manton, Thomas. *The Complete Works of Thomas Manton, D.D.* 22 vols. Reprint, Worthington, Pa.: Maranatha Publications, n.d.

Marot, Clément. *Les psaumes de Clément Marot.* Edited by S. J. Lenselink. Assen: Van Gorcum, 1969. This work is fundamental to an understanding of the Reformed practice of metrical psalmody.

Maxwell, Jack Martin. *Worship and Reformed Theology: The Liturgical Lessons of Mercersburg.* Pittsburgh: Pickwick Press, 1976.

McDonnell, Kilian. *John Calvin: The Church and the Eucharist.* Princeton, N.J.: Princeton University Press, 1967.

McKee, Elsie Anne. *John Calvin on the Diaconate and Liturgical Almsgiving.* Geneva: Librairie Droz, 1984.

McKim, Donald K. "Death, Funerals, and Prayers for the Dead in Calvin's Theology." In *Calvin Studies VI.* Edited by John H. Leith. Davidson, N.C.: Colloquium on Calvin Studies, 1992.

McLelland, Joseph C. *The Visible Words of God: An Exposition of the Sacramental Theology of Peter Martyr Vermigli.* Grand Rapids: Wm. B. Eerdmans Publishing Co., 1958.

McMillan, William. *The Worship of the Scottish Reformed Church: 1550–1638.* London: James Clarke & Co., 1931.

M'Crie, Thomas. *The Life of John Knox.* Glasgow: Free Presbyterian Publications, 1976.

Menoud, Philippe. "Les Actes des Apôtres et l'Eucharistie." *Revue d'histoire et de philosophie religieuses* 33 (1953): 21–36.

Miller, Ross. "Calvin's Understanding of Psalm Singing as a Means of Grace." In *Calvin Studies VI.* Edited by John H. Leith. Davidson, N.C.: Colloquium on Calvin Studies, 1992.

──────. "Music and the Spirit: Psalm-Singing in Calvin's Liturgy." In *Calvin Studies VI.* Edited by John H. Leith. Davidson, N.C.: Colloquium on Calvin Studies, 1992.

Miller, Samuel. *Thoughts on Public Prayer.* Philadelphia: Presbyterian Board of Publications, 1849. This is a fundamental work for understanding the worship of American Presbyterians.

Millet, Olivier. *Calvin et la dynamique de la Parole. Essai de rhétorique réformée.* Paris: H. Campion, 1992.

Moeller, Bernd. *Johannes Zwick und die Reformation in Konstanz.* Quellen und Forschungen zur Reformationsgeschichte, vol. 28. Gütersloh: Gerd Mohn, 1961.

Moore, George Foot. *Judaism in the First Centuries of the Christian Era.* 2 vols. New York: Schocken Books, 1971.

Mulhaupt, Erwin. *Die Predigt Calvins, ihre Geschichte, ihre Form und ihre religiösen Grundgedanken.* Berlin: W. de Gruyter, 1931.

Müller, Johannes. *Martin Bucers Hermeneutik.* Quellen und Forschungen zur Reformationsgeschichte, vol. 32. Gütersloh: Gerd Mohn, 1965.

Nettl, Paul. *Luther and Music.* Translated by Frida Best and Ralph Wood. Philadelphia: Muhlenberg Press, 1948.

Neuser, Wilhelm H. *Die reformatorische Wende bei Zwingli.* Neukirchen-Vluyn: Neukirchener Verlag, 1977.

Nevin, John Williamson. *The Mystical Presence.* Philadelphia: J. B. Lippincott, 1846. A more recent edition can be found in John Williamson Nevin, *The Anxious Bench: The Mystical Presence.* New York: Garland Publishing, 1987.

Oberman, Heiko A. *Luther: Man between God and the Devil.* New Haven, Conn.: Yale University Press, 1989.

──────. *Die Reformation von Wittenberg nach Genf.* Göttingen: Vandenhoeck & Ruprecht, 1986.

Oecolampadius, John. *Antwort auff Balthasar Huobmeiers büchlein wider der Predicanten gespräch zuo Basel, von dem Kindertauff.* Basel: Andreas Cratander, 1527. The three works listed here on baptism make clear that the so-called "regulative principle" is not Reformed in origin but rather Anabaptist.

──────. *Apologetica Ioann. Oecolampadii de dignitate eucharistiae. . . . Antisyngramma.* Zurich: Christoffel Froschauer, 1526.

──────. *De genuina verborum Domini: Hoc est corpus meum iuxta vetustissimos authores expositione liber.* Strasbourg: n.p., 1525.

──────. *De risu pascalis Oecolampadi ad V. Capitonem theologum epistola apologetica.* Basel: J. Froben, 1518.

──────. *Ein gesprech etlicher predicanten zuo Basel, gehalten mit etlichen bekennern des widertauffs.* Basel: Valentine Curione, 1525.

──────. *Form und gestalt wie das Herren Nachtmal, der kinder Tauff, der Kranken haymsuochung, zuo Basel gebraucht und gehalten werden.* Basel: Thomas Wolff, 1526.

──────. *Vnderrichtung von dem Widertauff, von der Oberkeit und von dem Eyd. . . .* Basel: Andreas Cratander, 1527.

Old, Hughes Oliphant. "Biblical Wisdom Theology and Calvin's Understanding of the Lord's Supper." In *Calvin Studies VI.* Edited by John H. Leith. Davidson, N.C.: Colloquium on Calvin Studies, 1992.

──────. "Bullinger and the Scholastic Works on Baptism: A Study in the History of Christian Worship." In *Heinrich Bullinger, 1504–1575, Gesammelte Aufsätze zum 400. Todestag.* Edited by Ulrich Gabler and Erland Herkenrath. 2 vols. Zurich: Theologischer Verlag, 1975.

──────. "Calvin as Evangelist: A Study of the Reformer's Sermons in Preparation for the Christian Celebration of Passover." In *Calvin Studies VII.* Edited by John H. Leith. Davidson, N.C.: Colloquium on Calvin Studies, 1994.

————. "Daily Prayer in the Reformed Church of Strasbourg, 1523–1530." *Worship* 52 (1978): 121–38.

————. "The Homiletics of John Oecolampadius and the Sermons of the Greek Fathers." *Communio Sanctorum. Melánges offert á Jean-Jacques von Allmen.* Edited by A. de Pury. Geneva: Labor et Fides, 1982.

————. "John Calvin and the Prophetic Criticism of Worship." In *John Calvin and the Church: A Prism of Reform.* Edited by Timothy George. Louisville, Ky.: Westminster/ John Knox Press, 1990.

————. *Leading in Prayer: A Workbook for Ministers.* Grand Rapids: Wm. B. Eerdmans Publishing Co., 1995.

————. "Matthew Henry and the Puritan Discipline of Family Prayer." In *Calvin Studies VII.* Edited by John H. Leith. Davidson, N.C.: Colloquium on Calvin Studies, 1994.

————. *The Patristic Roots of Reformed Worship.* Zürcher Beitrage zur Reformationsgeschichte. Zurich: Theologischer Verlag, 1975.

————. "The Reformed Daily Office: A Puritan Perspective." *Reformed Liturgy and Music* 12, 4 (1978): 9–18.

————. *The Shaping of the Reformed Baptismal Rite in the Sixteenth Century.* Grand Rapids: Wm. B. Eerdmans Publishing Co., 1992.

————. *Themes and Variations for a Christian Doxology: Some Thoughts on the Theology of Worship.* Grand Rapids: Wm. B. Eerdmans Publishing Co., 1992.

Owen, John. *The Works of John Owen.* 16 vols. Edited by William H. Goold. Reprint of the Johnstone & Hunter edition, 1850–53. Edinburgh: Banner of Truth Trust, 1976. Owen represents the left wing of the Puritan Movement. His thought did much to shape the liturgical practice of later Anglo-Saxon Protestants.

————. "A Brief Instruction in the Worship of God." In *The Works of John Owen,* vol. 15. Edited by William H. Goold. Edinburgh: T. & T. Clark, 1862.

————. "A Discourse Concerning Liturgies and Their Imposition." In *The Works of John Owen,* vol. 15. Edited by William H. Goold. Reprint of the Johnstone & Hunter edition, 1850–53. Edinburgh: Banner of Truth Trust, 1976.

————. A *Discourse of the Work of the Holy Spirit in Prayer (1662).* In *Opera.* Edited by Russell. London: 1826. Reprinted in *The Works of John Owen,* vol. 4. Edited by William H. Goold. Edinburgh: Banner of Truth Trust, 1976.

Ozment, Steven. *The Age of Reform (1250–1550): An Intellectual and Religious History of Late Medieval and Reformation Europe.* New Haven, Conn.: Yale University Press, 1980.

————. *The Reformation and the Cities.* New Haven, Conn.: Yale University Press, 1975.

Palmer, Benjamin Morgan. *Theology of Prayer as Viewed in the Religion of Nature and in the System of Grace.* Richmond: Presbyterian Committee on Publications, 1894.

Parker, T. H. L. *Calvin's Preaching.* Edinburgh: T. & T. Clark, 1992.

————. *John Calvin: A Biography.* London: J. M. Dent & Sons, 1975.

————. *The Oracles of God: An Introduction to the Preaching of John Calvin.* London: Lutterworth Press, 1947.

Patrick, Millar. *Four Centuries of Scottish Psalmody.* London: Oxford University Press, 1949.

Payne, John. *Erasmus: His Theology of the Sacraments.* Richmond: John Knox Press, 1970.

Perkins, William. *The Art of Prophesying or a Treatise concerning the Sacred and Only True Manner and Method of Preaching.* London: F. Kyngston for E. Edgar, 1607. Perkins was one of the most influential Calvinist theologians of his day.

————. A *Discourse concerning the Gift of Prayer.* London: Printed by T. M. for Samuell Gellibrand, 1655.

————. *Exposition of the Lord's Prayer*. London: John Lagatt, 1626.

————. A *Faithful and Plaine Exposition Upon the First Two Verses of the Second Chapter of Zephaniah*. London: T. Creele for W. Welby, 1605. This is in effect a work on the theology of worship.

————. *The Work of William Perkins*. Edited by Ian Breward. Appleford: Sutton Courtenay Press, 1970.

Peter, Rodolphe. "L'Homiletique de Calvin." *Supplementa Calviniana. Sermon inédits* 2: xlix–lxi.

————. "Rhetorique et Predication selon Calvin." *Revue d' histoire et de philosophie religieuses* 55 (1975): 249–72.

Potter, George R. *Zwingli*. Cambridge: Cambridge University Press, 1976.

Preston, John. *Grace to the Humble as Preparation to Receive the Sacrament*. London: Thomas Cotes, 1639.

————. *The New Covenant, or the Saint's Portion*. London: J. Dawson for Nicholas Bourne, 1630.

————. *A Preparation to the Lord's Supper: Preached in Three Sermons*. London: John Dawson, 1638.

————. *The Saints Daily Exercise*. London: W. I. & Nicholas Bourne, 1629. Reprint, Norwood, N.J.: Walter J. Johnson, 1976. This is an important work on the discipline of daily prayer.

Proctor, Francis. A *New History of the Book of Common Prayer*. Revised and rewritten by Walter Howard Frere. London: Macmillan, 1949.

Ratcliff, Edward C. "The Liturgical Work of Archbishop Cranmer." *Journal of Ecclesiastical History* 7 (1956): 189–203.

Ray, Richard. "John Calvin on Theatrical Trifles in Worship." In *Calvin Studies VI*. Edited by John H. Leith. Davidson, N.C.: Colloquium on Calvin Studies, 1992.

Reed, Luther D. *The Lutheran Liturgy*. Philadelphia: Fortress Press, 1947.

Richardson, Cyril C. *Zwingli and Cranmer on the Eucharist*. Evanston, Ill.: Seabury-Western Theological Seminary, 1949.

Ridley, Jasper G. *Thomas Cranmer*. Oxford: Clarendon Press, 1963.

Rordorf, Willy. *Sunday*. Translated by A. A. K. Graham. Philadelphia: Westminster Press, 1968. This is a work of major importance for the restoration of Reformed worship.

Rordorf, Willy, et al. *The Eucharist of the Early Christians*. Translated by Matthew J. O'Connell. New York: Pueblo Publishing Co., 1978.

Rorem, Paul. *Calvin and Bullinger on the Lord's Supper*. Bramcote, England: Grove Books, 1989.

Rous, Francis. *The Psalms of David Set in Meter, Approved by the Westminster Assembly*. London: Printed by J. Young for P. Nevill, 1643.

Schmidt, Leigh. *Holy Fairs*. Princeton, N.J.: Princeton University Press, 1990.

Scholl, Hans. *Der Dienst des Gebetes nach Johannes Calvin*. Zurich: Zwingli Verlag, 1968.

Schweibert, Ernest G. *The Reformation*. 2 vols. Minneapolis: Fortress Press, 1993.

Schweizer, Eduard. *The Lord's Supper according to the New Testament*. Translated by James M. Davis. Philadelphia: Fortress Press, 1967.

Sehling, Emil, ed. *Die evangelische Kirchenordnungen des 16. Jahrhundert*. Leipzig: O. R. Reisland, 1902–13, and Tübingen: J. C. B. Mohr (Paul Siebeck), 1955–63. Of particular interest are the liturgical documents of Augsburg, Kempton, Lindau, and Memmingen, found in volume 12, and the volume dedicated to the documents of Hesse.

Shepard, Thomas. *The Works of Thomas Shepard*. 3 vols. Boston: Doctrinal Tract & Book Society, 1853. Reprinted. New York: AMS Press, 1967. Of particular interest are his works on the Sabbath and the church membership of children, and his passages on prayer and on preaching in *The Parable of the Ten Virgins, Opened and Applied*.

Smyth, Charles Henry. *Cranmer and the Reformation under Edward VI.* Cambridge: Cambridge University Press, 1926.

Spurgeon, Charles Haddon. *Communion Sermons.* Nashville: Abingdon Press, ca. 1940.

Staehelin, Ernst. *Das theologische Lebenswerk Johannes Oekolampads.* Quellen und Forschungen zur Reformationsgeschichte, vol. 21. Leipzig: M. Heinsius Nachfolger, 1939.

Stauffer, Richard. "Un Calvin Méconnu; le prédicateur de Genève." *Bulletin de la Société de l'histoire du Protestantisme français* 123 (1977): 184–203.

———. *Dieu, la Creation et la Providence dans la Prédication de Calvin.* Bern: P. Lang, 1978.

Steinmetz, David C. *Calvin in Context.* New York: Oxford University Press, 1995.

Sternhold, T., and I. Hopkins. *The Whole Booke of Psalms Collected into English Metre by T. Sternhold, I. Hopkins and others.* London: John Daye, 1562.

Stephens, W. P. *The Holy Spirit in the Theology of Martin Bucer.* Cambridge: Cambridge University Press, 1970.

Sturm, Klaus. *Die Theologie Peter Martyr Vermiglis während seines ersten Aufenthalts in Strassburg, 1542–1547.* Neukirchen-Vluyn: Buchhandlung der Erziehungsverein, 1971.

Tate, Nahum, and Nicholas Brady. *A New Version of the Psalms of David Fitted to Tunes Used in Churches.* London: T. Hodgkin, 1698.

Tennent, Gilbert. *Twenty-three Sermons upon the Chief End of Man, the Divine Authority of the Sacred Scriptures, the Being and Attributes of God, and the Doctrine of the Trinity.* Philadelphia: Printed and sold by William Bradford,1744.

Tennent, Gilbert, et al. *Sermons on Sacramental Occasions.* [Boston: Printed by J. Draper for D. Henchman, 1739.]

Thompson, Bard. *Liturgies of the Western Church.* Cleveland: World Publishing Co., 1961.

Torrance, Thomas F. *The School of Faith and the Catechisms of the Reformed Church.* London: James Clarke & Co., 1959.

Trinterud, Leonard John. *The Forming of an American Tradition: A Reexamination of Colonial Presbyterianism.* Philadelphia: Westminster Press, 1949.

Tylenda, Joseph M. "Calvin and Christ's Presence in the Supper—True or Real?" *Scottish Journal of Theology* 27 (1974): 65–75.

Vajta, Vilmos. *Luther on Worship.* Translated by U. S. Leupold. Philadelphia: Fortress Press, 1958.

van de Poll, Gerrit Jan. *Martin Bucer's Liturgical Ideas.* Assen: Van Gorcum, 1954.

van Lodenstein, Jodocus. "A Communion Sermon, Introduced and Translated by Iain S. Maclean." In *Calvin Studies VI.* Edited by John H. Leith. Davidson, N.C.: Colloquium on Calvin Studies, 1992.

Vermigli, Peter Martyr. *Defensio doctrinae veteris et apostolicae de sacrosancto Eucharistiae sacramento.* Zurich: Christoffel Froschauer, 1559.

———. *A discourse or traictise of Peter Martyr Vermill . . . wherein he openly declared his . . . judgment concernynge the Sacrament of the Lordes supper.* Translated by N. Udall. London: R. Stoughton, ca. 1550.

———. *Most Godly Prayers Compiled Out of David's Psalms by D. Peter Martyr.* Translated by C. Glemhan. London: W. Seres, 1569.

———. *The Oxford Treatise and Disputation on the Eucharist, 1549.* Translated and edited by Joseph C. McLelland. Peter Martyr Library, vol. 7. Kirksville, Mo.: Sixteenth Century Essays and Studies, 2000. Vermigli's work on the Eucharist deserves careful study. He gives us a particularly thorough interpretation of the sacrament. This new translation will advance the discussion considerably.

———. *Sacred Prayers, Drawn from the Psalms of David.* Translated and edited by John Patrick Donnelly. Peter Martyr Library, vol. 3. Kirksville, Mo.: Sixteenth Century Essays and Studies, 2000.

————. *Tractatio de sacramento Eucharistiae, habita in celebrima Universitate Oxoniensi . . . Ad hec Disputatio de eodem Eucharistiae sacramento in eadem Universitate habita. . . .* London: R. Wolfe, 1549.

Wainwright, Geoffrey. *Doxology: The Praise of God in Worship, Doctrine, and Life.* New York: Oxford University Press, 1980.

Wakefield, Gordon S. *Puritan Devotion.* London: Epworth Press, 1957.

Watts, Isaac. *A Guide to Prayer.* In *Opera,* vol. 3. Edited by George Burder. London: J. Barfield, 1810.

————. *Hymns and Spiritual Songs.* 3 vols. London: J. Humphreys, 1707.

————. *The Psalms of David Imitated in the Language of the New Testament.* In *Opera.* Edited by George Burder. London: J. Barfield, 1810.

Welker, Michael. *What Happens in Holy Communion.* Translated by John F. Hoffmeyer. Grand Rapids: Wm. B. Eerdmans Publishing Co., 2000.

Whitaker, Edward Charles. *Martin Bucer and the Book of Common Prayer.* Alcuin Club Collection 55. Great Wakering: Mayhew-McCrimmon, 1974.

White, James. *Introduction to Christian Worship.* Nashville: Abingdon Press, 1980.

Willison, John. *Five Sacramental Sermons,* 1722. In *The Practical Works of the Rev. John Willison.* Glasgow: Blackie & Son, ca. 1817.

————. *The Practical Works of the Rev. John Willison.* Glasgow: Blackie & Son, ca. 1817.

————. *A Sacramental Catechism.* Originally published in 1720. Reprint, Morgan, Pa.: Soli Deo Gloria Publications, 2000. The several works of Willison on the Lord's Supper are among the best statements of Reformed eucharistic piety.

————. *A Sacramental Directory,* 1716. In *The Practical Works of the Rev. John Willison.* Glasgow: Blackie & Son, ca. 1817.

————. *Sacramental Meditations,* 1747. In *The Practical Works of the Rev. John Willison.* Glasgow: Blackie & Son, ca. 1817.

————. *Treatise Concerning the Sanctification of the Lord's Day,* 1712. In *The Practical Works of the Rev. John Willison.* Glasgow: Blackie & Son, ca. 1817.

Yoder, John H. *Täufertum und Reformation im Gespräch.* Basler Studien zur Historischen und Systematischen Theologie, vol. 13. Zurich: EVZ-Verlag, 1968.

————. *Täufertum und Reformation in der Schweiz I.* Schriftenreihe des Mennonitischen Geschichtsvereins, vol. 6. Karlsruhe: H. Schneider, 1962.

Zurich Letters. Edited by Hastings Robinson for the Parker Society. 2 vols. Cambridge: Cambridge University Press, 1842–45.

Zwick, Johannes, "Bekantnuss der zwoelff Artickel des Glaubens von Jesu Christo, zu dem allmaechtigen Gott im Hymel." In *Monumenta Germaniae Paedagogica,* vol. 23. Edited by Ferdinand Cohrs. Berlin: A. Hoffmann & Co., 1900–1907.

————. "Das Vatter unser in frag und betswyss für die jungenn kind ussgelegt ouch den alten nit undienstlich." In *Monumenta Germaniae Paedagogica,* vol. 23. Edited by Ferdinand Cohrs. Berlin: A. Hoffmann & Co., 1900–1907.

————. *Nuw gsangbuchle von vil schonen Psalmen und geistlichen liedern. . . .* Zurich: Christoffel Froschouer, 1540. This hymnbook, drawn together for the Reformed church of Constance, is one of the most important documents for the history of Reformed liturgics. Zwick's preface is particularly interesting.

Zwingli, Ulrich. *Action or Use of the Lord's Supper.* Zurich: Ch. Froschauer, 1525. Translated by Bard Thompson. In *Liturgies of the Western Church,* by Bard Thompson. Cleveland: World Publishing Co., 1961.

————. *Of Baptism.* Library of Christian Classics, vol. 24. Philadelphia: Westminster Press, 1953.

————. *Of the Clarity and Certainty of the Word of God.* Library of Christian Classics, vol. 24. Philadelphia: Westminster Press, 1953.

————. *On the Lord's Supper.* Library of Christian Classics, vol. 24. Philadelphia: Westminster Press, 1953.

————. *Refutation of the Tricks of the Catabaptists.* In *Selected Works,* edited by Samuel Macauley Jackson. Philadelphia: University of Pennsylvania Press, 1972.

————. *Selected Works.* Edited by Samuel Macauley Jackson. Philadelphia: University of Pennsylvania Press, 1972.

Index

Printed in the United States
203630BV00004B/91-126/A

9 780664 225797